the **Digital Big Bang**

the DIGITAL BIG BANG

THE HARD STUFF, THE SOFT STUFF, AND THE FUTURE OF CYBERSECURITY

Phil Quade, CISO, Fortinet

The Digital Bing Bang: The Hard Stuff, the Soft Stuff, and the Future of Cybersecurity

Published by
John Wiley & Sons, Inc.
10475 Crosspoint Boulevard
Indianapolis, IN 46256
www.wiley.com

Published simultaneously in Canada

ISBN: 978-1-119-61736-5
ISBN: 978-1-119-61738-9 (ebk)
ISBN: 978-1-119-61740-2 (ebk)

Manufactured in the United States of America

For general information on our other products and services please contact our Customer Care Department within the United States at (877) 762-2974, outside the United States at (317) 572-3993 or fax (317) 572-4002.

Wiley publishes in a variety of print and electronic formats and by print-on-demand. Some material included with standard print versions of this book may not be included in e-books or in print-on-demand. If this book refers to media such as a CD or DVD that is not included in the version you purchased, you may download this material at http://booksupport.wiley.com. For more information about Wiley products, visit www.wiley.com.

Library of Congress Control Number: 2019943278

V10012623_081219

*To my family, Yvonne, Bennett, Kristen,
and Jackson Quade, who are
"the fundamental elements" of my life.*

—Phil Quade, CISO, Fortinet

ABOUT THE AUTHOR

Phil Quade is the CISO of Fortinet. Quade brings more than three decades of cyber intelligence, defense, and attack experience, working across foreign, government, and commercial industry sectors at the National Security Agency (NSA), and partner organizations such as US Cyber Command, the CIA, and others.

Quade has responsibility for Fortinet's information and product security, leads strategy and expansion of Fortinet's Federal and Critical Infrastructure business, and serves as a strategic consultant to Fortinet's C-Level enterprise customers. Prior to Fortinet, Quade was the NSA Director's Special Assistant for Cyber and Chief of the NSA Cyber Task Force, with responsibility for the White House relationship in cybersecurity. Previously, Quade also served as the chief operating officer of the Information Assurance Directorate at the NSA, managing day-to-day activities associated with the protection of classified information systems. He held a variety of roles earlier in his tenure at the NSA, including head of the Information Operations Technology Center's Advanced Technology Group, professional staffer to the US Senate, detailee in the Office of the Director for National Intelligence, cryptanalyst, and computer scientist.

CONTRIBUTORS

Thad Allen

Ed Amoroso

Colin Anderson

Dan Boneh

Scott Charney

Michael Chertoff

Roland Cloutier

Tim Crothers

Michael Daniel

Erik Devine

George Do

Taher Elgamal

Jay Gonzales

Daniel Hooper

Chris Inglis

Michael Johnson

Mo Katibeh

Kevin Kealy

Peter Keenan

Simon Lambe

Shannon Lietz

Mike McConnell

Chris McDaniels

Kevin Miller

Theresa Payton

Dave Rankin

Chris Richter

Hussein Syed

Brian Talbert

Renee Tarun

Ken Xie

Michael Xie

ACKNOWLEDGMENTS

Although I am the named author of this volume, this book is the result of a much broader team effort. This book would not be possible without the contributions by leaders and experts in the field. All of the contributors are big thinkers and good cybercitizens—colleagues who give their time and energy to advancing the science of cybersecurity and who make our digital universe a better place.

I would first like to thank Ken Xie and the entire Fortinet team for supporting me in creating this book and providing me with the opportunity to explore and write about these topics.

And I especially want to thank Sandra Wheatley-Smerdon, my work colleague, who was instrumental in launching this exploration of the "big history" of cybersecurity.

CONTENTS

INTRODUCTION

"The most fundamental forces of cybersecurity are speed and connectivity. Our solutions must support and leverage these forces."

Phil Quade,
Fortinet

"Embracing cybersecurity as a science can be an incredibly powerful and effective way to underpin innovation."

Phil Quade,
Fortinet

Humankind experiences some of its greatest disappointments and disasters when we fail to acknowledge the fundamentals of physics and chemistry. As we solve problems and improve technology, we must work with, not against, the foundation of the laws of mass, force, energy, and chemical reactions—laws that began with the cosmic big bang.

Like the physical world, cybersecurity has its own set of fundamentals: speed and connectivity. When organizations ignore these fundamentals, distracted by sophisticated marketing or new products, we suffer the consequences. We end up with solutions that solve only part of the problem or that simply stop working (or stop us from working when put to the test of real-world conditions).

That's partly because, to date, cybersecurity has been treated as *a cost of doing business,* as opposed to *a foundational set of primitives and rules* that are leveraged to achieve greater things. To build a cybersecurity foundation that will work now and continue to work in a world exponentially faster and more connected, we must start treating cybersecurity more like a science. We must understand its fundamental elements and how they interact.

The early Internet, constructed decades ago to serve a small, tight-knit and primarily academic community, was built upon principles of game-changing speed and a deep understanding of the importance of connectivity. Security and privacy were not needed for that first small group of trusted users and thus were not part of the original design requirements. Although security and privacy have demonstrated their importance in today's blisteringly fast, global network, they have not kept up as the Internet has matured.

While we are exponentially more connected than at any other time in history, with nearly instantaneously accessible information at our fingertips, the cyberadversaries—not the defenders—are the ones who have mastered speed and connectivity to their advantage. Speed and connectivity serve us well as communication building blocks, but too often have failed us in cybersecurity, because we have failed to establish the foundation of cybersecurity upon those fundamental elements.

In a hypercompetitive business landscape, not only do cybersecurity fundamentals protect you and make you a much less attractive target to bad actors, but they also cast a halo of protection across all the individuals and organizations to which you are connected.

When we build our cybersecurity based on a complete understanding of fundamental elements and how they can work together, we can inspire and encourage scientific revolutions and evolutions in cybersecurity that will make us much better off.

We are on the verge of a new understanding of a basic element of human society. Just as the world has understood that economic security has been highly dependent on a stable flow of fossil fuels and that national security is dependent on safeguards for nuclear weapons, today we understand that, in our hyperconnected world, there is no global security without understanding and mastering the science of cybersecurity.

But the real historical analogy of cybersecurity, the story of the digital big bang, starts much earlier. Let's rewind nearly 14 billion years to the Big Bang, the beginning of the universe as we understand it today.

"The good thing about science is that it is true whether you believe it or not. That's why it works."—*Neil deGrasse Tyson*

THE COSMIC BIG BANG: THE BIRTH OF THE PHYSICAL UNIVERSE AND THE HUMAN SOCIETY THAT EMERGED

At the beginning of time as we know it, around 14 billion years ago, energy and matter were born in a moment of unfathomable brilliance. Those core building blocks combined into atoms, followed by even more complex assemblies (molecules) just a few hundred thousand years later.

Billions of years later, after countless stars were born and died out, our solar system was formed from the remnants of furnaces of those long-dead stars. Physicists and chemists study the big bang's fundamental elements and their interactions in part to explain what things are made of and how they behave.

Some of those complex configurations coalesced into what we call *life*. We study life and how it evolved from its most primitive state to discover where we come from and to help us thrive within our given universe, not fighting mother nature.

The human life that eventually emerged from among this plethora of creatures eventually formed complex rules and societies that evolved in a broad set of stages or ages. Yuval Noah Harari in *Sapiens* cited them as follows:

- The Cognitive Revolution (c. 70,000 BCE, when Homo sapiens evolved imagination)
- The Agricultural Revolution (c. 10,000 BCE, the development of agriculture)

- The unification of humankind (the gradual consolidation of human political organizations toward one global empire)
- The Scientific Revolution (c. 1500 CE, the emergence of objective science)

In each of these ages, humans made relatively large leaps forward in understanding their environment and, at times, directly shaping it.

THE DIGITAL BIG BANG: THE BIRTH OF THE DIGITAL UNIVERSE

If we take on the mindset of a cybersecurity historian, we can look at the big picture in the same way and attempt to understand what is driving it forward. Consider these observations:

- While it took billions of years for the physical world we know to create and sustain human life, it took just 50 years from the beginnings of the Internet as ARPAnet in 1969, for the explosive forces of digital speed and connectivity to transform human society.
- Ninety percent of all the data in the world ever created was generated in the last two years. Bang!
- The Internet itself—a vast and hyperconnected data transmission system—now creates *2.5 quintillion* bits of data per day. I don't even have a fathomable analogy to characterize how much that is—but it's 18 zeros.

Digital technology has come to enmesh and propel nearly every aspect of modern life, from the operational infrastructure that keeps our cities and towns powered and functioning, to the now almost entirely digitally driven systems of global finance, security, and energy production. The rapid transference of digital information is how we connect, communicate, and—in many ways—sustain human life, order, and a tentative semblance of peace on Earth.

Our opportunity is to describe how the digital big bang progressed over time, understand its significance, and do something smart and productive about it.

THE SCIENTIFIC REVOLUTION

After the cosmic big bang, billions of years passed before humans came along and eventually started trying to make sense of the whole thing.

In human history, the most recent and most significant age is the Scientific Revolution, not so much because of what it achieved, but because of what it left behind. It was in the Scientific Revolution that we finally admitted that *we didn't know everything*. The admission of ignorance advanced the pursuit of knowledge and reason. It allowed us to define the modern laws of physics and chemistry; to explain, in a data-driven way, how nature's fundamental elements interact; and to discover the perils? of ignoring those laws. It incentivized us to fill in gaps in our data collection that we didn't feel obliged to before.

For example, the maps of the world from 750 years ago had elaborate drawings of mid-ocean whirlpools and sea monsters—here be dragons—mid-continent mountain ranges, and other physical phenomena. Faulty thinking, and the desire to warn of the dangers of sea exploration, led mapmakers to fill in what they did not know.

In contrast, the maps of the Scientific Age were drawn with large blank areas, showing where we had no data. It was not until we admitted that we in fact had very little idea what was beyond the horizon, or mid-ocean or continent, that we began exploring those areas and filling in the missing pieces that led to a much better understanding of our world.

The pull of curiosity about basic principles reduced the fear of the unknown and prompted the physical world's golden age of scientific education.

Now we must make the same leap in cybersecurity. We need to stop quaking at the cyber threats—real and imagined—and get down to the business of defining how to navigate and master those threats.

THE BANG BEGINS

A masterpiece of international collaboration, the Internet has its roots in the desire to share computing and information resources and the US Department of Defense's goal of establishing connectivity via computers in the event of a nuclear attack that destroyed telephone systems.

On October 29, 1969, the first message was sent over what would eventually become the Internet. Meant to be the word "login," the letters "L" and "O" were sent from researchers at UCLA to a team at Stanford. Then the system crashed. (We'll pause while you chuckle about that first crash.)

When it was constructed and deployed, the Internet served as a communication platform for a tightly restricted group of specific users.

With the advent of packet switching—the division of information into smaller blocks to be transmitted and then reassembled, pioneered as a Cold War strategy—that communication became a viable, though intensely limited, reality.

WHAT WE GOT RIGHT

Internet pioneers got speed and connectivity right—the digital big bang's equivalent of matter and energy. Their goal was a secure, distributed widespread computer communication system, and they achieved that goal.

WHAT WE GOT WRONG

Because the digital transmission of information was so restricted in both users and data, the use of ARPAnet was governed by a shared sense of trust that was informed and enforced by security clearances, professional accountability, and total lack of anonymity.

AN UNWARRANTED ASSUMPTION OF TRUST

With this assumption of trust, things went off-kilter. That assumption thwarted the parallel development of security, particularly trustworthy authentication, that could have supported the speed and connectivity that would make the Internet transformational.

With the passage in 1992 of the Scientific and Advanced-Technology Act, research and academic institutions started using this early Internet. Security shortfalls were generally understood, but the circle of institutions that had access remained small and tight-knit. It wasn't until 1993, and the release of the first web browser that Internet access became mainstream. At that point, both the Internet and its security, or lack of security, achieved greater significance.

The assumption of trust that was still deep within the DNA of the Internet became a huge problem the moment the public could go online. On an increasingly vast and anonymous network, that trust soon transformed from guiding philosophy to greatest weakness. As more people arrived, the Internet quickly became a newly discovered continent of naïve users, systems, and networks to be exploited and hacked for digital fraud, grift, or simply to prove it could be done.

Since those first hacks, the field of cybersecurity has struggled to catch up and compensate. Mitigating the weakness—the wrongful assumption of trust and the lack of strong authentication—while still balancing the essential benefits and fundamentals of speed and connectivity, remains an enduring challenge of cybersecurity today.

AN HONEST ASSESSMENT OF THE CURRENT STATE

For all the stunning power of its speed and the vastness of its data, the Internet is shockingly fragile and fallible. We're propping it up, sometimes with ridiculously complex schemas and other times with little more than digital Popsicle sticks and Elmer's glue and, for high-end applications, duct tape.

The Internet is fast, anonymous, powerful, and profitable—all factors that have accelerated its use and deployment—while at the same time prone to malicious exploitation, with terrible potential for criminality and sabotage. The continuing series of breaches of organizations of all levels of sophistication shows what a huge problem we have.

WHAT CYBERCRIMES EXPLOIT

Perhaps what is most amazing (or at least ironic) about cyber-crime is how this masterpiece of technological collaboration and human connection is so often exploited to gratify human impulses. Distributed denial-of-service (DDoS) attacks, phishing emails, and ever-evolving scams manipulate recipients for the purpose of mass theft and extortion. From data corruption to identity theft, malware to man-in-the-middle attacks, the crimes that cybersecurity must mitigate and prevent run a gamut that only seems to get broader. Attacks are not only launched by criminals but also by rogue nation-states. Over time, these attacks become more destructive and less difficult to perpetrate.

The widening breadth of cybercrime is a direct reflection of our expanding global attack surface—and the increasing commodification of threat. The digital criminal barrier for entry that individuals and organizations alike must defend against is lower than ever. Today, it can be as easy to purchase a cyberattack as it is to buy a cup of coffee, and often even cheaper. We must defend ourselves from near constant silent digital attacks on the fabric of our societies, all roiling beneath the surface of an increasingly interconnected world.

Today, there is little difference between cybersecurity and national, even global, security. As we have seen time and again in reported malicious cyber activity—often in chilling reports of narrowly averted attacks—we can be reached at the most foundational levels by nearly anyone, from anywhere.

WHAT WE CAN GET RIGHT NOW

With so much at stake, it's time to borrow a page from the Scientific Revolution:

Scientific Revolution	Cybersecurity Scientific Revolution
▣ Admit our ignorance (redraw the earth's maps).	▣ Acknowledge what we got wrong (authentication).
▣ Use steadily increased strategies for becoming masters of our physical domain (sail oceans, fly planes, explore space).	▣ Implement steadily stronger strategies to become masters of the cyber domain.
▣ Replace fear with curiosity.	▣ Replace outmoded assumptions and strategies with rigorous fundamental strategies that build up to advanced strategies.

We need to stop expecting our network operators to continuously run ahead of ever more sophisticated attacks. You can't outrun the speed of light.

We can achieve better cybersecurity by thinking like physicists and chemists, by postulating and outlining the theorems and proofs necessary to master the cyberspace domain. As critical as these fundamentals are, though, they can easily be overlooked or forgotten by a digital culture that looks myopically to the near future, placing short-term gains ahead of long-term stability and sustainability. Cybersecurity is a marathon—not a sprint.

As our connectivity expands and deepens, the strength and intractability of these fundamentals only becomes more apparent. And more necessary.

With the exponential increase of digital connectivity, cyber-physical interfaces (in the Internet of Things), and machine learning and artificial intelligence, it is more important than ever to treat cybersecurity as a science and a business enabler, as opposed to simply a cost of doing business.

We must reveal the connection between fundamental scientific principles and cybersecurity best practices. What are the foundational primitives and rules that would have been beneficial to have at the beginning of the Internet? How would things have been different if they had been in place? How can we create a better form of cybersecurity based on the nature of fundamental forces and accurate assumptions?

Embracing cybersecurity as a science can be an incredibly powerful and effective way to underpin innovation. It will enable us to focus on effectively leveraging the Internet's forces of speed and connectivity as well as one more unchangeable force that we'll talk about later in this book: the fallibility and needs of humans.

It is a bold goal to attempt to make cybersecurity more scientific, but in our view, it is achievable with the right vision and engineering. By doing so, we can further extend the power of speed and connectivity to thrive within the digital world. Rather than suffering through the cosmic big bang's equivalent of the melting of our planet by the death of our sun billions of years from now, let's understand, define, and work within the laws of the science of cybersecurity.

THE DIGITAL NUCLEUS

As mentioned earlier, the most fundamental forces of cybersecurity are speed and connectivity. Our solutions must be built to support and leverage these forces.

Although security has historically slowed things down, security without speed is a losing proposition. Similarly, security is only as strong as the weakest link in the chain, so security must enable connectivity—specifically, an integration of your defenses to leverage your strengths. This is a far better core strategy than the common alternative: expecting your weakest point to be better than the adversary's strongest methods. To achieve not only optimal but even basically functional cybersecurity, we must have speed, connectivity, and integrated cybersecurity.

In the pages that follow, we will explore the scientific forces of speed and connectivity that must shape our approach (see Figure 1). We must show how to harness and amplify these forces with cybersecurity that offers greater degrees of precision to counter the increasing sophistication of threat actors and cybercriminals.

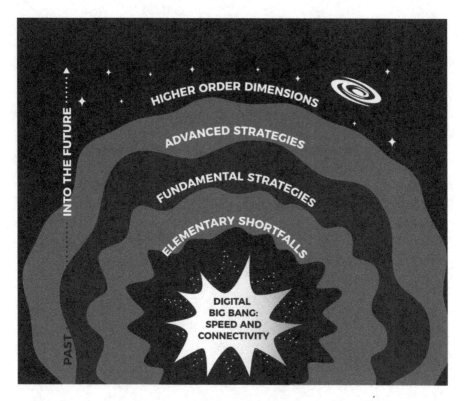

Figure 1 Speed and connectivity form the nucleus of the digital big bang.

We will explore how we can create a more scientific approach to cybersecurity, based on accurate assumptions. We will probe the essence of the modern problems we face and see how lessons from the world of science extend to cyberspace, leading us to certain inevitable mind-expanding conclusions about the very nature and order of how cybersecurity must evolve.

This book is divided into parts. Part I explores the digital nucleus of speed and connectivity.

Part II details the elementary shortfalls in the areas of authentication, patching, and training, and Part III discusses fundamental strategies of access control, cryptography, and segmentation.

Part IV covers advanced strategies, including visibility, inspection, and failure recovery, and Part V lays out higher-order dimensions we must account for, including complexity management, privacy, and human frailty.

In keeping with the spirit of the Internet's invention, this book is a collaborative effort. For each of the topics mentioned, we will hear from some of the leading experts in cybersecurity today, across industries and disciplines, as they come together to offer their insights.

We define success as enabling a pace of innovation in the field of security that outruns the inevitable attempts by adversaries to do their dirty deeds.

It is our hope that by focusing on the fundamental and foundational principles of the science of cybersecurity, this book will empower those who fight the battles to achieve more effective, efficient, and consistent victories for many years to come.

the **Digital Big Bang**

BINDING STRATEGIES:
THE CORE OF CYBERSECURITY

The central parallel between the cosmic big bang and the digital big bang rests in their origins. The cosmic big bang unleashed the two central forces of matter and energy, inexorably connecting them in a way that has shaped and driven our entire existence. The invention of the Internet harnessed technological innovation to weld speed and connectivity—the central forces of the digital big bang equivalent to matter and energy—as a means of communication so powerful it has the potential to change the future of the human race.

Because speed and connectivity are the two primary elements of the Internet, harnessing their strengths and managing their risks must be the primary elements of any effective security strategy.

But too often cybersecurity is at odds with speed and connectivity.

THE NEED FOR SPEED

The Internet created a game-changing means to increase the velocity of information and the speed at which business can be done—to send data faster, accelerating the rate at which we can connect and communicate with others. Remember the days of sending data on disks through the mail? From those early academic uses, that connection has grown. Now the connection includes large-scale business and personal interests, contains our most sensitive health and financial information, and falls within the private and public sectors. Or we may use that connection for sheer entertainment.

The velocity with which we can now send and receive even massive amounts of data is staggering and getting faster every day. We can search for obscure facts, with answers in seconds; communicate in real time with people all over the world; and buy products with one easy click. Regardless of their use and application, today's systems of digital data transmission were designed to be faster than any other means at the time, and they have consistently exceeded that goal.

But to date, that speed has been a problem for defenders. Defensive systems often leach CPU cycles, forcing communication to slow down. When that happens, users often will simply turn off security features, leaving the network and its data vulnerable to attackers. To succeed, our security strategies must be based on leveraging that core philosophy of doing things at Internet speed.

THE DRIVE TO CONNECT

The Internet's creation was a testament to the power of collaboration. Researchers realized that they could achieve more insightful results by comparing and combining their efforts and getting access to remote computing resources.

The resulting architecture was designed around rich and resilient connectivity. As it matured, the Internet fulfilled deep needs for speed and connectivity—organizational, financial, physical, mental, and even emotional—which catalyzed its unprecedented proliferation.

But that highly desired connectivity also opened the door to attacks. Attackers soon learned that they could use connectivity to their advantage to achieve a malicious effect without being near their actual target. Adversaries now can launch attacks from multiple places, focusing their multifaceted barrage on points of weakness. Perhaps it is the central dilemma of cybersecurity: if you can connect with everybody, you can be reached by anybody.

Defenders should take the same architectural approach: design security that leverages connectivity.

HARNESSING SPEED AND CONNECTIVITY

Just as the cosmic big bang's fundamental forces of energy and matter must be carefully managed to achieve intended results, so too must speed and connectivity in the digital universe. For example, a split atom can do one of these two things:

- Blast and heat whole cities—Generate cool air in the summer and heated air in the winter via clean electricity from nuclear power plants
- Heat and blast whole cities—Generate fire and concussion via a nuclear weapon

Cybersecurity implementations must be efficient enough to enable both the highest possible safe speed at all times and the maximum reach and scope of connectivity.

Trying to build cybersecurity solutions that do not maintain speed and connectivity will fail, like an engineer who tries to ignore the laws of physics and chemistry. Just as the communication infrastructure of the Internet is based on a connected fabric of fast communication mechanisms, the security fabric that underpins communications also must be based on an integrated security strategy. Because speed and connectivity are the two primary elements of the Internet, harnessing their strengths and managing their risks must be the primary elements of any effective security strategy.

1
SPEED

Speed must be viewed and treated like the fundamental element it is. But by its very nature, security slows things down. When you're in the security business, you're fundamentally in the business of slowing people down, and that's a horrible business to be in. Security must harness the power of speed to secure information while protecting against cyberattacks at the same rates.

Simply put, all cybersecurity must be extremely fast.

Security without speed is a losing proposition. In fact, slow security is often no security. Good security strategy must be based on leveraging speed, specifically

- Raw speed to detect and mitigate attacks in real time
- Processing capacity with more sensors, more data, and more insights to parse data more efficiently and find the smallest anomalies in system functionality

- Forward compatibility to create the headroom to implement future solutions that could involve even greater speed

Good security strategy must achieve these goals with as little impact as possible on the speed users have come to expect and demand. That's because in addition to the operational reason for speed, there is a practical reason: Users aren't willing to wait.

A consistent consequence results from that user impatience paired with cybersecurity techniques that don't feature speed as a fundamental component: Slow security solutions get shut off, either because they are too cumbersome or because they simply can't keep up. A security solution that lacks speed and thus is turned off provides zero benefit. Thus, slow cybersecurity techniques become greater impediments than benefits.

If organizations are forced to adopt tools that do not meet the needs and standards of fast data transfer, the odds are that not only will those organizations become less safe, but they will carry that lack of safety to every point of connectivity they share, endangering other organizations.

Acknowledging the inherent conflict between security and speed requires us to strategically design how, where, and when to slow things down, while maintaining and preserving as much velocity and efficiency as possible.

When it comes to cybersecurity, without speed, there is nothing. Users will, however, embrace a solution with speed as its key component.

SPEED: THE NUCLEUS OF THE CYBERFRONTIER

Roland Cloutier, ADP

Context is king when providing tangible models of reference to complex issues like cybersecurity. Even as security practitioners, we are faced with an onslaught of information, intelligence, data points, and other exceptional information with a need for action or decision, but we often lack the availability of context to make sense of the environmental settings that help us make great decisions.

WHAT DO WE MEAN BY SPEED?

As we begin to discuss speed as a binding strategy and guiding principle for approaching cybersecurity, we must take the time to truly understand the implications and context of the meaning of speed as a multifaceted component of the threat, of what we are protecting, of how we protect, and of the impact on our ability to be successful.

Speed is in fact at the nucleus of the cyberfrontier. As a term, it can be considered a noun (the rate at which something is measured for movement) or a verb (describing an action of movement). In either case, when linked to the defense of technology, it is speed that dictates our plans, actions, and, often, outcomes. It is speed that supports measures of priority along with residual risk measures. And it is speed that impacts basic program considerations such as cost, services, and urgency.

We'll now explore key areas of speed as a binding strategy and the key strategic elements that you can focus on to help you make better decisions, deliver better results, and have a greater impact in protecting your charge.

HOW SPEED IMPACTS SECURITY

Living in a digitally connected ecosystem of business, societies, and global economies that operate at the speed of light means that the factors and issues that determine how and what we protect are like a living, breathing organism. It is always thinking, consuming, and growing in many different ways. First, the environment you work in is not a controlled and managed architecture of systems and software encased in a protected data center with limited exposure. From the interconnection of data platforms between organizations to the extended components of the Internet, and even through the introduction of self-learning and decision-making software, digital infrastructures and operations are affected by the speed at which the globe is connected. To further complicate these scenarios, the human element cannot be forgotten. Decisions and actions made by humans can readily and starkly change the environment you protect through a limitless number of potential social and physical interactions.

Speed is also a critical element in the pace of change. Technology from a pure business asset perspective is often measured in years. Today, however, through the adaptation of advanced technology for criminal means, some cyberdefensive technologies may have a realistic effectiveness of only less than a year, and in some cases, days. The speed of the threat actor, your own technology environment, and your ability to defend it is entirely predicated on the speed of change. That pace of change also includes the necessary changes to our speed of making decisions. The critical actions of stopping, impeding, disrupting, and responding to cybersecurity risk and events that affect privacy in a digital world force us to make rapid and accurate decisions never required in previous decades. New methods of data acquisition and analysis for decision support are critical aspects of creating these new strategies for success in a digital age.

Finally, speed is a significant financial lever. Beyond the normal cost considerations of time to acquisition, time to deployment, and other accounting mechanisms that manage the total operating cost of programs, projects, and operations, the reality is that the speed of the next generational digital economy and the infrastructures you protect will essentially shorten the lifespan of any given technology or capital investment in your cybersecurity defense architecture. Technology in a normalized information technology portfolio is rationalized into a three- to five-year investment with a depreciation scheme that has been the standard for multiple decades. However, with the advancement of the criminal use of technology, protective and defense technology lifespans have been greatly reduced.

Through artificial intelligence (AI) and machine learning (ML), and the use of intelligence services, criminals can now identify, recalculate, and react to technology in record time, sometimes reducing the expected lifetime of a cybersecurity asset and investment from years to months or even days.

This chapter focuses on strategies to understand, plan for, and affect the impact of speed on how you think about and execute your responsibilities in defending your business or agency.

THE STRATEGIC IMPERATIVES

You may think that to align to the change in speed, you simply have to move and act faster. Although in some cases that is true, there are better ways to approach operational acceleration and excellence in the face of dynamic change than fighting speed with more speed. How we think, act, and instrument our protection portfolio and operations are all key aspects in making this dynamic shift to operational enablement in the age of speed. The reality is that the world, technology, and threats will only continue to gain momentum, and if the only tool in your toolbox is an ability to run faster, you'll soon realize the limits of that way of thinking. Strategic imperatives such as risk, intelligence, transparency, and action-based decision making are additional tools that when learned, practiced, and mastered will create new capabilities that are far more effective and sustainable than speed itself.

THE PURPOSE OF YOUR MISSION

Before you can decide how to best apply your newfound strategic tools, you must know the "why" of the "how and when" you will need to use them. Every business, industry, and organization is different. The reasons you need to protect your organization and how you protect it are important. Why you do what you do feeds into your organizational risk appetite, defines your value at risk, and informs key decision-making points such as the level of accuracy needed versus speed and financial investments. Working through a normalized risk process, or even something as simple as sitting down with your business leaders and discussing the downstream residual impact of cybersecurity failure, will help inform and shape your mission parameters. Are you part of critical infrastructure? Would intellectual property loss ruin your business? Can your business eco-system outside your control cause irreparable damage? These questions and many others should be the foundational elements of how you describe your "business of security" and what your mission focus is. In turn, as you begin to consider the implication of the speed used against you and the speed that will help you accelerate your effectiveness, a deep understanding of your mission imperatives in alignment with the following five critical areas of planning will ensure your success in the hyperconnected and hyperspeed world in which you operate:

1. Understand your environment. Your success depends on your direct ability to succeed within the environment in which you operate. To do that, you need to understand your environment through transparency, knowledge, and access. This includes crucial elements such as understanding your critical assets, a holistic understanding of the resources and technology deployed through a comprehensive configuration management database (CMDB), and data flow diagrams that detail how information flows through your business. Just as important is the understanding of your third-party ecosystem, your supply chain, and how your services are in effect an integrated component of your customers' supply chains. Your ability to quickly understand the impact of any given event through this level of transparency is a fundamental component to being able to think and act quickly.

2. Drive safely at high speed. Your business success depends on speed to market and speed to respond. Your job is to get everyone there safely. This sense of speed enablement, or acting like the brakes on the car so your business is confident to go faster, requires a mature risk process. Effective risk programs have tiers of risk considerations and actions that create broad bands of flexibility and enable decision making based on preselected and informed risk formulas that serve as guiding principles. Spending time developing those mechanisms and allowing them to mature, educating your business, and just as importantly, educating your team will empower and enable all levels of the organization to recognize and facilitate business-based risk decision making at speed.

3. Plan ahead. Your opposition is well funded, utilizing capabilities and decisioning guiderails that are faster than yours. As in an old-fashioned gunfight, the first one to put lead on the target wins. This means that you need to be comfortable with rapid decision making based on accumulated knowledge rather than absolutes and have a "gun belt" of premade decisions, actions, and plans on your side. For instance, if you have a ransomware incident that is less than x% contained, do you shut down your data center? If you are suffering a financial crimes attack, will you call law enforcement, and if so, what agency and what is their number? Simple efforts such as tabletop exercises or defining preplanned partners significantly add to your ability to react fast in times of crisis. Prepositioned decision making agreed to by your leadership also ensures that your business will understand, support, and expect clear action and leadership from you when needed.

4. See the big picture. You need over-the-horizon threat modeling. I think everyone would agree that seeing a speeding train coming at you is better than getting run over by one. Unfortunately, too many people concentrate too myopically on their own operating environment and never look up long enough to see the train coming down the tracks. The use of intelligence services, information-sharing partnerships, and other mechanisms that give you a view outside your business into adjacent industries, like competitors or aligned ecosystems, are great ways to measure and prepare for the potential impact of issues not yet affecting your business. This greatly enhances your time to prepare, plan, and react to situations and opportunities that too often are missed because of insular behaviors.

5. Make the most of limited resources. Managing a business with limited return on investment (ROI), no profit, and smaller teams takes a different approach. Not every industry has the mission criticality of a nuclear power plant or the financial resources of the financial sector, and most of us never will. But just because we can't build large operating teams doesn't mean there aren't methodologies we can put forth to make us more nimble and adaptable. For instance, sometimes less is more. Often, many of the services we use are not employed on a constant basis, and

thus the costs associated with maintaining them or the skills needed to maintain them are wasted. Why not consider third-party contracting support for those services? And that's not just for limited services. If there are opportunities to leverage or utilize an ecosystem of providers to deliver core services at a lower cost, or to use automation and cloud-based services to maintain a more current and manageable portion of your operations, why not consider them? Sometimes, using simplified capabilities rather than an entire offering allows you to have those capabilities most necessary to react fast for the most critical issue, while maintaining a profit and loss (P&L) reasonable for your business.

THE SCIENCE OF RACING: ACCELERATION, DECELERATION, HARD BRAKING, AND KNOWING WHEN TO APPLY EACH

The natural attraction of humans to speed has been a part of our history from the time we could walk upright. Whether by foot across land, in boats on the water, or being pulled by an animal, speed was a part of our ancestors' survival plan, social fabric, and continuing intellectual quest. In modern times, billions of dollars are spent on the sport of racing just about everything. But one of the most complex integrations of speed and humans is that between human and automobile. Whether it is for the sport of a high-speed thrill around a track, across the land in amazing road races, or as a part of our survival on the part of those who protect society by driving fast to protect and save lives, people have gotten good at driving automobiles fast.

As with anything else, there is a science, skill, and methodology to manipulating a vehicle into speeds faster than the norm, and the failure of not understanding that typically has a devastating effect. For example, not understanding at what point of a curve to accelerate or brake can cause you to roll your vehicle, not understanding the dynamic force of an object in motion will cause you to lose control, and not understanding acceleration inertia delay will cause you to lose your race.

In cybersecurity, the same is true of a leader managing the objective of being effective in the face of speed. There are tools, skills, and a science to creating an effective approach to enable organizations to move fast and defend against an ever-changing opponent. Many elements can assist you in delivering against that objective, but the following are practical skills that you can start using today.

ELEMENTS OF FORCE MULTIPLICATION

The military has been using the term *force multiplication* since the beginning of organized military doctrine hundreds of years ago. The concept is relatively straightforward: Apply additional assets to your common core operating capability (people), and it accelerates and expands their effectiveness. For example, give an army the asset of intelligence, and its operating impact will be greater than it was before it had that information. Give ground forces the capability of GPS location, and they will be faster and more accurate than they were with the same amount of core resources prior to that technology.

As a practitioner in digital infrastructure leadership, you can enable your organization to strategically focus on the need for speed through the same use of force multiplication. By aligning to the elements of speed that most affect your mission scope, you can add levers that will multiply the abilities of your resources. Perhaps it's intelligence, automation, or new technology. In some cases, it may be the use of a third party or the ability to have access to data. Whatever it is, you have an opportunity to manipulate and accelerate your current capabilities to meet the need for speed through the simple application of resource elements, resource combinations, and resource alignment.

Inertia

Books have been written on the laws of motion, and great strides in science have been gained through the study of motion and speed. The fundamental laws of motion still apply, and the truth of the principle that "things in motion stay in motion" is undeniable. In the context of speed, cybersecurity, leadership, and your job, the ability to act fast starts with the basic ability to act. In this arena, inertia is counter to growing in capability and speed over time. Often, we wait too long to enable our organizations with capabilities because of limited funding, resources, or just wanting a plan that is 100 percent complete every time. This approach is not helpful, nor is it necessary, because it will inevitably result in being too late to begin to create a necessary capability at the time it is most needed.

A simple tool in the development of operational effectiveness in the face of speed is to create supporting services, resources, and capabilities aligned with the scope of your mission that will be most applicable in the core areas of prevention, detection, response, and recovery. The idea is not to create these capabilities at 100 percent, but rather to have a baseline operating framework, knowledge, and understanding that can be refined and used over time. By maintaining this aggregate line-level capability, ensuring you and your organization understand it, adding it to your concept of operations, and knowing not only how it is applied but how to grow it, you can implement resources faster than if you were starting from scratch. Even though they may be minimal in normal operations, your ability to grow them fast and apply them faster will be significantly greater than if you had to start from the beginning.

Prioritization

A key capability often missing in an organization's ability to execute at speed is its ability to prioritize. Although in our world, many if not most things seem to be equally critical, the reality is that there is always a pecking order and prioritization of action and attention, and recognizing that is crucial to making smart, informed, and rational decisions that enable speed. As an operational leader, you should always have these three priority lists on hand, updated, and ready to use in your decision-making process:

Critical Asset Protection Priorities. These are the assets, systems, processes, or functions that run your business. If you had only $100.00 to spend, what would you spend it on? This discussion should be inclusive of your business to ensure you understand what it takes to go to market, what enables your business to operate, and what key assets hold the most value to your company.

Risk Prioritization. This list is all about your focus. What projects are most critical to resolve your value-at-risk? Where can you deprioritize to affect other priorities, and where can you move resources to scale faster?

Urgent Action Defense Protocols. These are pre-negotiated/ decided actions for when things go wrong. In layman's terms, which part of the body can I cut off to save the head? When catastrophic issues occur, timely decisions are necessary to prevent further catastrophe. Who can order the shutdown of a business line, and when? What thresholds require automatic action, such as turning a data center dark? Who has the authority to call law enforcement if needed? The most critical part is to get these hard-to-make decisions on paper, including what would trigger them, and ensure agreement across the entirety of the business on how to execute them.

GETTING ON THE HIGHWAY AND GETTING UP TO SPEED

In an era in which digital enablement means digital impact at breakneck speeds, it is hard to forget that the bad guys only need to get it right once, and we are responsible for getting it right every time. The education, innovation, planning, convincing, implementation, and management of "all of these things" that enable us to protect our businesses or agencies (especially at scale) don't lend themselves to the term *speed*. But that is exactly how we must retool our thinking and operations to ensure the digital success of a very digital economy. Through the five-step methodology of Learn, Test, Accelerate, Validate, and Repeat, we can continue to inch ourselves toward a more progressive capability that includes speed as a binding strategy to success.

Learn

Understand your organization's ability to adapt to and operate within strategies that incorporate speed as a fundamental requirement, and work those job functions and requirements into every job description. Create opportunities for education, practice, and innovation for speed in delivery, change, response, and, just as importantly, decision making.

Test

Test your processes to ensure that they meet the speed requirements your mission prioritizes and your operating environment requires. Until they are put to the test, theories are just theories. Unless you test, stretch, and ensure your ability to adapt and respond at speed, you will be operating on false expectations, which never has a good outcome.

Accelerate

Incrementally add capabilities to drive acceleration. Perhaps it's the use of automation in data collecting, or the use of automated analytics to churn through that data. Maybe it's shedding old technologies, programs, or services that are not part of your priority list that enables you to act faster. Whatever it is, first understand why you are making the change and then create a measure to ensure that the change is meaningful and effective. Finally, hold yourself and your organization accountable to maintain that new capability.

Validate

Validation is the art of putting it all together. Once your organization is educated, instrumented, and ready to operate at high velocity, it's time to validate it. There is nothing that stops a potential disaster from occurring in real time better than conducting tabletop exercises (TTXs) of issues, incidents, decision making, or just about anything that happens in your business or agency. In fact, not only are these great learning and adjustment opportunities, but they are also incredible team-building exercises. Knowing that I can trust my skills and the skills of those with whom I work instills a tremendous amount of confidence, which in turn helps us all run, act, and execute faster.

Repeat

Nothing in this new digital business ecosystem is stagnant. "Complacency kills" is one of the first things that military and law enforcement officers are trained on. If your situation is changing but your tools, technologies, practices, and capabilities are not, you will be at the losing end of any battle. Avoid complacency by implementing a life-cycle approach to reviewing and improving on your adaptation toward becoming a speed-based organization.

OPERATING LIMITS FOR YOURSELF AND OTHERS

None of this happens in a vacuum. Your ability to apply these principles, operate in a speed-enabled environment, and deliver services in a next-generation digital ecosystem depends on people. Part of your growth, and that of your business, will be to understand the strengths and weaknesses of people and their ability to execute and adapt over time. Speed has no place if it is not integrated as a binding component of your strategy, because an organization that attempts it without a thoughtful, purposeful, and well-planned approach will fail.

Finally, base your success in cybersecurity operations on an advantageous application of speed in how you think, understand, plan, and execute to the digital world around you.

ABOUT THE CONTRIBUTOR

Roland Cloutier – SVP and CISO, ADP

As staff vice president and chief security officer (CSO) of ADP, Roland Cloutier brings understanding and knowledge of global protection and security leadership to one of the world's largest providers of human capital management solutions. With over 25 years of experience in the military, law enforcement, and commercial sectors, Cloutier is a leading expert in corporate and enterprise security, cyberdefense program development, and business operations protection. At ADP, Cloutier has functional and operational responsibility for cybersecurity, information protection, risk, workforce protection, crisis management, and investigative security operations worldwide.

Prior to ADP, Cloutier served as vice president and CSO of EMC, where he spearheaded protection of its worldwide business operations, including leadership of all information, business risk, crisis management, and investigative security operations across commercial and government sectors. He served as vice president of cybersecurity at AimNet Solutions. He has more than 14 years of experience in the military and federal law enforcement in global aerospace protection, fraud and diversion investigations, and special event protection, including an assignment at the 1996 Olympic Summer Games in Atlanta.

IS SPEED AN ADVANTAGE?
IT DEPENDS ON THE CONTEXT

Scott Charney, Microsoft

An old adage warns, "He who hesitates is lost." Put another way, speed is essential. Indeed, speed is most often viewed in a positive light, connoting everything from exhilaration (fast cars), to competitive advantage (faster stock trades), to greater efficiency (airplanes over buses). Yes, there may be drawbacks ("haste makes waste"), but forward we rush.

In information technology, speed is often synonymous with increased productivity. Moore's law, which noted that the number of transistors in a dense integrated circuit doubles approximately every two years, permits us to process more data in less time. Faster transmission speeds, from fiber to 5G, give us access to larger datasets in less time. Machine learning and AI permit us to leverage these other technologies and promise decisions that will be both better and faster.

While this paints a rosy picture, there is another adage about speed, one that conjures up notions of risk. Although it may be true that "he who hesitates is lost," we are often cautioned to "look before we leap." That is, we need to slow down and be more cautious when making decisions.

So, should we in fact look before we leap, even if those who hesitate are lost? Which piece of conventional wisdom is correct? Clearly, quickly embracing new technology can yield terrific benefits, even if new risks must be managed at the same time. But can speed be cause for alarm?

Which adage is correct depends on context, and in this regard, it may be helpful to consider three different, albeit simplified, scenarios. The first involves credit applications in which older processes are made more efficient through modernization; the second involves unlocking new, transformative capabilities through the introduction of autonomous vehicles; and the third involves international affairs and the potential use of autonomous lethal weapons.

CONTEXT: CREDIT APPLICATIONS

In the area of financial transactions and the issuing of credit cards, we once asked humans to collect and analyze datasets and then make a binary decision about whether to grant credit. Two of these tasks—collecting and analyzing data—might be relatively time consuming and labor intensive, even if making the actual credit decision was relatively quick. In a post-computerized world, the process may be far more thorough (involving more data), happen far more quickly, and may all be done by machine. Simply put, greater connectivity, faster transmission and processing speeds, and machine algorithms have streamlined the process, resulting in faster and potentially more accurate decisions at lower cost. Yes, there are challenges with this approach, ranging from privacy concerns to biased datasets to faulty algorithms, but with appropriate controls and oversight, the risk is manageable.

More than just increasing transaction processing, the speed with which data can be collected, analyzed, and acted on may serve to protect both consumers and banks. For example, by more quickly analyzing spending patterns, banks can more quickly detect anomalous transactions and alert consumers of potential fraud. Perhaps more interestingly, banks themselves benefit from new computer security protections, particularly as they embrace cloud-based services. The reason is simple: In the cloud, we can harness new security capabilities that reduce security response times so that they more closely track the speed of malware distribution. This is best explained by example. Defenders of networks have long highlighted the importance of information sharing. Using the Financial Services Information Sharing and Analysis Center (FS-ISAC) as an example, if Bank A sees an attack, it notifies the ISAC. The ISAC notifies other banks, which then look for indicators of compromise on their networks. Other sectors have ISACs as well.

Although this model works well, it has challenges. First, it requires information sharing, which happens well in some sectors but not as well in others. Second, information distribution and analysis can take time. Third, the information may not flow to all players (for example, in the case of the financial sector, smaller banks may be less engaged). By contrast, as banks move to the cloud, the speed of response can increase dramatically. For example, Microsoft's Advanced Threat Protection strips attachments from emails, runs them in detonation chambers, and looks for malware. If found, that malware can be searched for throughout the cloud. This means if Bank A is attacked, all other banks—and other customers outside the financial sector—can quickly be protected from that attack. Simply put, protections can be broadly deployed to more entities without information-sharing delays. Moreover, as more customers move to the cloud, the amount of telemetry increases and protections improve. Thus, in the context of these financial transactions, speed provides significant benefits.

CONTEXT: AUTONOMOUS VEHICLES

Autonomous vehicles, which have started cruising the streets of major cities, offer a long list of benefits, including safer streets, more efficient use of vehicles leading to less congestion, increased mobility for seniors, and more. Data collection and analysis speeds are again critical, especially as vehicles analyze data on roads crowded with other cars, bikes, pedestrians, and traffic lights. It is also important that such technologies leverage the cloud (where data from multiple sources can be stored and analyzed) but also make "local" decisions without the latency caused by transmitting data to and from the cloud (this is called the "intelligent cloud/intelligent edge" model).

At the same time, we will be presented with new risks as the technology matures and perhaps comes under attack. Indeed, as of December 17, 2018, the California Department of Motor Vehicles had received 124 Autonomous Vehicle Collision Reports, and there have been reports of researchers hacking automated vehicles. Still, while autonomous vehicles may not be completely "safe," they will, if correctly designed, undoubtedly be "safer": Autonomous vehicles can process data far more quickly than humans, they will not panic in an emergency situation, and they are unlikely to be distracted by cell phones.

CONTEXT: AUTONOMOUS LETHAL WEAPONS

It is in the third scenario, international relations and autonomous lethal weapons, that speed may pose risks to humanity itself. That is a dramatic statement to be sure, but one that is not alarmist when the future of technology is considered in a military context.

The problem is that human thinking and the processes humans have established to manage their international affairs do not map to Moore's law—we do not become exponentially faster over time.

In the last century, intercontinental ballistic missiles shortened military response times from days to minutes. Since then, the introduction of cyberwarfare capabilities has arguably reduced response times further. As General Joseph Dunford, the outgoing Chairman of the Joint Chiefs of Staff, noted in 2017, "The speed of war has changed, and the nature of these changes makes the global security environment even more unpredictable, dangerous, and unforgiving. *Decision space has collapsed and so our processes must adapt to keep pace with the speed of war* [emphasis added]." To take advantage of the remaining decision space, Dunford noted, there must be "a common understanding of the threat, providing a clear understanding of the capabilities and limitations of the joint force, and then establishing a framework that enables senior leaders to make decisions in a timely manner." This suggests the need for greater pre-decisional planning, from collecting better intelligence about adversaries' capabilities and intentions to better scenario planning so that decisions can be made more quickly.

At the same time that we attempt to adapt, we must also grapple with a fundamental question: As the need for speed increases, will humans delegate decision making—even in lethal situations—to machines? That humans will remain in the loop is not a foregone conclusion. With the creation of autonomous lethal weapons, some countries have announced new policies requiring a "human-in-the-loop" (see Department of Defense Directive Number 3000.09, November 12, 2012). Additionally, concerned individuals and organizations are leading calls for international treaties limiting such weapons (see https://autonomousweapons .org/). But as we have seen with cybersecurity norms, gaining widespread international agreement can be difficult, particularly when technology is new and countries do not want to quickly, and perhaps prematurely, limit their future activities. And as we have seen recently with chemical weapons, ensuring compliance even with agreed-upon rules can be challenging.

THE RISK

The risk here is twofold. The first relates to speed: If decision times collapse and outcomes favor those who are willing to delegate to machines, those who accept delay by maintaining adherence to principles of human control may find themselves disadvantaged. Second, there is the reality that humans will, over time, come to trust machines with life-altering decisions. Self-driving cars represent one example of this phenomenon. At first, self-driving vehicles required a human at the wheel "for emergencies." Later, automated vehicles with no steering wheel and no human driver were approved. While this may be, in part, because humans have proven to be poor at paying attention and reacting quickly in a crisis, experience and familiarity with machines may have also engendered complacency with automated vehicles, much as we have accepted technology in other areas of our lives. If this is correct, then humans may ultimately conclude that with decisional time shrinking, machines will make better decisions than the humans they serve, even when human lives are at stake.

ABOUT THE CONTRIBUTOR

Scott Charney – Vice President of Security Policy, Microsoft

Scott Charney is vice president for security policy at Microsoft. He serves as vice chair of the National Security Telecommunications Advisory Committee, as a commissioner on the Global Commission for the Stability of Cyberspace, and as chair of the board of the Global Cyber Alliance. Prior to his current position, Charney led Microsoft's Trustworthy Computing Group, where he was responsible for enforcing mandatory security engineering policies and implementing security strategy. Before that, he served as chief of the Computer Crime and Intellectual Property Section (CCIPS) at the U.S. Department of Justice (DOJ), where he was responsible for implementing DOJ's computer crime and intellectual property initiatives. Under his direction, CCIPS investigated and prosecuted national and international hacker cases, economic espionage cases, and violations of the federal criminal copyright and trademark laws. He served three years as chair of the G8 Subgroup on High-Tech Crime, was vice chair of the Organization of Economic Cooperation and Development (OECD) Group of Experts on Security and Privacy, led the U.S. Delegation to the OECD on Cryptography Policy, and was co-chair of the Center for Strategic and International Studies Commission on Cybersecurity for the 44th Presidency.

22

2
CONNECTIVITY

> "The convenience of IoT devices comes at a cost: a vastly expanded attack surface."
>
> *Brian Talbert,*
> *Alaska Airlines*

> "The drive to connect is an unstoppable force within cyberspace."
>
> *Chris Inglis,*
> *Former Deputy Director, NSA*

Enabling and protecting safe connectivity is the core mission of cybersecurity. At its most basic definition, cybersecurity is about allowing or denying access to information. That is how information is protected. And while the extraordinary adoption of the Internet may certainly have been powered by recognition of the incredible benefits of connectivity, it comes with risk.

The triumph of collaboration and connectivity coded into the core of the Internet has been manipulated to attack it. As the connectivity of the early Internet broadened—and with it, new targets—so too did the breadth and depth of the attacks. Every cyberattacker has at least one substantial advantage. As Sun Tzu succinctly stated in *The Art of War*, "In conflict, direct confrontation will lead to engagement and surprise will lead to victory." Threat actors can choose when and where to strike.

When they do attack, they strike from multiple places, focusing their multifaceted approaches on your points of weakness—discovered through relentless attempts to breach the infrastructure that houses whatever data is most valuable for their own intent.

Each attacker may learn from other attacks about what worked, what didn't, and where the valuable data resides. This is one reason attackers often hold an advantage over defenders.

An integrated defense—a staple of high-end security strategies in all other areas and fields of protection—is an often-neglected cybersecurity fundamental. Too many point solutions offer insufficient defenses that leave the network vulnerable once penetrated. Maginot Line–style defenses, no matter how sophisticated, that focus only on keeping attackers out of the network are doomed to fail just as their namesake failed in 1940—only much, much faster.

The necessity of connectivity mirrors the importance of speed in cybersecurity: Less integration creates more vulnerabilities. For effective cybersecurity, defenders should take the same integrated approach as the architects of the early Internet did (and the attackers who soon followed). The architecture that underpins security must match the cooperative fabric of flexible integration mechanisms of the Internet as a whole. Cybersecurity architects must design security that leverages the connectivity of all defensive components. By leveraging the connectivity among defensive components, defenders can field an entire team of security players from within and beyond their organizations.

Just as security must utilize and enable speed, it must also have and empower strong connectivity.

With properly designed security, defenders can achieve the core mission of cybersecurity: Enabling and protecting safe connectivity and allowing or denying access to information. Defenders who adopt such an integrated defense will gain an advantage.

MANAGING THE INTENSIFYING CONNECTIVITY OF THE IOT ERA

Brian Talbert, Alaska Airlines

Over the past several years, the reach, scale, and depth of digital connectivity has intensified so dramatically that it has fundamentally changed our conceptions and definitions of what being connected even means.

While many outside the fields of security and information technology still talk of greater levels of digital connection in the context of human beings communicating with one another, chief information security officer (CISOs) and their teams understand that that is merely a small, visible ripple on the very surface of today's hyperconnected world. Things and machines connecting with each other is the bigger picture of connectivity—which gets exponentially bigger each day and now borders on the immeasurable and the unimaginable. And, as many IT teams can attest, it is also increasingly unmanageable—at least by people alone, anyway.

That's because, as the Internet of Things (IoT) grows, the majority of connectivity today occurs between devices. With aims of greater efficiency, cost savings, and convenience, everything from cameras to lightbulbs to household appliances is being augmented with digital capabilities, allowing these things to connect to the Internet and to each other to share relevant information.

It is a level of new-normal functionality that creates a momentum powered by consumer demand: As more smart devices are manufactured, more people come to expect a new device to have that capability. And more companies scramble to enhance their product lines with technology—whether or not they have experience with it.

Today, the IoT comprises more than 8.4 billion devices—with a projection of 20.4 billion deployed by 2020.

What consumers and manufacturers often don't realize, though, is that the convenience of IoT devices comes at a cost. And that cost is a significant one: A vastly expanded attack surface comprising millions of devices with minimal security—manufactured by companies with little experience in securing digital technology.

Many IoT devices can be easily compromised to gain access to a network, or they can be chained together to create a huge increase in attack power. Layer in cloud services for managing these devices, and what results is a level of vulnerability that is ripe for attack. Because of the minimal security of the devices themselves, that attack can be incredibly destructive with little expertise required. You don't need to be a civil engineer to topple dominos, and you don't need to be a master cybercriminal to harness the IoT into a botnet.

Take the Mirai botnet, for example. In October 2016, a massive denial-of-service attack left most of the East Coast of the United States without Internet access. The attack was so large and so disruptive—a digital tsunami of 1.1 TB of data per second—authorities first suspected it was an act of war by a rogue state or enemy nation. It turned out to be a couple of college kids with novice-level hacking skills and the desire for more competitive advantage in Minecraft.

And *that* gives an indication of the scale, power, and risk of today's landscape of connectivity.

Mirai harnessed the combined power of IoT devices—specifically routers, cameras, DVRs, and printers—by scanning for open ports, then taking over the devices with a few lines of code that cycled through 61 common unchanged default passwords. In the first 20 hours, it captured 65,000 devices—doubling the amount every 76 minutes, growing to a peak of up to 300,000 infections. All told, 164 countries were hit.

As the IoT continues to spread, IT teams are now faced with two primary connectivity challenges within their organizations. They must contend with devices brought in by casual end users, such as connected speakers that someone puts on their desk. And they must also secure business-use devices such as security cameras, office equipment, and facility equipment.

As enormous a challenge as this presents, it is important for IT teams to recognize that for the most part people are not using these devices with disregard for security. It is a new technology, and people simply don't know the risks it presents. Still, regardless of intent, IT has to treat every device as untrusted until it is verified.

These results create issues of incredible complexity and scale. With the IoT, as the surface area grows, it also becomes less and less defined. It is difficult to discern where a network begins and where it ends when literally thousands of devices can access it—and it also serves as an access point to anyone who can surpass the limited security of the devices.

Unfortunately, in such a complex and expanding environment, many organizations simply lack the visibility needed. As a result, they don't know what they don't know, much less how to secure everything they can detect.

As this new reality intensifies, it will create a primary need for better tooling for visibility; network access controls; and stronger threat detection, prediction, and response capabilities. But even with all these important defenses in place, it is not enough. The IoT is simply too vast to be managed and mitigated by people alone.

As the scale increases and vulnerabilities become more complex, the standard manual human security operations center or threat defense responders will no longer be a viable first line of defense. Success will depend on deeper machine intelligence and automation. That said, investing in the technology is only a small part of the solution—and even then, it requires a great deal of insight and understanding of the network and the greater connectivity landscape to design a model that is appropriate.

To create scalable and sustainable solutions, it's important to recognize that these problems are organizational—not individual or team-based. Before designing security strategies, executive leadership needs to fully understand the importance of addressing the problem systematically, with a cross-functional, cross-divisional program.

This program will have to include good security policies and architecture review processes. But it will also have to address the new reality that software engineers and application developers can no longer assume that they are building on top of a naturally secure and private underlying network. Secure coding practices must become so deeply ingrained in the philosophy, processes, and deployment pipelines that they simply become a part of the natural practices of the developer. The bar is high here, and these individuals must understand everything from user authentication to data obfuscation and secure data transport. Organizations will quickly see the need to develop repeatable patterns with consistent, standardized, and reusable security code libraries.

In short, addressing the connectivity challenge will require even deeper levels of cooperation and collaboration across an organization, from the coding level up. And to do that effectively requires both funding and expertise. As many CISOs and their teams know, this is a square one reality that they must advocate and evangelize to decision makers in the C suite, and even to the board of directors.

As daunting as organizational and cultural change can be, it is important to start where you are and move forward from there. If a company doesn't have experience and expertise in these areas, there may be an inclination to delay planning. But it is better to take modest first steps rather than to do nothing. External assistance from a trusted adviser will often prove valuable, even if only to provide a roadmap that an organization can follow. Find those outside experts and advocates as necessary and then scale their services to fit the budgets available. If nothing else, doing so will begin to build the network of strategic partnerships that will become increasingly needed and valuable.

Funding limitations are a reality all CISOs and their teams must contend with, but the cost of securing the enterprise is too often considered just on the basis of hard allocations—the tools, time, and resources needed. Intangibles and opportunity costs must be considered as well. Is the return on the investment of resources to build that next application feature greater than the costs of an inevitable breach and the reputation and brand harm it has created? These can be complex and challenging questions for any organization, but they are the types of questions that all companies should become more comfortable answering.

And they pale in comparison to the complexities and challenges of ever-expanding and complicated networks, sprawling outward with more and more consumer-level devices. The longer an organization delays, though, the more difficult the path forward could be.

The telltale sign of a need to focus on these areas is the recognition that you haven't already. Too many companies use a breach as an indicator—perhaps not understanding the substantial risks involved. If you are not already implementing secure coding practices, if you are not already looking for the presence of unauthorized IoT devices joining the network, you are already behind the curve. It's almost a certainty that you have devices and code that are easily compromised. The fact that you don't know for sure indicates how great the risk can be—and reveals how critical visibility, and the insights it provides, is to strategically managing and mitigating the intensifying levels of connectivity in the IoT era.

ABOUT THE CONTRIBUTOR

Brian Talbert – Director of Network and Connectivity Solutions, Alaska Airlines

Brian Talbert leads the Network and Security Engineering division of Alaska Airlines. Brian is responsible for the strategic direction and platform development that secures the infrastructure responsible for flying 33 million passengers per year to over 115 destinations. In the 20 years prior to Alaska Airlines, Brian worked for leading service providers and enterprises building solutions and organizations that drive information security technology.

CYBERSPACE: MAKING SOME SENSE OF IT ALL

Chris Inglis, Former NSA Deputy Director

Cyber. Few words enjoy more widespread use across languages and cultures. Used variously as a noun and an adjective, it conveys more meaning in five letters than the vast majority of its counter-parts in any language. As a direct consequence of the varied uses of the term, many discussions involving cyber fail in the simplest goal of human communication, namely to ensure that the participants understand or mean the same things in their attempt to communicate.

To that end, this section lays out a foundation for understanding the essential elements of cyber as a literal place—hereafter referred to as cyberspace. Of note, the term *cyberspace* includes, but is not limited to, the sum of hardware, software, and interconnections that are collectively referred to as the Internet.

One of the most important things that the curiosity-minded pioneers of the Scientific Revolution did was to intellectually (and sometimes literally) peel apart a common thing—a leaf, a parasite, a hillside—to better understand what it was made of and how its parts were connected, trying to understand how each layer worked and helped govern the whole.

THE CASE FOR CYBERSPACE AS A DOMAIN

Various writers have argued that cyberspace is not a domain, since it is man-made and therefore lacking in the enduring and unchanging properties inherent in domains resulting from immutable laws of nature, time, and space. The case for cyberspace as a domain is found in the simple fact that, on the whole, it has unique properties that can be understood, or purposely altered, only by studying cyber as a thing in its own right. It is a center point that is the result of integrating diverse technologies and human actions, while it also serves as a resource enabling widespread collaboration and integration.

TEASING OUT THE CONSTITUENT PARTS OF CYBERSPACE

Mention the term *cyberspace* in any otherwise polite conversation and the mind's eye of the listener immediately conjures up a jumbled mess of technology, wires, people, and communications racing across time and space or stored in vast arrays of storage devices. The resulting rat's nest of technology, people, and procedures then offers such a complicated and undistinguished landscape that, within the context of the conversation, further use of the word *cyber* could mean anything, and often does. It is important, then, to tease out the constituent parts of cyberspace to describe their characteristics, their contribution to the overall effect, and their relationship to each other. This, in turn, will yield a taxonomy or roadmap that allows focused discussions about discrete aspects of cyberspace that can be considered in the context of the whole.

This section attempts to describe, in context, discrete facets of cyberspace along the following lines: Physical geography, communications pathways, controlling logic and storage, devices, and people. It's important to note that cyberspace is not actually built this way, any more than a human being grows from embryo to adult according to the taxonomy laid out in *Gray's Anatomy*. But the understanding of the unique characteristics of cyberspace and how it is likely to operate under various scenarios is the goal here, not a description of how to build it anew.

THE BOOKENDS: GEOGRAPHY AND PEOPLE

Like any domain, cyberspace is sandwiched between the earth that hosts it and the people who would use it. Given humankind's long experience with both (that is, geography and people), this fact is both a source of comfort and a vexation. To see why, we need only consider each in turn.

The Geography Layer

Human knowledge of geography often informs an understanding or sense of how things move from one place to another and how authorities for various activities are allocated across vast stretches of geography. What schoolchild has not memorized the axiom that the shortest distance between two points is a straight line? However comforting the thought, cyberspace is only vaguely aware of the rule, finding it inefficient to blindly route communications around the globe based solely on the physical distances involved. To wit, an email being sent from New York to San Francisco in the middle of an American workday will compete for bandwidth with the massive flows attendant to financial trades and transfers, logistical coordination among shippers and suppliers, personal communications, and even the latest YouTube craze-du-jour of cats playing pianos, and might be sent from New York to San Francisco through other countries.

Software running on the millions of computers controlling the storage devices and pathways of cyberspace constantly senses the status of various routes, sometimes sending communications around the planet on pathways that are underutilized to arrive at a destination only miles away in the shortest time possible. Not understanding the informal but influential rules that inform cyberspace routing means users may be forever surprised at the paths their communications take and where they may actually reside while being stored until the owner accesses them. In most cases, this counterintuitive phenomenon represents a user-preferred feature, in that the details of routing and storage are handled automatically without requiring the user to master and direct complex aspects of technology, communication routes, and traffic flows. But the downside is obvious for users who assume that their data is safe from prying eyes or other risks because it is stored or routed through technologies and routes that are wholly within the users' field of view.

Experience in the geography layer also informs a sense of who is responsible for what. Cyberspace cannot ignore the reality that laws, policies, and treaties that govern human affairs are almost always tied to geography. This reality becomes particularly challenging when trying to sort out which laws pertain to property that is shared across countries or, more significantly, what jurisdiction pertains to an activity that crosses space and time in milliseconds, only to take a different route seconds later.

A case in point helps to illustrate this challenge. If a person in country A (for instance, the imaginary nation of Inglisia) hacks into a computer in country B (the imaginary country of Quadeland) and uses that hacked machine to attack computers in a third country (the United States), then which laws and property rights pertain? Can the victim who owns the US-based machine reach out and hack back at the machine in Quadeland? If so, do the laws of the United States or Quadeland apply? What if the victim is a resident of a fourth country? In this way, rules based on geography quickly break down and require a model that allows users to work across borders, a model that must satisfy the highest common denominator of the expectations of privacy, due diligence, and other user expectations embodied in the laws of the various jurisdictions. The issue of jurisdiction in cyberspace is only now being reconciled to the physical (based on geography) and practical (how it really works) realities of cyberspace.

The People Layer

The top layer reflects the fact that people are an integral component of cyberspace. Indeed, people (rather than technology) explain the dynamic, ever-changing nature of cyberspace as users employ its various capabilities in ways that depart from, and even confound, the expectations of component, software, and system designers.

There are several important implications attendant to this layer of the model under discussion. First, while constitutions, laws, and policies typically allocate rights to people based on their citizenship or physical location, cyberspace allocates access and privileges based on the identities formed and authenticated in cyberspace. The old joke of one dog saying to another that "on the Internet, no one knows you're a dog" remains truer than not across broad swaths of the domain. Although there is often a reconciliation of a person's status between the physical and virtual worlds, cyberspace rules prevail in the determination of privilege in accessing resources in and through cyberspace. This reality makes the application of laws defined in the physical world to its cyberdoppelgänger challenging, especially when identities in cyberspace are spoofed or are indeterminate as a result of the users' employment of applications designed to cloak their identity so that their actions can be taken without attribution (sometimes referred to as "anonymity" features). This is not to say that the distinctions defined in the physical world do not matter, or that they do not have jurisdiction in cyberspace, but merely that it is often difficult, and sometimes impossible, to identify users or assign attribution within the current capabilities of cyberspace. This difficulty has significant implications for any desire to attribute actions in cyberspace so that identification of who took a certain action can be achieved and serve as a basis for meting out the appropriate rewards or consequences attendant to the action.

The Circuit Layer

The circuit layer of the model depicts the literal pathways that communications take to make their way from one place to another within cyberspace. Taken together with the geography and people layers of the unfolding model, this layer represents the sum total of what would have once been referred to as the telecommunications domain.

Long before the advent of the computers, sophisticated software, and ubiquitous wireless devices that power today's Internet, the telecommunications domain offered a simple and reliable means for a given communication to be sent and received across far-flung stretches of the earth. In that day and age, the flow of communications was still directly and manually controlled by human beings. A person would literally choose whether, when, and how a message would be sent by dialing a phone, faxing a message, or keying a microphone to initiate a communication. The communication would then flow from one location to its destination along a generally straight line, often a dedicated path (or link), and would be immediately received by the intended recipient on the other end. In effect, the communication would be manually pushed from one location to another and would be at risk of disclosure to a third party only during the time it was in transit. Before and after the transmission, the communication would reside in a sanctuary of sorts: In a person's mind, in a desk drawer, or if need be, in a safe.

As the Internet began to spread its web using these same methods of communication and as the means of transmission, storage, and presentation to communicants around the world increased exponentially in variety, scope, and scale, the telecommunications domain was transformed in several important ways.

First, decisions about when and how communications would flow across the spaces between two communicants were delegated to computers embedded with increasing regularity in communication and storage devices.

Second, communications were *stored* for later retrieval by intended recipients or as "on the web" resources for the sender. Some readers may recall that the initial novelty of email was less in the fact that it connected two people living great distances from each other than in the fact that it allowed people to communicate without both having to be "on line" at the same time. The communication would simply wait for the intended recipient to request access to the stored communication—forever, if necessary.

Finally, the richness of communications steadily increased to the point that a given communication began to represent more than a simple reflection of thoughts or values held outside the domain. The communication, in transit or stored, began to be valuable in its own right, often as a unique representation of thoughts, wealth, and treasure. Financial transfers, cash accounts, corporate secrets, and pictures are now all stored, *often with no backup in the physical world*, in cyberspace. Gone are the days when colored rectangles of paper, printed stock certificates, and passbooks served as the primary means to represent financial assets (it is likely that the term *passbook*, in wide use throughout the 1970s, is completely unknown to those born thereafter). Passbooks have been replaced by ones and zeros that are stored, traded, earned, and lost in cyberspace alone.

The Control Logic Layer

The control logic layer represents the logic embedded in the billions of devices, computers, and other smart components comprising the physical infrastructure of cyberspace. While the spread and ubiquitous presence of this logic make it impossible to literally observe a physical manifestation of this layer, its effect is no less real and is, more importantly, essential to an understanding of the behaviors of cyberspace's fundamental properties. Indeed, the extraordinary efficiency of cyberspace in routing, storing, correlating, and rerouting increasingly massive and complex flows of information is almost wholly dependent on the delegation of these tasks to the logic embedded in this layer.

This is the layer that makes it possible for computers to interact with one another without human interaction as they make the myriad choices needed to sustain coherent and orderly interactions among billions of human and machine users interconnected through cyberspace. The result gives rise to what is increasingly referred to as the Internet of Things, or IoT: Machines interacting with other machines, all programmed to anticipate and exceed the expectations of people who have little direct involvement with, or even understanding of, the technological complexities involved.

The Device Layer

The device layer completes the model. This is perhaps the most visible component of cyberspace, since devices connect users to the services available within and from cyberspace. They include personal computing devices, smartphones, desktops, tablets, and navigation units—an ever increasing and diverse mix of hardware, software, and ubiquitous apps. Their role is to capture, present, and manipulate information according to the user's preferences and the designer's specifications. Importantly, the latter of these two influences is not always evident, as these devices capture and transmit information far beyond the communications themselves in order to better enable the routing, storage, and recovery of the data entrusted to them by their owners (for instance, the so-called metadata, which includes routing information and other attributes such as geolocation, the specifications of operating and system software being employed, and so forth).

And as these devices become increasingly mobile (keeping the people who employ them connected to cyberspace and its panoply of services, regardless of the location of either the device or the user), the once straightforward task of associating a device with a person or a location has become a much more complicated affair. Attendant changes in the underlying economic model of how service providers charge for their wares have enabled even greater user and device agility by replacing per-call and location-based charges with flat-rate plans that simply charge users for access to global communications services anywhere in the world. Legal regimes that determine privacy rules or the status of property rights based on the physical location of a device now have to sort out the complex reconciliation of the data, device, and person, which may be actively and richly associated with one another, despite their being physically located in three (or more) disparate locations. Coupled with the reality of one person employing multiple devices, often concurrently, the actions associated with a single individual may be manifested in cyberspace as a collection of personas operating simultaneously in multiple locations across the planet. The consequence is a legal regime dependent on tenuous mapping of the physical to the virtual world, and there is ambiguity about which nation-state's rules should be employed in determining what constitutes reasonable behaviors and acceptable consequences for exceeding them.

THE IMPORTANCE OF THE VERTICAL AND THE VIDEO

As imperfect as any static representation of cyberspace might be, the model is now complete. The components of the model have been layered in a manner that presents the whole of cyberspace as if captured in a still photograph. But although it is useful to consider any particular layer in isolation in understanding the building blocks of cyberspace, its operations can only be understood by analyzing the interaction of and between the layers as users and processes leverage cyberspace to achieve their end purposes. To wit, whereas it is easy to perceive that cyberspace enables one user to communicate directly with another (an activity that may be perceived to take place horizontally across the people layer of this model), the reality is that users interact with their devices. Those devices connect to one another using communication pathways heavily influenced by controlling logic and so forth, thus effecting a flow of data and actions that is more vertical than it is horizontal—up and down the layered stack. And although it is tempting to consider cyberspace as being principally comprised of the technology components of the stack (the middle three layers), the whole can only be understood by considering these layers and their intimate relationship with the outer two layers: People and geography.

Insofar as a hinge makes little sense in the absence of both the door and the wall, so it is with cyberspace and its intimate weave of people, technology, and geography. It is also impossible to exaggerate the dynamic and roiling nature of these vertical connections as communications, transactions, modifications, and additions surge up and down, to and from, across the length and breadth of cyberspace. The result is very much like a living organism, varying in character and scope from moment to moment, defying all attempts to statically define its character or its properties. This latter point has significant implications for security insofar as the constant creation and lapse of connections combines with the inexorable transformation of software, hardware, and user behaviors to make the task of defending cyberspace quite literally the defense of a moving target. And so it is that the metaphor of a video constitutes a truer character of the result than does a still photograph. Put another way, the dynamic and ever-changing interactions between the layers must be considered to understand and, more importantly, predict the true nature of cyberspace in action.

IMPLICATIONS

When considered as a whole, the model offers a means to understand properties that derive from the interaction of the constituent pieces. Four key attributes come immediately to the fore:

More than Technology

As tempting as it is to think of cyberspace as technology alone, it is impossible to understand, predict, or meaningfully influence its operations without considering the impact of people, geography, and the policies and practices that attend to them.

Characterized by Convergence

Cyberspace is characterized by a massive convergence of people, technology, and data on an exponential scale. The model would suggest that this convergence occurs on any given layer and between all the layers. More importantly, when you connect to cyberspace, it may be understood that the whole of it connects to you. Security professionals strive to reduce or mitigate unwanted connections, but the drive to connect is an unstoppable force within cyberspace. This leads to the increasing use of the term IoT to describe a seemingly inexorable trend to connect everything to everything—refrigerators, cars, power plants, and more—all connected to, in and through cyberspace. As a result, system designer and user choices about whether and how to connect must be driven by an up-front consideration of the implications of convergence versus an approach that says "I'll solve that problem when I get to it" (users *get* that problem when they connect to it). Furthermore, as previously noted, convergence and geography do not easily mix in a world that applies distinct and different rules based on physical location. Cyberspace will require both collaboration and normalization across these boundaries, though clarity on the part of those wielding jurisdiction based on geography regarding locally expected behaviors and consequences would be a valuable down payment to reconciliation across locales.

Wealth, Treasure, and More

Cyberspace quite literally contains—more than simply referencing or coordinating the management of—wealth and treasure. And given the enormous efficiencies offered in synchronizing the aspirations and actions of both people and systems, cyberspace is increasingly used to coordinate and carry out essential functions of critical systems, from electrical power generation to financial markets to diplomacy, collaboration, and even the conduct of war. As noted by Dr. Mark Hagerott of the United States Naval Academy's Cyber Center, a transformation in human affairs is taking place in which *sensing, thinking,* and *acting,* even in physical space, are increasingly delegated to the web of hardware and software serving human endeavors across the length and breadth of cyberspace. Humans' natural desire to impose rational controls on the result will succeed only if we move beyond creating rules about technology to crafting broader rules of governance for the interaction of people, technology, and systems (taking into consideration rules and policies rooted in geography).

Ever Changing, Never Secure

The impressive performance of technology in massively improving processing power, bandwidth, and user experience across the past 50 years of the silicon revolution is widely understood as an iconic representation of the times (sometimes referenced as Moore's law for hardware, but there have also been exponential improvements in software, visualization, and the collaboration that collectively aids in pushing cyberspace capacity to new heights). Less well appreciated is the fact that changes in features, capabilities, and behaviors are driven as much or more from the bottom up as from the top down by a virtual army of entrepreneurs. The result of this and unsynchronized changes in user behaviors and software (which often lag behind or precede changes in hardware) make it almost impossible to define and impose a comprehensive and enduring description of how things behave, let alone work, in cyberspace. This can rightly be considered a feature for those who await the next marvel from their favorite technology providers, but this same attribute makes the prospect of defending the wealth and treasure held within cyberspace, and the critical systems and processes dependent on the resilience and integrity of cyberspace, a virtual tail chase. Every change to technology, software, or user behavior portends a possible tear in the fabric of security overlaying the whole. The reality of this inexorable and unsynchronized change offers a fundamental choice as to whether security will be considered as a primary or a secondary feature in the continued transformation of cyberspace. This author suggests that it must be the former and that the security implied by the services of confidentiality, integrity, and availability must be thoroughly considered when any technology, service, or capability is being designed or introduced. Moreover, security must consider all of the contributing factors, encompassing all five layers of the model. Issues of policy, law, and ethics attach to the people and geography layers, which cannot be separately defined from the middle three (technology-only) layers.

But although the challenge of securing cyberspace may be a bridge too far, it is a domain of extraordinary interest that can and must be made defensible and, in turn, *actually* defended and supported through the employment of means and methods both in and outside of cyberspace itself. Useful analogs may be found in other complex manmade systems, such as those employed by the aviation industry, which has, over time, introduced a system of both technology innovation and governance that fosters continued transformation and capacity generation while imposing a requirement that the security implications of each new addition be considered and thoroughly engineered up front and by design, rather than after the fact. Cyberspace would do well to emulate this approach, though the immediate problems will be that domains do not govern themselves and that the present roles and responsibilities for driving and implementing security solutions remain fractured across organizations and sectors.

As stunning as the changes wrought by cyberspace have been to date, trends suggest an even greater transformation ahead. The pace will only increase anywhere and, increasingly, everywhere on the planet. And while the cyberspace domain can and must continue to be an engine of innovation and a means of global collaboration in support of private or public interests, the opportunities afforded by these trends must be accompanied by the exercise of responsibility across engineering, operations, and governance in fair measure to the value that is derived from, stored in, and leveraged from cyberspace.

ABOUT THE CONTRIBUTOR

John C. (Chris) Inglis – Former NSA Deputy Director

Chris Inglis is a former deputy director of the National Security Agency, currently serving as the Looker Distinguished Visiting Professor of Cyber Studies at the United States Naval Academy. He began his career at the NSA as a computer scientist in the National Computer Security Center and was promoted to the agency's Senior Executive Service in 1997. While at the NSA, he served in a variety of senior leadership assignments, including eight years as its chief operating officer, responsible for guiding strategy, operations, and policy.

A 1976 graduate of the US Air Force Academy and retired Brigadier General in the US Air Force, Inglis holds advanced degrees in engineering and computer science from Columbia University, Johns Hopkins University, and the George Washington University. From 2014 to 2018, Inglis served on or co-chaired Department of Defense Science Board Studies on cyber-resilience, cyberdeterrence, and cyberstrategy. He is a member of the Strategic Advisory Groups for the United States Strategic Command, the Director of National Intelligence, and the National Security Agency. Inglis is a managing director at Paladin Capital Group and serves on the boards of FedEx, KeyW, and Huntington Bank.

ELEMENTARY SHORTFALLS:
THE THINGS WE DIDN'T GET RIGHT AT THE BEGINNING

Because the Internet represents one of the most astounding innovations in the history of human evolution, its originators are often so revered that their staggering shortsightedness gets a pass. But when we pause to reflect, it is baffling that such visionary computer scientists—whose insights into the power and possibility of digital connectivity were powerful enough to change the course of history—could overlook or not address the most basic question about their invention: what if this really catches on?

It is sadly ironic that the three things that cause the most havoc in the cybersecurity domain are ones that network operators have the most control over.

UNANSWERED QUESTIONS

Today, nearly every cybersecurity expert and executive is living in the havoc of the answer. When a communication platform designed by and for a tight circle of academics and engineers is rapidly expanded for global public use by billions of people, incredible challenges result, along with fundamental questions that should have been more effectively addressed.

For example, authentication. If this really catches on:

- How will it be possible to authenticate who is who and what is what?
- How can we validate the identity of users to dictate and restrict their access across this vast network?
- How will we authenticate software to operating systems, operating systems to hardware, or software to software?
- In a system structured around the principle of trust, what happens when nothing is trustworthy?

For example, maintenance. If this really catches on and spreads beyond the confines of high-level military and academic use cases:

- Who will be the police, the doctors, the civil engineers, and the maintenance workers?

- How will we be able to recruit, train, and consistently, methodically advance the skillsets of the workforce necessary to ensure proper functioning of this innovation?
- How will we tier, organize, and classify this workforce—and what are the potential ramifications of a vast, hyperconnected system without sufficient human resources to protect and maintain it?

For example, protection. In this digital utopia of human connection:

- Do we risk it becoming a digital dystopia—a collapsed information state that creates a vacuum for the most unscrupulous?
- Could we be creating a model of extremely efficient contagion—a volatile potential chain reaction of fraud, grift, and vulnerability?
- How will we be able to identify vulnerabilities and provide the necessary solutions to mitigate them?
- How will we distribute those solutions, who will implement them, and how can we ensure that it is done correctly?

These unaddressed questions led to inherent vulnerabilities that are built into the DNA of Internet security. In turn, the vulnerabilities have led to repeated patterns of compromise, settling for some measure of security so as to achieve satisfactory performance. The result has been deep-seated weaknesses that have shaped the tangible paradigms of digital compromise. As we will see in the next three chapters, these fundamental structural flaws form the common denominators of nearly all attacks and create the most intractable challenges in the cybersecurity domain.

The greater, overarching trajectory of cybersecurity becomes clear when we analyze what happened when these deep-seated weaknesses proliferated across the global Internet.

- If fixes are ignored or fumbled, will the liabilities remain contained within the confines of those who didn't make the suggested improvements?
- Or, in a hyperconnected system, will one individual or organizational error create a foothold and safe haven from which to attack others?

Network operators need not be exquisitely insightful at guessing foreign threats or omnipresent in detecting network intrusions. As the chapters in Part II make clear, if they master the issues of authentication, patching, and user training, they can develop a cybersecurity strategy that will succeed.

3

AUTHENTICATION

> "The truth is, we actually enjoyed a higher degree of authentication in the past using a physical signature or a stamp than we do today in the digital world using ones and zeros."
>
> *Mike McConnell,*
> *former Director of*
> *National Intelligence*

> "We will soon no longer be able to trust the network itself without modern authentication."
>
> *Shannon Lietz,*
> *Intuit*

Authentication is the security process that validates the identity of an individual, system, or entity. From the very beginning of the Internet—in both philosophy and digital infrastructure—authentication was a neglected necessity. This neglect created a pervasive weakness that has metastasized into the primary methodology for hackers to access protected data.

As the Internet began and developed within an isolated community—shaped by principles of trust governed by tightly controlled access—it is understandable but agonizing to modern security practitioners that trustworthy authentication, for instance, lagged behind. Why focus on authenticating users when everyone on the burgeoning networks had security clearances and tightly specific, highly visible approved uses?

- Lack of trustworthy authentication has been the bane of security since the Internet's inception.
- Authentication needs are many: People to hardware, software to operating system, operating system to hardware, hardware to hardware, software to software.
- Trustworthy authentication remains elusive. Failed authentication is the common denominator found in nearly every digital breach, crime, and exploitation, from theft and harassment to state-sponsored espionage and terrorism.

When approaching cybersecurity as a science, we must account for the evolution of scientific thought. That evolution represents the refinement of science—in terms of both the scientific process itself, as well as the information and facts it reveals.

Consider that for more than 1,500 years, astronomy was based on Ptolemy's theory of geocentricism—the theory that the sun, stars, and all other planets revolved around Earth. While it is easy in hindsight to dismiss the theory, it is important to recognize that the world's most respected minds, including Plato and Aristotle, based their work on this now-dismissed theory.

It wasn't a lack of intelligence or insight that enabled the acceptance of geocentricism. Instead, it was the central mistake that drove the theory, and then the centrifugal force of common knowledge that perpetuated it. It wasn't until Copernicus published *On the Revolutions of Heavenly Spheres* shortly before his death in 1543 that adoption of the heliocentric model started. And it still took over a century for the idea to gain broader support, finally allowing for much more significant advances in astronomy.

In the same way, cybersecurity must rigorously identify faulty premises so that we do not devote time, effort, and resources devising brilliant solutions that are doomed to fail. One of the clearest examples of a central mistake in cybersecurity is inadequate authentication.

Until we solve this problem—effectively authenticating people to machines, software to hardware, processes to operating systems, and more—we will forever be compensating for this vulnerability with other essential strategies and mechanisms.

Those mechanisms and strategies include segmentation, cryptography, and access control, which we'll cover in Part III of this book.

The challenge, as we will see time and again, is speed—both keeping pace with the velocity of threat evolution and delivering authentication solutions that maintain the speed and volume at which digital communication, particularly enterprise-level business communication, now occurs.

The good news is that security techniques like multifactor authentication greatly increase the odds of thwarting an initial breach. The chilling bad news about authentication is the power of its domino effect. One slapped-together phishing email with just a few lines of code, one clumsy click on a criminal's link, can expose and offer up extraordinary amounts of personal information at both the individual and organizational levels.

Let's start at the most basic.

Imagine the trove of personal data housed in your email account, some of the most sensitive and identifying information about you and many people you know—all stretching back years. This might include bank accounts, medical records, Social Security numbers for yourself and your family, tax documents, and more.

A single guessed or grifted password unlocks it all. And once attackers have gained access, their ability to commit far more informed, sophisticated, and targeted attacks against every connection in that archive of information increases exponentially. Current statistics estimate that one out of every 131 emails sent globally contains malware or malicious links. It takes only one to enable a breach.

Now imagine you are not an individual but an organization—with 100 or 1,000 or 10,000 employees. All of these users have email accounts, laptops, tablets, smartphones, and other mobile devices that provide points of entry to access the most mission-critical data on your network, from onsite servers to multiple-cloud networks.

For those cybersecurity experts and executives tasked with preventing attacks at the enterprise, national, or even global security levels, authentication—at speed and scale—remains one of the greatest challenges. There is a reason that phishing, spear phishing, whaling, SQL injection, distributed denial-of-service (DDoS), brute-force, and man-in-the-middle attacks are increasing—in both frequency and damage.

With stronger authentication, we can fight back.

AUTHENTICATION, DATA INTEGRITY, NONREPUDIATION, AVAILABILITY, AND CONFIDENTIALITY: THE FIVE PILLARS OF SECURITY

Mike McConnell, Former Director of National Intelligence

In 1994, I had been the director of the National Security Agency (NSA) for just over a year when the creators of Netscape turned the old and complex system used for logging onto and communicating across networks into the World Wide Web. Almost overnight, this was possible because international radio-based communications (mostly satellite) were replaced by submarine fiber-optic cables (circa 1990), which could handle not only voice and data, but also the exploding demands of network (think Internet) traffic. These networks were made possible by digital processing (computers and routers) with dramatically increased processing speeds. Today, more than 95 percent of Internet traffic is transmitted via fiber-optic cable.

Up to that point, the NSA had primarily focused on the interception and analysis of radio wave communications being transmitted through the atmosphere between antennas by foreign intelligence targets. That meant scanning the right frequency, in the right place, and in the right—frequently short—timeframe. Everything had to be timed and aligned to capture communications.

When fiber wireline network communications exploded, intercepting data expanded from capturing data in motion (the transmission of data from antenna to antenna) to also include data "at rest," where it was stored digitally, not printed on paper and stored. Since organizations now stored that information digitally in a computer, it became vulnerable even while "at rest." This meant changing how and where we could gather foreign intelligence.

Fortunately, at the time, the NSA had the highest concentration of PhDs in math and computer science in the country, focused on things like cryptography, math, security codes, code breaking, and code making. And at that time, we had more compute power than the rest of the world combined. So we soon realized that we could access information stored on computers via the Internet.

Although this idea was intriguing, it had some challenges. US law stated that data collected on foreign targets in the atmosphere above the United States was free game because there was no expectation of privacy. So we could intercept foreign target data moving from one antenna to another at will. But as the Internet exploded, our foreign targets began communicating via email over fiber-optic lines rather than radio waves. And at that time, according to the Foreign Intelligence Surveillance Act, collecting that data, even from a foreign target in the United States, required a warrant.

We responded by focusing on network exploitation techniques to access data at rest in a foreign country. The objective was to get into a network, locate a device of interest, take the target information we needed, and then get out. That was how signals intelligence developed in the 1990s. Since one of the NSA's two primary missions is to break code to exploit foreign targets, we found it relatively easy to open a computer, take data, and leave no fingerprints.

But the other side of the NSA's mission is to make code: To secure all classified information to make sure a foreign entity couldn't break in and take our data. In the Computer Security Act of 1987, Congress tasked the NSA with providing the code to protect all classified information, while the National Bureau of Standards, which in 1988 became the National Institute of Standards and Technology (NIST), was given the mission to protect the government's unclassified information. No federal agency is responsible for securing the information of the critical infrastructure in the private sector.

But the shift to digital fiber wire line communications didn't just impact the government. Critical infrastructure and data, such as those managed by our private financial sector, began to be exposed as well. Nations can't function without banks, because nations must have a trusted medium of exchange and a trusted system to manage them for business and society to function effectively. Disrupting banking services would have serious national consequences.

With the explosion of information technology and digital processing, the banking industry was moving to an environment in which they stored wealth as ones and zeros, and transactions occurred at the speed of light. In a brief period, the United States became the most vulnerable nation because we were the most dependent on new digital infrastructure.

With that realization, I began to focus on the "make-code side" of the NSA's two primary missions to understand how we could secure those critical infrastructures—such as finance, energy, transportation, and telecommunications—that the government had identified as being vital to the continuing functioning and well-being of the nation.

I sat down with my cybersecurity mentor to better understand what the next steps should be. He said, "Mr. Director, you probably don't fully understand this, but you also are responsible for the integrity of the National Nuclear Program and the integrity of the communications system that manages our nuclear weapons." I choked back a gasp and said, "Well, I guess I didn't fully understand that." He said, "Let me take you through the basic building blocks of information security and tell you why they're important to give you a better understanding."

THE FIVE KEY ELEMENTS OF CYBERSECURITY

He then listed five ideas that form the backbone of cybersecurity: Authentication, data integrity, nonrepudiation, availability, and confidentiality.

My mentor then asked me what the most critical thing for securing the Nuclear Command and Control system was. I said, "Confidentiality, scrambling text, and keeping it hidden." He said, "Wrong. Let's go back to the beginning. The single most important aspect of the integrity of Nuclear Command and Control is *authentication*." I said "All right, you're going to have to explain this to me."

He explained, "The only person in the US government who can give an order to execute a nuclear attack is the president of the United States. If you're on a submarine at sea or buried in a missile silo and you get the order, what's the most important thing you need to know? That the order is authentic and is coming from the president of the United States. There's a system for verifying that. If the order is given, you break open a packet of codes, and the code that came with the order has to match what you're holding in your hand." With codes and encryption, we achieve mathematical certainty.

He then asked me what the second most important thing was. I said, "It has to be scrambled text." He said, "No. The second most important is data integrity. Once the missile operator has authenticated that launch code, what if some actor or error changed just one digit or moved a decimal point to the right or left in your target designation? You just struck the wrong city. Data integrity ensures that nothing has been changed in a transaction because, with proper encryption, operators can verify it with mathematical certainty."

"What's third?" he asked. "Well, now I'm going to guess confidentiality," I replied. And once again, he said, "Well, you're going to be wrong. The next thing is nonrepudiation." He explained, "Imagine that the president gives the order for a nuclear strike, the act is carried out, and Congress later discovers that the president made a mistake. Nonrepudiation means he could not say it was not him. It means you can't repudiate the fact that you gave that order."

I then said, "Since you've given me the list of authentication, data integrity, nonrepudiation, availability, and confidentiality, I'm guessing that availability is next, meaning that a process is not only always available but that it operates the same way for infinity." I was correct. And then he said something I will never forget. "In Nuclear Command and Control, we don't even worry about confidentiality. In fact, we may want the other side to know, so an order may even be sent in the clear."

And that was my introduction to information security.

That was when I began thinking about information security for the first time. In the military, we used secret key encryption and codes that required looking things up and verifying them. But in the early digital world, we were all logged onto the Net using computers to send information, including data of immense value, using ones and zeros that represented wealth or the results of research and development or intellectual property or proprietary business information. All that valuable data was moving across the network, and most organizations hadn't even thought about the concepts of authentication, data integrity, and nonrepudiation.

That's when I also began to realize that the country was incredibly vulnerable because there was no way to apply the national security approach to the private sector. But the private sector owned and operated 90 to 95 percent of the telecommunications and information systems in the country.

The economist in me then started to think about this lesson in terms of banking. If you're moving $100 million from Tokyo to New York, the authentication part of that transaction is vitally important. Are the sender and receiver really who they say they are? This means authentication is essential. You can make the same argument for data integrity. You don't want to move a digit because $100 million will suddenly become a billion. And finally, nonrepudiation becomes essential because once the two parties move that $100 million, you don't want the receiving party to say it wasn't they who received it.

The challenge is that we are still vulnerable to those same digital risks today. I believe we need a national consensus and set of prescriptive strategies—driven through legislation, regulation, or policy—that can guarantee authentication, data integrity, and nonrepudiation of our information systems protected by valid encryption. What those three components provide is mathematical certainty about the validity of the information and attribution. Whether this is considered in terms of access management, identity management, or access control, it is setting up a system where the identity of the parties is confirmed and there is attribution that can achieve mathematical certainty. Organizations can add confidentiality if that is a priority. Using proper encryption provides these attributes and makes it much more difficult for a criminal or a nation-state to access vital information.

THE ART OF COMMUNICATIONS

All transactions can be simplified to two or more entities needing to communicate, understand, and accept the information. It could be a military order, a banking transaction, a request for a contract, or a major engagement between two businesses. These communications can be considered in four dimensions: To communicate, to exploit (access) the communications, to defend the communications, and finally, to degrade or destroy the communications.

First, the goal is for those entities to share information, understand it, evaluate it, and then make some decision about it, whether in person or over great distances.

The next element is the act of intercepting that communication to know what the parties are talking about. The purpose could be sinister, it could be legal, and it could even be self-defense.

But regardless, the goal is to understand those communications by intercepting and possibly decrypting them.

Today, for example, China is actively engaged in a massive exploitation effort. They access computer systems to steal source code, research and development information, and business plans. Some estimates value that trade theft at between half a trillion and a trillion dollars a year. And because they have a larger and cheaper workforce, not bearing the costs related to research and development puts China on a path to becoming the world's largest economy. Accordingly, with a plan to invest in technology to get ahead, China could lead the next industrial revolution in areas like artificial intelligence, cryptography, information processing, nanotechnology, 3D printing, and so on. These efforts to exploit systems for economic gain are critical elements of China's stated goal of outstripping the United States in the global marketplace. And left unchecked, these activities will have a debilitating effect on the United States because our primary capability is innovation and creativity.

This activity is why the third element—that of defending communications—is so critical. In addition to code breaking so that you could read someone else's mail, we need to improve our efforts at code making to keep others from reading our mail.

And now, there is a fourth element of communications, which is to not only exploit a system for passive analysis but to damage or destroy data and other critical resources. It has driven the creation of the cyberwarfare capabilities by nation-states.

ACHIEVING INFORMATION INTEGRITY

If an outsider can enter an information system and extract information without attribution or authentication, nations, businesses, and individuals are at risk. Whether it's in the context of the president ordering a nuclear attack or the legitimate recording of a transaction to move $100 million from Japan to New York, authentication, data integrity, and nonrepudiation are essential.

The question is, how do you achieve and maintain information integrity? Part of the challenge has been getting the Executive Branch and the Congress to think about the magnitude of the problem we face. We need policies and legislative frameworks that enable us to establish the same level of authentication, data integrity, and nonrepudiation for the digital world that we currently have for a face-to-face interaction that requires a driver's license or a passport for authentication. The truth is that we enjoyed a higher degree of authentication in the past using a physical signature or a stamp than we do today in the digital world using ones and zeros.

Another part of the challenge is that not everyone has the same objectives when it comes to these issues. Of the five permanent nations in the United Nations Security Council, the United Kingdom, France, and the United States want to use the Internet for the free exchange of ideas and creativity to inform their citizens, facilitate commerce, and make the world a better place. The other two permanent members, China and Russia, however, want to monitor their citizens and control their access to information, which also allows them to grade how well their citizens adhere to the party line.

How do we establish a global capability to ensure authentication, data integrity, and nonrepudiation to encourage the free and secure flow of ideas when some nation-states clearly operate with different objectives? Banking has probably done the best job as a sector. They have created an information sharing and analysis center, and the information security officers of the top ten banks all know one another and have a forum to exchange ideas. Not only does that approach need to be replicated across other sectors, but it also needs to be automated so that organizations can exchange threat and vulnerability information at network speed.

The more significant challenge is that as technologies and networks converge, different sectors will no longer be able to manage their security in isolation. Once you can drive a smart car into a smart city, a fantastic array of devices will begin interacting. Navigation, the ability to tie banking information to toll roads or parking, real-time access to road condition information, and rerouting traffic and lighting to address busier areas of the city all require an ability to authenticate across all those elements seamlessly. Digital businesses face the same challenges with technology-savvy consumers, cloud and Internet of Things (IoT) networks, the convergence of IT and operational technology (OT), and smart devices that blend the personal and professional lives of users and are also loaded with hundreds of potentially exploitable applications.

Using an improperly authenticated and secured access point means that bad actors potentially have access to critical infrastructures and resources where they could degrade, change, or destroy critical information. That's what cyberwarfare is all about. Enabling and securing this new generation of interconnected systems will require not only legislation, but also the adoption of open standards and protocols that allow this process to occur more effectively, both between and across organizations. That's because everything will be on the same interconnected infrastructure, making authentication, data integrity, and nonrepudiation more critical than ever before.

ABOUT THE CONTRIBUTOR

Mike McConnell – Former Director of National Intelligence

After retiring from the Navy in 1996 as a vice admiral, McConnell joined Booz Allen and led the development of the firm's Information Assurance and Intelligence business.

Upon being asked by President George W. Bush in 2007 to become the second Director of National Intelligence (DNI), he served as the DNI, a position of cabinet rank, and a member of the White House National Security Council under Presidents Bush and Obama. In 2009, McConnell returned to Booz Allen as an executive vice president to lead the firm's Intelligence business. He retired from Booz Allen in July 2014, and currently serves as a senior executive adviser.

McConnell's career spanned over 45 years, focused on international and foreign intelligence issues. His focus since his service as director of NSA in 1992–96, has been to improve the cybersecurity posture of businesses and government agencies around the globe to better protect them from hackers, criminals, terrorists, and nation-states focused on economic espionage or destruction of vital data. He continues to work closely with the Department of Defense, the Department of Homeland Security, and the National Security Agency.

AUTHENTICATION AND MODELS OF TRUST

Shannon Lietz, Intuit

When networks first arrived, authentication began as a relatively straightforward process. Things were either inside or outside the perimeter. It was simple. A short time later, it was easy for adversaries to breach the common network, so firewalls became a necessity. Soon after that, virtual private networks (VPNs) were born. Today, networks are much more interactive and complicated, and require multiple levels of authentication to access resources. They require separate authentication for most resources. Some users complained about the resulting productivity challenges, and single sign-on was created to lessen the problem. But now, applications require authentication to each other to achieve more complicated operations. And finally, we have to contend with the IoT. Sadly, that's just the beginning.

Even the concept of access has become very complicated. For example, people are now replacing the key-based locks on their homes with digital door locks. They want to see who is coming to the door before answering it. They want to prevent packages from being stolen, so they provide a special access code to the delivery service. They want the digital lock to notify them with a message and maybe a photo or video clip when a family member leaves or returns. And they want to be able to remotely lock and unlock the door and turn the alarm on and off.

This level of access control and enablement was never possible before recent innovations in smart home technology. All of this flexibility is possible because a digital key is fundamentally different from a physical key. However, it also introduces new risks. Extending trust while addressing new risks requires pairing digital locks with additional tools, such as digital cameras, motion-activated lights, and an integrated digital alarm system. This notion of pairing controls to safely extend trust is critical for understanding authentication. Authentication now requires tools and technologies to enhance identification verification, with controls such as device identification, multifactor authentication, quarantines, monitoring, tagging, and dynamic encryption being just a few examples of these newly required elements. The fact is that simple authentication alone is no longer enough. The game has changed, and it is time to level up.

THE POWER OF PAIRING AUTHENTICATION WITH ACCESS KEYS OR TOKENS

Pairing authentication with access keys or tokens that provide different access rights allows an organization to create a perimeter with authentication, even where a traditional border may no longer exist. The network edge has become elastic and permeable, making traditional edge-based security less effective. When properly applied, however, authentication, paired with other technologies, can serve as a sort of firewall that can help secure perimeterless environments.

The impact of such an approach is difficult to overestimate. Modern or trust-based authentication enables us to build more responsive environments; extend security controls deeper into the network; and develop better, more personalized applications so that we can accomplish more. To scale to the next level of interoperability and interconnection, however, you need to build an inherent trust capability into the fabric of the network.

BROKERAGE CAPABILITIES

To accomplish this, modern authentication also requires brokerage capabilities that can assert and broker on behalf of those people and things that require authentication. This goes beyond simply granting or denying access, extending deeper into why access was granted, the degree to which access should be applied, and when access levels should be adjusted. For example, when a device is behaving well, it's allowed to achieve new levels of trust to perform certain actions. When it's not, it's no longer allowed to do them. This is simple. But what if we were to pair access with keys or tokens that are asserted to enable more specific interactions, such as exchanging access on behalf of a user with better, more fine-grained intention derived by application needs and usage? In this case, authentication itself is not so much about understanding who you are and whether you should have access but extends further into the ecosystem that supports you.

In this way, the digital ecosystem originates from the combination of authentication and digital rights management that has become ubiquitous as technology becomes increasingly complex. Trust is developed based on the exchange of keys or tokens that the system grants *on behalf of* the end user and their intention. Having a set of keys that also extend to other devices, applications, and processes enables authentication to do more things for you. If a device or process has a key associated with your identity, as far as the network is concerned, that device *is* you, and you're going to be able to scale in ways that were never possible before.

By comparison, in the traditional monolithic approach to authentication, you might have navigated to a system, entered your password, and been granted access through a set of hard-coded permissions.

Today, that is not enough. You might have hundreds of authentication keys associated with your identity and a set of intentions that you want to enable on your behalf. You might have a single password or token to get access to those keys, but once you do, those keys decide whether or not you can access network resources based on a variety of factors.

And in some cases, developers are building applications that can make dynamic decisions about access, which means traditional authorization mechanisms are failing to keep up.

When you then tie these authentication keys to microservices, they can provide degrees of access to applications, workflows, or similar resources based on trust. And because you have so many more authentication keys, you also have many more on/off switches that enable you to do your job without compromising the integrity of the network, even if a particular key needs to be turned off for some reason.

Beyond access to resources, authentication can also extend to services and capabilities so that we can interact with our digital world outside of the confines of a specific organization. Essentially, zero trust environments are critical to modern authentication paradigms. This requires dynamic authentication keys connected to a fluid number of grants and parameters so that we can access resources and conduct transactions across the hyperconnected digital environments we are creating today, such as smart homes, smart cars, and smart cities. Of course, this is an emerging field, and it requires building an open key fabric of some sort that can easily span different networks and systems.

AUTHENTICATION BEYOND INDIVIDUALS

In particular, authentication has to extend beyond individuals. As networked devices become smarter, they can increasingly function autonomously *on behalf of* an individual or even groups of people. We will also see direct relationships between applications, directed by software, to provide specific, customized services based entirely on the identity profile that these devices represent. The implication is that we are going to need zero trust identity validation that can extend trust to more than just human beings by enabling scoped permissions to be carried as part of an identity.

Establishing and adopting open standards is crucial for making this shift to a new authentication paradigm. Projects like OpenID and OAuth are taking off because identity must extend beyond a specific network or network segment. Users want smart wallets, identity verification, and the ability to dynamically create contracts that travel with them between their work and personal lives. And although it might seem awkward, technology like blockchain may even play a role in how that's enabled. Blockchain may provide a way to deal with trust boundaries through a voting or crowdsourcing mechanism that enables different ways to establish trust. Ironically, the drive toward more personalized authentication, identity, access, and authorization is happening because, as networks grow and expand and interconnect, we will soon no longer be able to trust the network itself without modern authentication.

Once we can no longer trust the network, we need dynamic authentication keys, enumeration, and logging to protect individuals and their resources with what is, in effect, a very personal and mobile security blanket. If we no longer trust the network, that also means that we will need to fundamentally rethink things like SSL (Secure Socket Layer), TLS (Transport Layer Security), and similar network-based security functions that have enabled authentication in a somewhat lazy way. Enabling encryption to function as a next-level authentication capability will require it to operate in a way that is tied not to the network, but instead to the data and identities that it is enabled to share.

One way to approach this is by tying authentication to something like application-level encryption (ALE), which enables the application itself to decide what's encrypted, how it's encrypted, and how to protect data so that when it has to transit through a hostile environment, authentication can dynamically determine the scope of its encryption. On the other end of that connection, trust is what allows you to decrypt that information using modern authentication schemes. Of course, all of this will require adding new security features to consumer products based on open standards. The driver will be consumers demanding easier ways to hold and transmit sensitive data so they can do more with their digital capabilities, such as have software operate on their behalf. What is clear is that as everything becomes interconnected, authentication plays an increasingly essential role in security.

Customer-driven security has significant challenges. Paramount to the evolution of modern authentication, it must be simple—and mostly invisible—to the end user, while not sacrificing security. Among other things, this means we need to get rid of our current password-based access strategy as soon as possible. For too many years we have relied on human verification to access applications, and hackers have finally caught up with that strategy. We can spend time shifting to device identity verification, but they're going to catch up with that as well, and in a relatively short amount of time. Some signs of that are already occurring.

Consider all of the people logged into Facebook, LinkedIn, and Google who then use their profiles to log into other applications and services. This is an example of extending very fragile human-based identity in ways we never considered before. As you work your way through the identity space, it becomes apparent that trust is the only way forward.

BROKERAGES AS A SECURITY VERIFICATION ECOSYSTEM

We're going to have to switch to a security verification ecosystem where certified third-party brokerages can assert, identify, verify, and extend trust. These brokers will become the backbone of the interconnected ecosystems that we all work and live in by arranging higher levels of trust that enable us to take advantage of applications and services that now span environments.

As this scales out, we will soon be dealing with issues related to expansive levels of trust that extend in all sorts of directions we haven't yet conceived of. To achieve that, we must use an open consensus model to address the related challenges.

Collaboration is fast becoming a critical component of problem-solving today. Science has reached a point where individual expertise is no longer enough to push the frontiers of research to the next level. Likewise, addressing business issues in a world of hyperconnectivity, smart devices, and big data requires different teams to work together. That's why we see more and more DevOps and DevSecOps teams pushing collaboration to solve complex problems. And we are seeing a greater need to share, which is pushing the boundaries of business models and the authentication that supports them.

The minute you start pushing collaboration, however, the question becomes, "Who can you trust?" Collaboration and authentication go hand in hand. Solving a problem as part of an extended team will require individuals, devices, and applications to join a trust ring based on a variety of factors, such as identity and authorization credentials, combined with a crowd number score and even your apparent goal. Being able to authenticate through a system using a goal, and then finding other people with similar, related goals, will dynamically create rings of trust that will enable us to move even faster. Only those who are worthy of trust can participate in environments where collaboration is essential. I don't want to have to deal with individuals with counter goals until I am ready to test my ideas.

One of the biggest hurdles moving forward is that we have made authentication pretty complicated. It's identity. It's authentication. It's authorization. It's IdM (identity management) and IAM (identity and access management) processes. And this segmented way of thinking about authentication is going to interfere with our ability to create a mesh-based system that can open and lock circles of trust based on a dynamic set of requirements. That will require an authentication mechanism different from anything we currently have in place.

I've been doing a study on companies that have invested in higher-end, more advanced security versus those that have opted for more basic and traditional lower-end protection. The data so far is fascinating. Companies that invest in advanced security are not only realizing higher-end revenue through increased productivity and more effective collaboration, but they are also generating a more substantial stake in the industries in which they operate. I believe the future is very bright. However, only by leveraging mechanisms like authentication brokerages and trust models are we going to realize the potential of the interconnected world we are in the process of creating. The ability to adapt to and adopt these new models will determine which organizations and systems not only thrive, but actually survive.

ABOUT THE CONTRIBUTOR

Shannon Lietz – Head of DevSecOps, Intuit

Shannon Lietz is an award-winning innovator with over two decades of experience pursuing advanced security defenses and next-generation security solutions. As the DevSecOps Leader for Intuit, Lietz is responsible for setting and driving the company's security engineering strategy and cloud security support for product innovation. She is passionate about leading the charge for security transformation and change management in large environments, leveraging Agile and Rugged principles. Prior to Intuit, Lietz worked for several Fortune 500 companies, most notably Sony and ServiceNow, where she supported mission-critical teams engaged in advanced security programs. She was also a serial entrepreneur and is an avid blogger and evangelist for all things DevSecOps, HackerGirl, and Rugged Software.

4

PATCHING

"High-profile breaches fill the news, many directly related to poor patching discipline."

Chris Richter,
Former VP of Global Security
Services, CenturyLink

"We need to evolve the patching paradigm to make it less burdensome."

Renee Tarun,
Fortinet

Patches are fixes for known problems. Patches are small pieces of software rolled out by developers when they become aware, or are made aware, of a weakness.

Patching is the process of fixing these problems, and securing these revealed vulnerabilities to prevent exploitation. Patching is the first line of defense against what was famously dubbed by former Defense Secretary Donald Rumsfeld as "the known knowns."

As vigilant as cybersecurity professionals must remain to new, evolving, and emerging threats (the known unknowns and the unknown unknowns alike), the majority of cybersecurity attacks are the result of hackers exploiting vulnerabilities that are common knowledge but not patched.

Just as spacecraft designers are destined to fail if they ignore how the laws of physics (gravity, thermodynamics, acceleration, inertia, and so on) can degrade their design and its performance, so are those who ignore the "law" of patching. Failure to patch is self-destructive.

The expression *cyberhygiene* was invented to codify regular patching as comparable to taking a regular shower; it's basic behavior from which few are excused.

In the vast majority of environments, patching results in far more gain than pain. Take your medicine. Patch regularly and ruthlessly.

Patching is one vivid example of a security defense that teeters precariously on the fulcrum of basic human weakness. When developers release a software or security update, a bug fix, or a service pack, the release is essentially two-for-one: A highly specific warning that users are at risk and the solution to mitigate that risk at the same time. The fact that recipients then fail to install the patch—out of concern for business continuity, forgetfulness, or just the belief that cyberattacks happen only to others—is particularly troubling. Consequences are severe.

Some of the most destructive cyberattacks in recent memory, including Heartbleed, WannaCry, NotPetya, the Equifax breach, Spectre, and Meltdown, exploited vulnerabilities for which patches had already been issued. In other cases, attacks intensified because security patches were not installed even after the attacks became known.

Of course, patching at the network or enterprise level is a far more complex process than it is at the individual level. For understaffed, stretched, and strained IT teams, patching is a Sisyphean task, with thousands of boulders needing to be pushed up thousands of hills with grueling consistency. Even a smaller enterprise organization is often running a massive range of different software programs on different systems—some current, some legacy, some purchased, some built. All develop vulnerabilities that must be patched.

Like many other aspects of cybersecurity, patching demands difficult decisions and a coherent strategy to guide it. Without such a strategy, it would be difficult for an IT team to do anything other than patch—and still there would be vulnerabilities.

The difficulty of patching reveals the goalie position that IT and security teams are forced to play: Taking all the blame for the losses and getting little credit for the wins.

In a global economy with daily life dependent on a digital infrastructure far vaster than the human resources available to maintain and defend it, what we've learned about the failure to patch illustrates a troubling truth about the consequences of human frailty.

The human fallibility that drives the inability or unwillingness to patch systems is a symptom of larger issues and challenges that we must reckon with in a digitally driven world of ever-increasing size and complexity. To master cybersecurity, we must master the challenge of patching and develop security solutions that somehow overcome the human tendency to ignore the fundamental need to patch.

PATCHING: A GROWING CHALLENGE AND A NEEDED DISCIPLINE

Chris Richter, Former VP of Global Security Services, CenturyLink

Nearly all successful attacks and network breaches start by compromising a vulnerable system for which a patch or update has been available for weeks, months, and sometimes even years. And yet one of the biggest misconceptions about patching is that it's an optional task for protecting your organization from cyberattacks. Safeguarding networked resources from viruses and malware with expensive hardware and software technical controls seems to get a lot of attention, as well as a significant share of the security budget. But based on recent research, nearly half of all compromised devices typically have no malware on them at all. These systems were compromised merely to establish a network foothold, and they were exploited because of a vulnerability that could have been patched. Understanding and treating risks associated with vulnerabilities is essential.

Over the past few years, we have seen a considerable problem growing around the lack of consistency and discipline around patching. Part of the reason is that it is becoming more difficult to find security talent. There are far more job openings in cybersecurity than there are people to fill them. The individuals tasked with patch and device management and keeping track of patching schedules burn out quickly. It's mundane, repetitive, and not very exciting work, so it's hard to find individuals who will stick with it. In addition, patching and updating systems is hard to do, especially in a live environment, where the issue isn't just taking a potentially critical device offline so it can be updated, but also the impact on the business if that patch creates other, more severe problems. Some applications, for example, will simply stop functioning because IT didn't test the applied patch for compatibility with that application. But the more significant issue may be that it's also challenging to keep a regular patching program in place because of the rapid pace of change occurring in our infrastructures. Architectural designs change rapidly today, devices need patching, and patching can be a risk to uptime.

I've participated in those discussions about the challenges related to patching. "What happens if we lose our data because we failed to patch our devices? But then, what if the patch breaks our system and we're in a state of downtime for several hours or days? Will we get fined or lose customers? What would the impact be to our brand or reputation or bottom line? What is our responsibility to our shareholders?"

The advent of the Internet of Things (IoT) is making this problem even more challenging. I recently worked with one organization with over 100,000 IP addresses connected to virtual and physical appliances that they didn't know existed. If you don't know a device even exists, you're not monitoring it, and you certainly don't know you have to patch it. You also don't know what data is on it, what the value of that data is, where the device is located, or how old it is. All of those are risk factors that hackers can exploit.

Changes in the digital marketplace are compounding this problem, requiring organizations to move faster and do more with limited resources and less funding, especially in the security space. All of that combined creates a perfect storm through which an attacker can exploit these weaknesses. We've seen it time and time again. Wide-reaching hacks and high-profile breaches fill the news, many of them directly related to poor security governance and patching discipline.

ESTABLISHING A SECURITY GOVERNANCE FRAMEWORK

Of course, patching does not happen in isolation. It must be part of a larger security framework that includes different functions working together alongside patch management. Data discovery and asset discovery are critical components of any patch management program. The assets with the highest value need to have the most security controls built around them. But before you can protect those assets, you must first determine which systems have the highest importance, where they reside, what data resides on them, what other devices and applications connect to them, and the age and type of data they contain, all of which often can be difficult to ascertain. But that information is essential for establishing a priority-based system for patching, or even installing other security controls around them in case of a zero-day vulnerability for which there is no patch available.

Unfortunately, too many organizations don't have solid frameworks in place. And even if they do have a framework, it's something that they wrote up in the form of documentation and then filed away, never to be reviewed again. Thus, few organizations are really managing adherence to their security framework. It's often difficult for CSOs to reach out across the organization, understand where those assets are, classify them, and then establish a valuation of the assets so they can begin building controls around them. But the real work can start only after a framework is put in place.

A security governance framework doesn't have to be complicated. One that I like and many CSOs rely on is the NIST Cybersecurity Framework. It's written in plain English, not technical jargon. It's a good starting point, and it's free. However, even with that framework, you have to follow the guidelines and the principles, and that's where the work is. And it has to be able to adapt as the environment changes. It's a growing problem, because so many devices and applications are being connected and distributed across the network. Add multiple cloud environments and virtual devices and the problem grows exponentially.

Of course, one thing that is making patching more critical than ever is that the networks we are now defending look nothing like the ones from just a few years ago. It used to be that we could more easily protect unpatched systems or take our time patching devices because we had hidden them from outside malefactors. Back then, we didn't trust anything outside of the perimeter. But the perimeter is now pretty much gone, and if it does exist, it's so porous that you still have to assume that every system inside your organization is compromised in some way, whether or not you have patched it.

Another challenge I'm seeing is a decline in our ability to manage people and maintain the discipline needed to adhere to a security governance framework, including practices like patching. Consider the growth of shadow IT arising from a merger or acquisition. As different organizations bring their networks together, they inherit different types of frameworks, often along with lax security discipline in one area or another. These new networks may already be infected with malware or have poor patching policies of their own. But the business is being pushed by shareholders to grow revenue very rapidly, so the last thing management teams want to do is slow things down by imposing security rigor and discipline. When your organization sees security as getting in the way of revenue growth, it is difficult to succeed.

This common misunderstanding is why a security framework needs to become a central governing document for the entire organization and requires buy-in from the very top. That way, when you begin to expand networks or consolidate technology landscapes because of mergers and acquisitions, everyone is on the same page about converging and cleaning up security because you have already calculated those expenses into the cost of the transaction.

AUTOMATION AND PATCHING

One option for closing the gap in critical but tedious activities like patching is automation. Automation is going to play a vital role across IT, including in security. It's the only way that we're going to be able to keep up with the pace of change. But when it comes to patching, as stated earlier, one of the most significant concerns is that patches sometimes break applications. I have seen security professionals accept the risk of an unpatched system to keep an application running. Even experienced security professionals will evaluate the risk and determine the likelihood of a cybercriminal exploiting it, and then balance that against the risk of taking an application offline because the patch could break it.

You can and should automate patching on systems where the likelihood of the patch breaking an application is either minimal or not disruptive. But those systems that have critical applications, where the risk of disrupting data access or breaking the application will hurt the company more than a potential exploit, will be slow to adopt automation, if it is enabled at all. What it all comes down to is whether the risk is worse than going offline. Is the threat of a breach worse than a system going down altogether? That's part of the risk classification process. However, addressing those challenges goes beyond the scope of today's automation technologies.

I've seen patches bring entire global networks down. People were fired. Heads rolled. It hurt business and reputations. And it took a long time to recover. But that is often the result of poor patching discipline and failing to test a patch before you apply it to a production system. Security controls should never slow down business. (Availability is a part of the CIA triad, along with confidentiality and integrity.)

Still, failing to patch a system because you're worried that it will bring the application down is not a good excuse. The testing process should be running on a redundant, fault-tolerant system where you can test a patch before putting it into production. This requires placing critical applications or devices on a system that technicians or automation can leverage for patch testing. An automated system could even detect a failure and perhaps also consider options for resolving that issue. If not, it could flag it for a human being to resolve. This practice requires redundancy so that patches can be tested before applying them to production systems.

DEALING WITH UNPATCHABLE DEVICES

Increasingly, organizations are deploying devices that are simply not patchable. IoT devices, for example, have become a real challenge for many organizations. If patching is not an option, those devices must be isolated. You have to place them on discrete networks that are logically isolated from networks and virtual local area networks (VLANs) that hold critical data. The challenge is similar for IT/operational technology (OT) convergence. Industrial Control Systems (ICS) and Supervisory Control and Data Acquisition (SCADA) devices traditionally deployed on a completely isolated network are now being exposed to vulnerabilities because they are networked through IT.

But you have to start with a solid risk assessment from either internal or external qualified risk assessment experts who can crawl through data discovery and classification, network architecture, application location, use of cloud, access controls, and more. There's a long list of these things that every organization should evaluate. You then need to put in place an ongoing governance program (as a part of your security framework) for performing security checks and rechecking security postures and profiles.

Once that's in place, you'll understand what you need to patch, what you simply shouldn't worry about patching, and what applications and systems to isolate on separate networks for systems that are unpatchable.

ABOUT THE CONTRIBUTOR

Chris Richter – Former VP of Global Security Services, CenturyLink

Chris Richter is an independent cybersecurity consultant specializing in helping organizations build and adapt security frameworks to digital transformation initiatives. Richter has authored several IT security articles, is a contributing author to *Security 2020*, and frequently speaks at conferences on the topic of outsourced security services. Most recently Richter was CenturyLink's vice president of global security services and was responsible for the company's global managed and professional security services business. Prior to that he served as senior vice president of Security Services at Level 3 and vice president of Security Services at Savvis, a CenturyLink Company.

With over 30 years of experience in IT, Richter has held a number of leadership positions in managed security, IT consulting, and sales with several technology product and services organizations. By helping organizations rearchitect their risk management programs and security controls to outsourced, virtualized, and shared infrastructure services, Richter has helped numerous IT organizations lower their cybersecurity costs while improving their overall defense posture.

CONQUER OR BE CONQUERED

Renee Tarun, Fortinet

Like the universe that's constantly expanding, the cybersecurity landscape is constantly growing and changing. With the drive for a more interconnected world, the emergence of new advanced technologies, and the Internet of Things (IoT), more and more devices are connecting online at an unprecedented pace. This growth creates a bigger playing field for adversaries, as it broadens their access to potential attack vectors, including various security vulnerabilities or weaknesses within the application and system designs. Whether your organization is an academic institution, a private sector company, or a government entity, no one is immune to these vulnerabilities.

Zero-day vulnerabilities, or vulnerabilities that are unknown, receive a lot of attention in the media and from threat researchers. However, developing a zero-day attack is costly and time-consuming for the adversary. The reality is that most attacks don't require a tremendous amount of creativity or work on the part of the adversary. The majority of successful attacks today exploit known vulnerabilities in software and systems that are left unpatched, giving attackers the upper hand.

We need to change our strategy to give the good guys the advantage. We need to evolve the patching paradigm to make it less burdensome for organizations to patch their systems with speed and scale. This will require vendors and organizations to overcome many technical and cultural challenges, but it can be done.

For many organizations, the challenge with patching comes down to too many patches and too little time. The sheer volume of vulnerabilities discovered annually, along with the associated patches, numbers in the thousands and is constantly on the rise. This creates quite the quagmire for IT personnel, as patching is only one aspect of the myriad of activities they are responsible for to keep networks and systems operational.

Why do these vulnerabilities exist in the first place? The answer is simple: As long as there are humans in the loop, writing the software programs that computers must follow, there will always be a risk of vulnerabilities in the code.

IT STARTS WITH DEVELOPERS

Poor coding practices by developers result in security holes within systems and applications. In addition, most developers today rely on open source and third-party libraries to aid their development efforts. These libraries can often introduce vulnerabilities, and developers may be unaware of software updates for the libraries that they use, resulting in unpatched vulnerabilities throughout their applications.

To reduce the volume of vulnerabilities in their products, vendors and developers need to adopt proactive methodologies within their development life cycles. This starts by training developers on secure coding practices and how they can be applied to their development efforts. Also, numerous automated vulnerability scanners are on the market that can scan applications for vulnerabilities prior to their release. Additionally, quality assurance testing should include a security review along with the standard functionality review.

THE OPERATIONAL IMPACT OF PATCHING

Another patching struggle organizations face is, "If it ain't broke, don't fix it." There are several potential operational impacts caused by patching systems that are otherwise running normally that make organizations reluctant to patch. Vendors could help in a number of ways, as outlined next.

No Restart or Reboot Required

Deploying most patches requires stopping and restarting the application, or even a complete system reboot, to fully install the patch. With today's business demands of interconnectivity and "always on," it is becoming more challenging for organizations to take critical systems offline for any amount of time out of concerns for loss in revenue, customer service abilities, and overall decrease in productivity within the organization. Vendors need to design new methodologies for patch deployments that allow for patches to take effect without having to restart and reboot systems and applications.

Separate Patches from New Features

Most patches released by vendors include not only a fix for the vulnerability but also new or enhanced system or application features. Some organizations don't want to install the patch because the new features are unwanted or aren't compatible with other systems or processes. Some patches are very large, creating a performance strain on an organization's network. Vendors must shift away from the all-or-nothing approach to applying patches and identify ways to segment their patches to allow organizations to pick and choose which parts they want to apply (for example, security fixes versus new features).

Offer the Ability to Roll Back Patches

Despite all the testing that is done on a patch, it's nearly impossible to test against every single device and software configuration out there. As a result, patches intended to fix a system can inevitably end up breaking it. For example, industrial control systems often use legacy systems that are not only old but costly, so fielding a spare to test patches is not always feasible, making patching risky if something goes wrong. Similar to the rollback feature in databases that allows you to undo an operation and return the database to a previous state, there needs to be an easy mechanism to undo patches on an application or system if it has an unintended negative impact.

AN ORGANIZATIONAL PRIORITY

Vendors alone can't solve the entire patching conundrum. When vendors release patches, organizations must do their part by being proactive and ensuring that these patches are applied in a timely fashion, because the clock is always ticking for adversaries to exploit unpatched systems. Patching must be an organizational priority.

Everyone within the organization needs to understand the vital role patching plays in maintaining the stability of systems and preventing breaches. Patching does take time and resources away from other important projects, whose return on investment can be more immediate and easily codified, but organizations must consider the alternatives. The damage an adversary can do through these unpatched systems, and the cost associated with fixing that damage, can easily outweigh the resource costs that would be invested in patching.

Upgrading and replacing legacy systems that can't be patched may be well worth the investment to ensure the security of an organization's infrastructure. Regularly patching systems and applications must be ingrained in the culture of the organization and must be routine, just like system backups and keeping antivirus and antimalware up to date.

Organizations need to recognize the importance of patching by implementing the necessary business policies and processes in a way that can be measured. Having a well-documented and executive-endorsed vulnerability and patch management policy can provide an organization with a roadmap for addressing these issues. In addition, those within an organization who are responsible for patching must have the authority to do so. You can't hold system administrators accountable for patching, but then make certain systems "hands off" or excluded, especially when the applications and systems are at high risk.

All vulnerabilities are not created equal. Focus patching on the most critical assets and most heavily utilized systems. Patch applications at most risk of severe consequences, such as loss of confidential data, intellectual property, revenue, or reputation, first. Ensuring that backups are in place and patches are tested on noncritical systems before they are applied are other steps that organizations can take to reduce their exposure.

Patch management is a continual process that requires knowing what patches are available, knowing what patches are necessary for particular systems, ensuring they are installed properly and tested, and maintaining all the documentation associated with these procedures. Multiple vendors have technologies to help automate the patch management process. Organizations should evaluate these technologies to see what would be most effective for their environments.

DON'T LEAVE YOUR DOORS UNLOCKED

Having an unpatched vulnerability in a system is like leaving the door unlocked for a thief trying to break into your house. If you knew a thief was going to try to break into your home, you wouldn't leave your door unlocked. Similarly, patching is a must to prevent an adversary from using a vulnerability to break into a system. The decision to patch or not patch comes down to risk management.

It is probably one of the toughest decisions IT executives and system administrators have to make. On the one hand, patching can be very challenging, but on the other hand, it can be detrimental to the organization if they choose not to patch.

In today's environment, combating compromises and breaches requires a layered defense that includes good basic hygiene. Patching is an essential element of good basic hygiene. It's a never-ending process, but neglecting to patch can create the weakest link in a system's defenses. With disciplined focus and a little planning, patching doesn't have to be difficult. If you want to protect your organization, then make patching a priority—your revenue, brand, and reputation depend on it.

ABOUT THE CONTRIBUTOR

Renee Tarun – Vice President Information Security, Fortinet

Renee Tarun is the vice president of Information Security at Fortinet. She oversees security compliance and governance, enterprise security, and product security.

Immediately prior, she served as special assistant to the director of the NSA for Cybersecurity and director of the NSA's Cyber Task Force, in which she advanced the NSA's execution of its cybersecurity and cyber-related missions by acquiring, investing, and overseeing resources; defining and integrating mission capabilities; and shaping agency strategy and national level policy.

As the assistant to the chief operating officer of the Information Assurance Directorate at the NSA, her focus areas included strategy, planning, integration, and relationship management, in cybersecurity and related disciplines across the NSA and the Department of Defense (DoD).

Tarun also served as Senior Cyber Strategist in a joint DoD-DHS organization that orchestrated joint efforts in operational planning, policy, and strategy, for cyber issues across the US government.

She was the portfolio lead for the Protect Data and Networks and Operational Resiliency Portfolios for the Deputy Assistant Secretary of Defense for Information and Identity Assurance. Previous assignments include computer scientist, information technologist, and a variety of policy, programs, and resource jobs.

Tarun serves on the George Mason University Volgenau School of Engineering Advisory Board, creating synergy between the school and the professional community by addressing workforce development demands, industry expectations, and employment trends.

5

TRAINING

"One of the most significant challenges facing today's organizations is the cybersecurity skills gap."

Chris McDaniels,
CT Cubed, Inc.

"My approach is to promote the reality that we're all in this together, because we are."

Mo Katibeh,
AT&T

"Each person at every level brings something unique that enriches the team dynamic."

Dave Rankin,
Verisign

We need more cybersecurity workers. The proliferation of automation and artificial intelligence gives rise to a peculiar and ironic trope: "Digital technology is eliminating jobs," a refrain echoed across numerous articles, op-eds, and blogs.

But there is ample evidence that the innovations in AI and automation are driving greater value and opportunity for human insight and expertise, not less. In my view, technology is creating jobs, not erasing them. Many of those jobs remain vacant.

In no area is that more apparent than cybersecurity—where there are far more jobs than people to fill them. The unemployment rate in the field of cybersecurity is holding steady at zero percent, with no indicators that it will change—quite the opposite, in fact.

Each year, one million new cybersecurity jobs are created. Estimates project an increase to 5 or 6 million over the next few years. Recently, there was a 74 percent growth in cybersecurity job postings. Half of those positions went unfilled.

As the premium on cybersecurity talent increases, so do the costs. More powerful organizations are able to pay workers more, while smaller organizations are priced out—placing a greater strain on the teams they have and expanding the footprint for attack.

Those who constructed and maintained the small information platform now known as the Internet were PhD-level computer scientists and engineers. Little thought was given to the evolution and escalation of the need for expertise at all levels and skillsets.

As we hurtle faster toward an incredibly complex digital future, we need a model in which network security doesn't wholly depend on the wizardry of a small set of experts.

There is a lesson to be learned from the Middle Ages, when the guild model emerged—with craftsmen (and women) called apprentices, journeymen, and masters—to meet the talent needs for the technologies of the time. Needed were blacksmiths, locksmiths, weavers, builders, and many others. First recorded in the Roman Empire, the guild model was effective enough to survive the fall of Rome and to remain in place in some capacities today. A large number of apprentices learn from a smaller number of journeymen, and those journeymen eventually join the ranks of an even smaller number of masters.

And far from being a model that's barely hanging on in history's dustbin or only used by those who work with their hands, this model is used powerfully and effectively in some of the most important and sophisticated settings, including by operational technologists in critical infrastructure and in high-end cybersecurity organizations around the world.

We need to create a cybersecurity workforce guild that builds and sustains a workforce with tiers of mastery, growing over time and training talent to focus on the tasks at their level of expertise. Such a guild model simultaneously helps create social stepping-stones toward well-paying jobs for those without computer science degrees and increases the pool, and sophistication, of cybersecurity specialists in a field with chronic workforce gaps.

Cybersecurity masters would not be tasked with important but relatively easy day-to-day tasks of cybersecurity—that's an opportunity cost. Apprentices would not be expected to take on foreign intelligence services—not a fair fight. Apprentices would have the opportunity to learn and move up with the goal of eventually becoming masters. Such a cybersecurity workforce guild would create an enduring workforce, with each tier of expertise suited for its own tasks.

With a larger workforce that gains skills and advances to the next level within a cybersecurity workforce guild, we can overcome the challenges of a deeply understaffed industry. We can reverse the tide of escalating inefficiencies and ineffectiveness. We can thwart catastrophe.

FILL THE SKILLS GAP WITH AN ENVIRONMENT OF CONTINUAL TRAINING

Chris McDaniels, CT Cubed, Inc.

One of the most significant challenges facing today's organizations is the cybersecurity skills gap. There are too few qualified professionals to fill all of the available seats, and there isn't a suitable process in place to create them. To address this challenge, technical security training is a critical component of any business strategy, especially for a managed security service provider (MSSP), which needs a large, diverse, and skilled security staff. But the reality is, training is hard to do in any nonproduction or simulated environment. Frankly, I haven't seen many simulated environments that provide enough stimulus with a realistic problem set to provide high-quality training beyond what's needed for a tier-one or entry-level position.

Instead, what I've seen work well for training is starting with a foundational set of knowledge, vocabulary, and nomenclature that your analysts and engineers understand. That requires some book knowledge so that everybody is speaking the same language and is familiar with the same fundamental and foundational concepts. But the real training value comes from putting analysts or engineers directly into production environments where they need to solve actual problems under the mentorship of someone who has been there longer and who has achieved a higher level of proficiency. It is important to let people experience challenges, come up with solutions, and have mentors who can tell them, "Okay, everything up to this point in your thought process was good. Here's what you need to do." This type of mentoring (before they make a catastrophic mistake) is the best kind of training.

ADAPTING SKILLS TO NEW ENVIRONMENTS

Once an effective and ongoing training climate has been established inside your organization, new problems and challenges are easier to address. For example, when you have a new cloud problem set, the cloud may be newish but the underlying technologies are all still the same. You just don't have to deal with the physical parts of the problem anymore. Many skillsets transfer. For a savvy Linux systems administrator, administering a Linux server that happens to live in the comms closet of your branch office is not fundamentally different from administering a server that lives somewhere in Amazon Web Services (AWS).

The challenge lies in understanding the additional capabilities or limitations of a solution that has been adapted to a cloud environment. You need to focus on those differences, and having a flexible mentorship process in place means that everyone can get up to speed faster by leveraging the skills of the cloud experts on the team. This is a training strategy that I think most organizations overlook.

The most significant security technologies that we'll all be talking about five years from now haven't even been heard of today. And because the landscape is changing so quickly, you have to give people slices of time to go out and tinker with these new technologies as they are being implemented, and then come back and become the resident expert and mentor others when they encounter that technology.

FINDING THE RIGHT PEOPLE

When using this model, choosing the right people is more important than the education or certification they may have. You want people with a particular type of mentality who are curious and want to dive into new technologies. We are actively recruiting and retaining those people, and then we are making sure to give them time during their workday to go out and gain new knowledge, with the expectation that what they bring back to the broader audience of analysts and engineers will make everybody better.

We actively apply this approach to our apprentice program—we recruit people with absolutely zero requirements for any IT or cybersecurity experience. One of the most successful interns I've seen to date was actually a Lyft driver who gave a ride to the owner of an MSSP. In talking to the driver, the owner asked, "What do you do at home?" The driver responded that he had been working on Python. That piqued the owner's curiosity, and he asked what version he was using. The Lyft driver was stunned and wondered, "Who is this guy in the back of my car? And what's happening here?"

They talked for a while, and the driver explained that he had moved to Phoenix from Atlanta to get into cybersecurity because he heard there were some opportunities there but he didn't know exactly how to start. The owner asked for the driver's résumé, which he forwarded to me later that night. I called the guy, and he had what I thought was the right attitude. A few weeks later he was in a security operations center (SOC) in the apprentice program, starting to gain expertise.

I told him, "Everyone is going to look at you and say, 'This can't work. You don't have a computer science degree. You don't have years of experience.' But I want you to spend a week or two just shadowing some folks and look at all the different toolsets you're exposed to. In the end, you're going to pick one or two of them and we're going to have you dive deep into them and gain all the expertise you can."

This was not an academic environment. The advantage we had is that we managed production networks for some of the most critical networks in North America. Although we did not let this new recruit perform any task that could have an impact on a customer environment, the exposure he got was as realistic as possible. He was looking over the shoulders of experts who were managing real networks, doing real things with real users who had real missions and business operations they had to conduct.

At the end of the two weeks, he told me that he wanted to dive into a particular solution. He then spent the next month reading every bit of literature he could, running the solution inside an environment we set aside for him so that he could use more advanced features, and within 30 days he became extremely knowledgeable. He wasn't up there with our tier-three folks yet, but a lot of coworkers on his shift started to come to him if they had a question about that solution. And he gained real niche expertise that wasn't just book knowledge. He could actually employ the system in a way that made sense. And after he became proficient in that toolset, he moved on to the next one.

CHALLENGING SENIOR ANALYSTS

For our more senior analysts, the challenge is keeping them engaged. I believe a lot in the power of autonomy, so we give them time every week to invest in themselves by developing skills in new technologies. We also encourage them to automate and orchestrate as much as possible. I told our team that the first person who can completely automate themselves out of a job, I'll still pay anyway. That person can then do whatever they want to do. No one's taken me up on that just yet, but they're trying.

In the meantime, they're allowed to work on new concepts so that they understand all the different problems they might face in the engineering and analysis worlds. Even if a project ends without being successful, such as not being able to come up with a solution after spending time on it, we don't consider that a failure. We feel that an investment in learning something that did not solve the problem takes us one step closer to finding something that does.

BUILDING BROAD SKILLS

One reason we have adopted this model is because clients use so many different technology stacks that no single individual can be an expert in all of them. To address this challenge, we have designated customer subject matter experts (SMEs) and specific toolset SMEs. We also have a number of different divisions that all contribute to cybersecurity, such as a cloud-based security team; connectivity and endpoint SMEs; and network intrusion detection system (IDS), intrusion protection system (IPS), and next-generation firewall SMEs. And we encourage people to move around within the company if they've done as much as they can in the area they're in, or even if they're just looking for a change.

Another thing MSSPs do very well is to run a hybrid model in which they put physical analysts on a customer site where they walk around in the environment and integrate with that customer team. Most of their people start at an operations center in Las Vegas, Phoenix, or Portland, but when an opportunity opens up in San Francisco, Charlotte, or Los Angeles, they raise their hands to go be a field engineer. Some people do that for a year or two, and then they come back with a whole new perspective and skillset.

WHY THE APPRENTICE MODEL WORKS

This is a very different approach from the traditional academic model. One of the things that scares people away from the cybersecurity field is that they walk into a computer science or cybersecurity class, and the first thing they are hit with is, "Welcome to Cybersecurity 101. Today we're going to talk about hexadecimal addition and subtraction." And I cannot understand the logic behind that. I think it's the equivalent of wanting to learn how to drive a car and on your very first day the instructor says, "We're going take apart this engine, and look at how the pistons work."

What we're doing instead is using a classic training model that goes back hundreds of years and that follows a path from apprentice to journeyman to master craftsman. In that model, on the first day of driving school I start with, "Here's the steering wheel, here's the gas pedal, and here's the brake. And here's how you shift from park into drive. And tomorrow we're just going to drive in straight lines." That's the mentality we've taken with our apprentice program.

ENGAGING MENTORS

Initially, I got a lot of pushback from senior analysts who thought, "These new people are going to come in and they're just going to be a drag. I'm going to have to spend all my time babysitting them." My response was, "Name a repetitive task that you have to do 10 times a day or 10 times a week. Identify a task that is not really the best use of your talents."

They identify something that requires someone to manually perform a task that we can't automate. Most of the time, it's chasing down false positives because one time out of 100 it's not a false positive, so we can't automatically clear them.

Then I said, "What if we trained one of these apprentices to do just that?" And their reaction is, "I wouldn't hate that at all." Of course, for the first 10 or 1,000 times, they're performing that task in a fully supervised status. Then we come up with a success criterion, treat it as a trainable task, and sign them off when they have demonstrated proficiency so that they can do it in an unsupervised status. And once you get them spun up on that task, you move to the next task. Gaining practical experience on very small subsets of technology stacks is a critical component of any training program. You can't replicate that in a classroom environment.

DEFINING TIERS AND STAGES

This approach requires a lot of preparation. Training can't be haphazard, because you may get someone with a lot of small skills but no coherent understanding of the bigger issues. So we define what an expert looks like, and we break it down into consumable tiers and stages. A junior-level stage has three levels, and we document what we expect a junior-level-one person should be able to accomplish, and on to junior-level-two, and junior-level-three, and so on. They get lists of things they should be able to do, and they can either do them or not. It's pretty cut and dried. And then we do the same thing for middle and senior levels.

At the senior tier, we expect individuals to be able to handle just about any problem. They should be able to sit alone, unsupervised, manage a group of people around them, and handle any issues we have experienced as an organization. Even for problems we have not yet encountered, we expect them to be able to troubleshoot and find a solution. Once we start getting into the team leads and the manager positions, of course, things begin to get a little bit squishy. It's hard to give someone a task list for leadership or management ability. But you do have to have worked your way up through the junior tier.

Probably the most important takeaway from all of this is that for any training or internal management process to be effective, you have to define your problem at the outset, establish a clear path of development, and assign mentors at every step of the process. That's where a lot of organizations fail. They've inherited a system that's been there for a long time, it's pretty loose, and there's no meticulous documentation of what's required to do a job or what happens once you've met those expectations. Many just don't seem to have the discipline to pull something like that together, so they suffer from an understaffed and overworked team. And it's all because they don't have a process in place to solve the security skills gap problem for themselves.

ABOUT THE CONTRIBUTOR

Chris McDaniels – CEO, CT Cubed, Inc.

Chris McDaniels is the CEO of CT Cubed, Inc., a cybersecurity consulting company. Formerly the chief security officer of a nationwide managed security service provider, McDaniels is also a US Air Force veteran with over 16 years of cybersecurity operations experience defending enterprise networks. In addition to being a distinguished graduate and instructor of the prestigious US Air Force Weapons School's Cyber Warfare Operations Weapons Instructor Course, McDaniels holds a bachelor of science degree in computer science as well as a master of business administration. He has extensive experience leading cybersecurity operations, including directing the Intrusion Prevention and Response Flight for the US Air Force Computer Emergency Response Team. Before founding CT Cubed, Inc., McDaniels served as the Chief of Adversary Cyber Integration and Chief of Training of the US Air Force Red Team, instructing and training US Air Force, Joint, and Coalition warfighters by replicating current and emerging cyberspace threats.

EMPLOYEE TRAINING IS KEY FOR CYBERSECURITY

Mo Katibeh, AT&T

Ask any business leader what keeps them up at night, and I'd be astonished if cybersecurity wasn't one of their top responses. This isn't new; it has been true for years. But I think the thing that many are concerned about is a sophisticated attack that manages to bypass all of their elaborate security planning and technologies and bring their organization's operations to a staggering halt, not with the latest, most sophisticated attack, but with one innocuous but convincing email.

People are aware of scams and phishing, but they still click on malicious links and infected files (from people they don't know) or from extremely convincing "fake" emails from friends or colleagues. So why aren't companies doing everything they can to prevent this? Answers generally fall into one of three camps.

The first concern is that the efforts are too expensive. But the cost of a single successful attack on an unsuspecting employee can easily outpace the cost of any training program or technology you might implement. The second concern is that training takes too much effort. However, I believe that the security of your data and operations should be worth any effort. And as for the third concern, that such efforts don't work, I simply disagree. Here's a real-world example.

AT&T worked with a boutique financial services firm after it suffered a phishing incident. This wasn't just an instance of some unsuspecting user clicking on a cat video. It was well planned and executed. On the surface, the malicious email certainly looked like the real thing. It came from a high-ranking employee in a client firm, under the person's name and email address. The email was filled with personal details, making it sound legitimate. So, when the sender concluded the message by requesting a $100,000 transfer to an overseas account, it never occurred to anyone to question it. No one, that is, until the real client inquired two weeks later about an outstanding payment.

That cyberthief used a combination of a disguised email address and data gleaned from the employee's social media accounts to create a convincing request. As a result, an experienced investment manager unwittingly became an accomplice in a six-figure heist (AT&T Cybersecurity Insights Report, Volume 1). However, regular training on how to spot a phishing or spear phishing attack (which is what this attack turned out to be) and how to respond to out-of-the-ordinary requests, like transferring $100,000 to an offshore account, may have saved everyone a lot of time and money and frustration.

SECURITY EVERYWHERE

For security to be effective, it must be all-encompassing. It needs to reach all areas of the organization. Security is a huge concern for us at AT&T because we are a constant target. Every day, every hour, every minute, we face relentless attempts to disrupt our business, steal information, or otherwise wreak havoc on our network. Why? Who knows? It doesn't really matter! Whether it's hackers who want to make a name for themselves, who have been hired to steal trade secrets, or just who want to watch the world burn, our focus remains unchanged because the health of the company depends on it.

Protecting our diverse operations has required us to create multiple layers of security. We use advanced, connected technology to make our operations better and more efficient because businesses, consumers, and employees trust us to protect their data. We also work with companies to help them put together strategic plans for improving their own security posture and then help them execute against those plans. We help them recover from the aftermath of a cybersecurity incident.

The threats organizations face are myriad, and we are committed to helping them keep pace. And in our own organization, we do this through an employee training and awareness program

We may have already transitioned to a world in which the number of businesses that have suffered a cybersecurity incident is greater than the number of those that haven't. (In 2015, some 62 percent of organizations acknowledged that they had been breached. AT&T Cybersecurity Insights Report, Volume 3.)

THE SCOPE OF THE PROBLEM

If we're a target, that means our employees are targets. This is true for every organization, and it's where the conversation needs to change and evolve. The truth is that a critical piece of any cybersecurity risk mitigation strategy in any organization rests with employees. Multiple studies report that the vast majority of all breaches are linked to employee behavior. In fact, 91 percent of cyberattacks and resulting data breaches begin with a phishing email. (See https://cofense.com/enterprise–phishing–susceptibility–report.) Some 78 percent of employees do not follow security policies, according to the AT&T Cybersecurity Insights Report, Volume 1, and some 25 to 30 percent of employees still click on suspect links (AT&T Cybersecurity Insights Report, Volume 4).

However, email phishing is just the tip of the iceberg of the things that organizations and employees need to be concerned about. Shadow IT is a mysterious term for something people in your organization probably do every day. When employees want to get their work done, and they don't necessarily feel that they have all the tools at their disposal to do so, what do they do? They become proactive and download one. That's shadow IT.

Maybe it's another Internet browser because the corporate-approved browser doesn't work with a particular website or application. Maybe it's a file compression tool or photo editor. Or perhaps they need a way to transfer large files that exceed email attachment size limits. It doesn't matter.

What's important is that IT is unaware that employees are using these tools and online services. As a result, applying patches might not be top of mind for the user, and as a result, vulnerabilities creep in. What most organizations may not know is the scale at which this is happening. According to the AT&T Cybersecurity Insights Report, Volume 1, some 81 percent of line-of-business respondents admitted to using shadow IT in the past. And between 2013 and 2015, before shadow IT became as prevalent as it is now, the financial impact was estimated at $740 million (AT&T Cybersecurity Insights Report, Volume 4).

Social media usage presents another channel rife with phishing threats. It can also be used, intentionally or inadvertently, to broadcast company secrets to a broader, external audience. Likewise, increased employee mobility has become a growing source of vulnerability. The ability to work from anywhere and at any time is immensely important for productivity and efficiency, but the risks it can introduce are significant.

Part of both of these trends involves allowing employees to use their own devices for business functions. While mixing personal and business activities on a single device that is owned by the employee is becoming more common, doing so relinquishes control and introduces new risks. For example, using mobile devices to store unencrypted data can result in multimillion-dollar regulatory fines. Even worse, nearly 40 percent of users admit that their mobile devices have been compromised occasionally or frequently over the previous 12 months (AT&T Cybersecurity Insights Report, Volume 4).

EDUCATING EMPLOYEES TO REDUCE RISK

Of course, this makes it sound as if everyone on your payroll is a huge liability with the potential to expose your organization to unnecessary levels of cybersecurity risk. But I don't think that's the case. Employees shouldn't be seen as security liabilities. They should be perceived as valuable pieces of the puzzle who play an essential role in keeping your organization safe. You just need a strategy. However, when one wrong click can mean millions of dollars' worth of losses, no organization can do this alone.

What is it worth to build and implement a plan to educate your employees about cybersecurity risk? There's a good chance that whatever value you place on it, you're underestimating it. One prevented breach might save your organization not just a lot of money, but its brand value, reputation, and even its ability to survive.

I support an organization that has more than 250,000 employees worldwide. Many of them use mobile and connected devices, and many more of them use AT&T email. The number of endpoints and threat vectors could be multiplied tenfold. This is exactly why we engage our employees as a critical element of our overall security strategy.

It doesn't require a persistent hacker, trying for months to infiltrate an organization, for your organization to be at risk. It could just be one person's bad day. Imagine a top-tier employee who follows cybersecurity protocols to a T 99.9 percent of the time.

What if one day they skip their coffee and mindlessly click on a link they shouldn't? That one mistake could halt operations or trigger a months-long saga in which you spend resources on protecting and rebuilding your reputation in addition to funding investigations and forensics.

Preventing that sort of incident needs to start by understanding that your employees have skin in the game. Helping them realize that they are an essential part of the organization gives them a sense of ownership and responsibility that will often cause them to think twice before making a careless mistake. Making that happen requires an effective training and education program that provides employees with the opportunity to

- Understand, even at a basic level, what the threat landscape looks like and acquire good cybersecurity habits they can use to address those threats.
- Embrace their role in mitigating risks. Good security behaviors can't be something they feel is burdensome, or they won't practice them. They need to understand the context and significance security plays within their own specific roles, including an awareness that cybersecurity incidents that affect the organization also affect them.
- Practice effective cybersecurity-focused behaviors consistently and vigilantly so that they become muscle memory.

WE'RE ALL IN THIS TOGETHER

My approach is to promote the reality that we're all in this together, because we are. The cybercriminal community has an army, so we need an army. It also helps when tips and tactics extend beyond the workplace. We do all this by focusing on an approach that we describe as "engage while learning." We keep employees engaged with a regular cadence of interesting and relevant topics like detecting suspicious links, retaining sensitive documents, and practicing safe social media behavior that they can apply at work as well as at home.

For us, engaging our employees means including compelling visuals in videos and images. We've found success in including gaming elements to better engage our workforce with entertaining, actionable objectives. We also create posters, stage live events, and even have a relatable cartoon mascot who embodies everything we want to accomplish with the program.

The results speak for themselves. When AT&T launched the program, link phishing was our most common issue, as it is for most organizations. In the two years since our program launched, we've seen a significant decrease in phishing incidents, according to AT&T's CSO, Tony Tortorici.

But what works for us might not be the right prescription for every organization. Not everyone needs to prioritize the same threats, and not everyone needs to address the same issues. Company culture plays a huge role as well. Tone, regularity of communications, and content all depend on what's "normal" within your organization.

The threat landscape's perpetually evolving nature is what makes establishing foundational elements so important. It makes it easy to assess, reassess, and activate your strategy.

While a plan should be unique to your organization, we see and hear common threads from our customers who are able to make real headway in building a successful awareness program. Here are some of the approaches that are commonly implemented:

Start at the top

While you need to engage everyone for a training and awareness campaign to work, employee buy-in for security starts at the top. We see the most impact when CEOs, board members, and top executives all lead by example. They need to embrace the policies publicly, talk about them in ways employees can understand and relate to, and then practice what they preach. A vital part of making that happen is helping your executive team understand the true value of cybersecurity awareness and ensuring they are willing to carve out the financial resources and time required for effective training and awareness programs.

Share the security responsibility

The International Organization for Standardization (ISO), an independent standards organization, published recommendations for information security management systems (ISMSs) called ISO 27001. Part of that recommendation called for organizations to create a steering group that includes members from across your organization, including leadership. The ISMS document is a good place to start. The National Institute of Standards and Technology (NIST) also provides best practice guidelines.

Train your users

Security awareness courses to teach people about topics like how to avoid phishing attacks and safely use social media are a good starting point. However, for this sort of training to stick, it needs to be both engaging and relevant. You should also consider reinforcing training with an awareness campaign that includes a regular cadence of posters, email and other electronic messages, and even short infomercials that require a quick acknowledgment.

EDUCATE YOURSELF AND PASS IT ON

While this discussion has centered on businesses and their ability to prepare their workforce for cybersecurity threats and challenges, the conversation is actually much larger. These themes and behaviors can and should extend beyond the workplace. Bad actors looking to steal your information for their own gain often aim for soft targets, whether that is a huge enterprise, a small business, or you. In almost every case, humans turn out to be the weakest link in any security strategy.

Take responsibility for educating yourself on how to best avoid being a victim, and then share that information—and enthusiasm—with others. This approach can also save you a lot of headaches in your personal life, as I'm certain many identity-theft victims can attest. For example, my wife just texted me asking, "Hey, I just received the following message. Should I click on it?" And I told her, "Nope. Don't click. Never click."

Herd immunity is why many horrible diseases that have plagued humanity no longer exist. Everyone working together is still the best way to prevent many of the problems that plague our modern society. Inoculating our networks—and digital lives—from cyberattacks, however, will take a little more than a simple vaccine. It will require innovation, along with embracing and adopting new technology. But perhaps most importantly, it means learning. Learn how you're vulnerable, make simple behavior changes, and then share those insights with others.

ABOUT THE CONTRIBUTOR

Mo Katibeh – CMO, AT&T

Mo Katibeh's background includes his recent role as senior vice president, Advanced Solutions, at AT&T, where he oversaw business solutions for cybersecurity, digital, cloud, Wi-Fi, and field services solutions. As part of one of the fastest-growing managed security service providers, his security portfolio spanned solutions ranging from public safety solutions, virtualized security functions, and threat management to a full-service security consulting practice. In 2016, Katibeh's managed security solutions team launched Threat Manager, providing unique visibility into both known and new cyberthreats, and improving the speed of deploying security protections. In previous AT&T roles, Katibeh managed their digital strategy and platform, strategic technology planning for the global Wireline Network, the Mobility Radio Access Network, and AT&T's Domain 2.0 initiative; led the AT&T Northeast Construction & Engineering; and managed regional IT.

Katibeh was recently promoted to chief marketing officer for AT&T Business, a $71 billion business unit. He oversees business solutions for cybersecurity and cloud connectivity and is responsible for AT&T's business marketing organization for traditional telecom services as well as mobility and strategic services, such as Ethernet, IP networking, hosting, software-defined networking in a wide area network (SD-WAN), and applications services.

TRAINING IS A MINDSET

Dave Rankin, Verisign

The traditional idea of cybersecurity training is now evolving to meet the needs of an increasingly digital-based society. Knowledge, experience, and expertise are still fundamental, but qualities like critical thinking, natural curiosity, problem-solving ability, and diversity of thought are also crucial in the development of a cybersecurity professional. While all education is valuable, cybersecurity training should not be dependent solely on select certifications or specific degrees. Training begins with the mindset that each person at every level brings something unique that enriches the team dynamic.

The training environment should be a highly collaborative place where individuals feel free to ask meaningful questions, raise concerns, suggest alternative approaches, and present new ideas. A successful cybersecurity training program is one that trains the whole person as part of a team. It utilizes strong mentors and maximizes the strengths of each individual in a way that complements the team as they work together to protect the organization from security threats.

THE CHALLENGE OF SECURITY CERTIFICATIONS

As security began to rapidly rise to the top of corporate priorities in the 1990s, organizations quickly encountered a severe shortage of cybersecurity professionals. The individuals chosen to fill these new positions generally had previous IT experience, often as a system administrator or network engineer. But as cyberthreats escalated and malicious hackers honed their craft, a severe shortage of cybersecurity professionals with deep technical skills became evident. To fill the gap, the market created a certification-based approach to training.

Unfortunately, certification was often a false step in helping organizations find the most qualified candidates to manage the growing threat landscape. Employers began using recruiting practices that focused on certification status rather than experience. At that time, it was commonplace for someone working in a totally unrelated field to attend a cybersecurity boot camp that taught them little more than how to pass a certification test. This led to the hiring and placement of individuals with little to no cybersecurity experience into highly specialized security roles. Despite being certified as experts, many of them lacked real-world cybersecurity experience, a curious mindset, or the benefit of strong mentoring that is essential for success. Given our current reliance on a digital economy, the consequences of having inexperienced people leading the security of our critical infrastructure could be devastating.

A cybersecurity certificate on its own is not enough. Certifications need to be tied to experience. This connection is already a common practice in other professional fields. One example is the Project Management Professional® (PMP®) certification. In addition to passing a test, a PMP® certification requires a minimum level of education and a minimum number of years of experience leading and directing projects. Cybersecurity certifications should follow a similar path. A limited number of cybersecurity certifications have recently started including experience requirements, which is a step in the right direction.

Overall, we must shift our focus from the current "memorize and repeat" mantra for cybersecurity or vendor security certifications and instead focus on training the whole person. Certifications and experience help us to identify potential skillsets, but the overall mindset of a cybersecurity professional is often the determining factor in their success. Ideally, someone with a cybersecurity mindset has a strong curiosity, seeing problems as challenges and using a combination of logic and intuition to identify risks and develop solutions to neutralize threats. It is essential to nurture and develop these qualities with the help of strong mentors.

THE IMPORTANCE OF MENTORS

Organizations should not underestimate the importance of developing successful mentoring relationships within their security training environment. Training is a mindset for the trainers, too. Being a mentor means being willing to share the benefit of acquired knowledge and experience. Mentoring takes a significant investment of time and energy, but fruitful mentoring relationships are positive and rewarding for both participants. A successful mentoring program should lead to a culture shift that pays knowledge forward and values lifelong learning and constant professional development.

LEVERAGING IT EXPERIENCE

In the coming years, we face a tight labor market and a shortage of experienced cybersecurity professionals. Organizations find themselves trying to fill security positions that have been open much longer than other types of positions in the company. One way to address this shortage is to consider training candidates who already have experience in adjacent areas of IT. It is much easier to train someone how to troubleshoot a firewall if they already know routing fundamentals.

This cross-training strategy doesn't just apply to entry-level positions. Many of the skills developed in IT architecture and engineering already include security fundamentals. For example, The Open Group Architectural Framework (TOGAF) enables organizations to design, evaluate, and build successful architectures. A talented IT architect or engineer fluent in TOGAF principles should be able to successfully transition into the role of a security architect. A training mindset facilitates these transitions at both an individual and an organizational level.

Organizations must value mentorship and make cybersecurity a training priority, and individuals must harness their natural curiosity and practice thinking critically to help the security team solve complex problems.

DEVELOP CRITICAL THINKING

Cybersecurity training is more than just a set of items on a checklist and goes beyond merely teaching the nuts and bolts of security. Developing critical thinking skills is an essential element of a successful training mindset. Critical thinking skills enable people to solve complex and often unexpected problems. In security, that's what we're doing all the time, and we're doing it at a fast pace in an ever-changing threat landscape. That is why the now outdated "memorize and repeat" style of training is ineffective and may actually give a false sense of security readiness. Critical thinking courses often use the powerful examples of both the Challenger and the Columbia space shuttle disasters to emphasize the importance of moving away from "groupthink" to thinking critically. Organizations must give critical thinkers a voice to speak out about discrepancies, the power to ask hard questions, and the freedom to tackle old problems in new ways.

THE NEED FOR DIVERSITY

Diversity of thought is not just business jargon. It refers to the way people think and learn, based on their unique set of work and life experiences. Diversity within our security teams can be just as transformational as it is in any other kind of team. Diversity brings different perspectives, and with them, new ways of analyzing and solving problems. Training the whole person means embracing and cultivating these different ways of thinking and learning. Ideally, a security team consists of individuals with diverse educational and employment experiences that enrich and complement each other.

It is important for us not to limit ourselves to recruiting individuals with a computer science or technology degree. For example, someone with a marketing background who thinks creatively could be a valuable asset in developing and delivering end-user security awareness training. They could even market security ideas to the broader organization, including senior management or the board of directors. The key to training is to develop the whole person, building on their skillset and cultivating their natural abilities. Utilizing individuals in ways that showcase their strengths not only allows them to grow and succeed but may also offer a competitive advantage to the organization.

UNDERSTAND THE WHY

Cybersecurity experts need training and development beyond technical skills. Security professionals need to be able to communicate effectively with people from different areas of the business. It can be a common misperception that "no" is the only word the security department knows. "No" should not be an automatic response to a request unless it is unethical or illegal.

Repeated denials of security requests can place departments at odds in an "us versus them" scenario that ultimately decreases the organization's productivity. An important part of security training should be to develop collaborative working relationships throughout the business and with our business partners. We need to understand what our business partners' needs actually are so that we can find ways to secure them to the best of our ability.

It is important to explain the "why" as it pertains to security controls. Why is that particular security control important to the company, to the stakeholders, to the individual's role or function? What are the potential consequences? What are other solutions? With effective communication, cybersecurity professionals can go from being seen as a roadblock to being seen as a partner in the success of the business.

DEVELOPING THE WHOLE PERSON

Cybersecurity training is more than a certificate or a degree. It is a mindset, focused on developing the whole person, on maximizing their natural strengths and empowering them to participate and contribute to the team in innovative ways. It is about harnessing the power of mentors and developing lifelong learners who strive to stay current as technology rapidly evolves. It is about effective communication, being able to collaborate with other departments in the business to mitigate risks to an acceptable level. Overall, cyber-security training is about the members of your team, the attributes they bring to the table, and a focus on developing the whole person.

ABOUT THE CONTRIBUTOR

Dave Rankin –*VP*, Information Security — Verisign

As vice president, information security, Dave Rankin is responsible for enabling all aspects of Verisign's information security program, as well as information governance risk and compliance (GRC). Additionally, he represents Verisign in key forums focused on critical infrastructure and security. With over 25 years of experience spanning numerous technology disciplines, Rankin has a unique blend of business and IT expertise across multiple industries, including commercial, defense, military, finance, consulting, and training.

Prior to joining Verisign, Rankin spent nine years at Raytheon, where he served as CISO for two Raytheon businesses, as well as the CIO of Raytheon United Kingdom. He has held leadership positions at Ernst & Young, Computer Associates, and Fannie Mae. In his past work, he designed and implemented the IT security infrastructure of the Bahamas International Stock Exchange, enabling remote trading for the first time in the country's history.

Rankin is a United States Air Force veteran and founding member of the Department of Defense's first cyberinformation warfare squadron, focusing on protecting the IT security posture of the United States and forward deployed locations in the Middle East.

FUNDAMENTAL STRATEGIES:

PROVEN STRATEGIES THAT DON'T LET US DOWN

The intractable shortcomings and inherent challenges of authentication continue to provide a large opportunity for cybercrime. Until we can solve the authentication problem once and for all—effectively authenticating people to machines, software to hardware, processes to operating systems, and more—we will forever be compensating for this vulnerability with other essential strategies and mechanisms.

In the meantime, all is not lost. Cryptography, high-fidelity access control, and agile macro- and micro-segmentation can provide a substantial amount of cybersecurity. Each of these strategies is in a constant, rapid process of evolution and iteration to keep pace with the increasing sophistication of risks. All three have proven to be impressively resilient defenses against even the most skillful attacks. Encryption, based on hard-to-solve mathematical principles, is often used to help weed out people who try to falsely authenticate. Access control limits people to only the assets they need to do their jobs. Segmentation, based on well-constructed computer science implemented in firewalls, is used to put extra security around assets, since no one has successfully invented an impenetrable guard.

There are interrelationships among cryptography, access control, and segmentation that compensate for less-than-ideal authentication. All three are forms of controlling access. Further, cryptography extends beyond the obvious use (encrypting data) and also protects the mechanisms used within access control and segmentation.

Each of these fundamental strategies has been able to build from straightforward basics to solutions with intense levels of tactical sophistication. Together, they have been extraordinarily effective tools against cybercrime. But like all defenses, they weaken over time, especially in the face of rapid, consistent innovation. The first step to strengthening them is understanding why they are essential.

The backbone of the science of cybersecurity is built from cryptography, access control, and segmentation.

6

CRYPTOGRAPHY

"Agile cryptography is an imperative now—not in a decade or two."

Taher Elgamal,
Salesforce

"Even an error that leaks a small amount of information can be exploited by an attacker and result in a complete break."

Dan Boneh,
Stanford

Cryptography harnesses the most fundamental principles of mathematics to secure data. Cryptography is astoundingly strong, almost mystical, and enduring—its first use was recorded in ancient Greece.

Cryptography is the layer of protection that safeguards segmentation and plays a key role in allowing or denying access. It also plays a role in keeping information private, in detecting changes to information (integrity), and creating confidence in the identity of a person or process (authentication).

Viewed by many as arcane technology, cryptography is a powerful way of encoding information. All the computers on Earth today would have to spend longer than the age of the universe to brute-force a single correctly encrypted Triple-DES encrypted message.

But as quantum computing gets closer to becoming an operational reality, the protective power of important applications of cryptography will be lost. And if cryptography fails, so too will segmentation and access control.

Strong encryption, correctly implemented, is one of the rare silver bullets available to the security community.

Cryptography is based on certain mathematical properties that make it easy to compute one value, but really difficult to compute the reverse of it. An analogy for how encryption works can be easily found in a high school math class that has learned about prime numbers. It's pen-and-paper-straightforward to multiply two 9-digit prime numbers together, but extraordinarily hard to figure out what two unknown prime numbers were multiplied together to get an 18-digit number. Although creating that product is effortless, reversing the process is incredibly difficult.

Though there is a fundamental difference between the two main forms of cryptography used in data protection today—symmetric and asymmetric encryption—both leverage a mathematical technique that, when correctly implemented, creates something extraordinarily powerful.

Symmetric encryption allows senders and receivers to convey information privately to each other using a single shared secret key to scramble the data into forms that are meaningless to anyone else who doesn't have that key. Asymmetric encryption, often used to establish a secret key for symmetric encryption (and used for many other important purposes), employs a different technique: A "public key" is used by many to encrypt the data, but only a separate "private key" is able to decrypt it (that is, two different keys are used). A good analogy for asymmetric encryption is a combination lock: Anyone can close the lock (lock it) but only one person knows how to unlock it.

When correctly implemented and initialized, both forms of encryption are impressively resilient to brute-force attacks that try to crack them by cycling through all possible numeric combinations of the key that decrypts their ciphers.

How impressively resilient?

If a hacker were to obtain a computer sophisticated enough to launch a brute-force attack against a 128-bit key at the rate of one key per second, it would take approximately 149 trillion years to guess all possible keys necessary to crack the symmetric encryption. The universe itself is only 13.75 billion years old.

However, the accelerating speed and power of innovation can erode the protective power base of mathematical truths. What we once considered unshakable must now be reexamined. With quantum computing on the horizon—some estimates predict its arrival in 20 years or sooner—the deployment of formulas such as Shor's algorithm and Grover's algorithm could make asymmetric encryption far less secure.

As a science, practice, and discipline, cybersecurity has only a few silver bullets. For now, cryptography is the rare exception, a simple, powerful way to provide substantial protection against the torrential downpour of cyberattacks. But though cryptography remains one of cybersecurity's most powerful tools today, we must always prepare for the risks we will face tomorrow.

CRYPTOGRAPHY: THE BACKBONE OF CYBERSECURITY

Taher Elgamal, Salesforce

Amidst all the digital doomsday blogging about the impending chaos of data protection in a post-quantum world, it is easy to understand why some may think there is an hourglass slowly counting down to the inevitable moment when the information security we have come to depend on may be rendered obsolete.

But with some planning, and by using the same care and caution that scientists and mathematicians put into correctly designing and implementing strong cryptography, we can continue to leverage the goodness encryption brings to cybersecurity, even in the future with quantum computers.

There is no denying that quantum computing—which some speculate will be ready for initial adoption, at least by nation-states and the upper echelons of digital businesses, within 20 years—could undermine some of today's encryption standards. And though it's seemingly comforting to think that data coveted today, such as credit card numbers and expiration-loaded financial data, will be long obsolete by the time quantum computing is a reality, some will still be relevant—including Social Security numbers, mortgage and medical information, trade secrets, and proprietary information. So that means that encrypted data today, if stored for about 20 years, could be decrypted and compromised with a future quantum computer.

Either circumstance means that we should be planning for the future in which quantum computers exist.

But rather than devote inordinate amounts of attention to debating a potential impending doom, we should focus on actual cryptography challenges that are occurring now. Solving them makes us immeasurably more secure than we are today and will also inform and catalyze the development of the type of agile cryptography we need more and more.

Unfortunately, focusing on the current issues does not involve a "moonshot"—the kind of audacious, heavily branded external mission that delivers reputation equity whether or not it succeeds. Instead, it demands that we—both as an industry and as global users of digital information and connectivity—be internally reflective about how we protect and consume data. After all, genius is 1 percent inspiration and 99 percent perspiration. It would be wrong of us to project a kind of mysticism onto cryptography's formidable mathematical and scientific theory in order to absolve ourselves of the rigors of better understanding.

A GAIN THAT IS MORE THAN WORTH THE PAIN

It's helpful to look back to the beginning of cryptography's adoption as a fundamental aspect of cybersecurity—a process originally encumbered by the lack of financial incentive in developing cryptographic algorithms and made more efficient by the ease of following suit with the practices endorsed by standards organizations and adopted by the biggest companies of the era.

Unlike many fundamentals of cybersecurity, which have seemingly struggled to keep pace with the blistering velocity of data and threat alike, encryption has been at the core of data protection since the beginning of the modern Internet. And it has remained remarkably resilient against an intense rate of innovation.

But cryptography is also a highly specific and intensely idiosyncratic discipline that requires deep knowledge to implement and deploy correctly. And because it is such a specialized and complex mathematical science, that deep knowledge is held by a relatively small community of cryptographers.

That problem—a huge upside combined with a small number of experts—means that cryptography is too often deployed imperfectly by those less seasoned in the discipline and still appears to function appropriately. This creates serious vulnerabilities that are completely overlooked by those who consider cryptography to be magically impervious to breach, regardless of how it is deployed or implemented.

As a result, many chief information security officers (CISOs) are inadvertently—and unwittingly—implementing encryption in ways that fail to leverage the fundamental strengths of cryptography. This creates risk at the organizational level. To slow this unintentionally reckless implementation, it is critical to understand cryptography's strengths and its modern history alike.

From the very advent of cybersecurity, cryptography was one of the first tools to be embedded into Secure Sockets Layer (SSL), which is now called TLS. It was an enduring solution to a truism that still drives security today: The Internet's openness is also a weakness, and without encryption, there is no means to create confidentiality, integrity, and authentication. This core strength of cryptography is critical, of course—and it has received the majority of the focus in terms of both its valuation and its functionality. This is especially true in the post–General Data Protection Regulation (GDPR) era, as the concepts of confidentiality and privacy are increasingly perceived as being interchangeable (to the disservice of each, it is worth noting).

Confidentiality is important but by no means the most critical aspect of encryption. As a security feature, integrity is often more important. If you received a financial transfer of $10,000, it could be understandably inconvenient or uncomfortable to have that transaction lack privacy. But it would be a different problem entirely if that transfer lacked integrity rather than confidentiality—if, for instance, a zero was removed and you received $1,000 instead. Extrapolate that out to, say, the majority of global currency in a digitally driven financial system for just a glimpse of the scope of the impact of weak integrity.

Equally important is authentication. While privacy is central to secure personal and business communication, it is critical to know that you're communicating with the right party. If you are not, the confidentiality of the communication doesn't matter—and could, in fact, intensify the risk.

It's the encryption algorithms used for integrity, authentication, and to establish confidentiality—called "asymmetric encryption algorithms"—that are most at risk for quantum computing attacks.

BUILDING ON A STRONG FOUNDATION

The beauty of cryptography is that theoretically (which is perhaps the most important adverb in all of cybersecurity), it provides all three critical aspects of security: Confidentiality, integrity, and authentication. As a mathematical theory, cryptography is extremely powerful. But as a quick glance at the most infamous of breaches will prove, the implementation of cryptography is extremely difficult to get right. And when done incorrectly, it creates a house of cards of unprotected data that can topple with shocking speed and scale.

Heartbleed, the massive 2014 compromise of a security vulnerability in the OpenSSL cryptography library, is perhaps the most notable example. Neither a virus, as it was at times wrongly identified, nor a failure of the cryptography itself, Heartbleed was a programming error that exploited the implementation of the use of cryptography to render it toothless.

It is hard to imagine a more dramatic way to learn a lesson, but even so, some organizations—even major ones—are still not aware of the threats to their cryptography from side-channel attacks and programming errors.

There are many probable reasons for this. One is the overvaluing of cryptography's mathematical strengths in a way that makes its implementation seems less critical than it is—which is a serious error. Not only is implementation what determines the strength of the encryption itself, but cryptography is deceptively challenging and should never be done by anyone other than an expert. There are a thousand different ways to implement cryptography, but only one way to do it correctly. You can write code that implements the mathematics of a cryptographic algorithm, and it will work in the sense that it will encrypt and decrypt correctly. But its security assurance will likely not be as strong as intended, creating vulnerabilities that can be exploited and even making it possible to extract the core secret—the cryptographic key—out of a running system.

In the physical world, an analogy might be designing a rocket that has enough thrust to leave Earth's orbit but making engineering errors in the building of the rocket that cause it to fail to achieve enough speed. Alternately, you might build an exquisitely engineered rocket whose designed thrust levels are inadequate to escape Earth's gravity.

Compounding that challenge is the fact that cryptography programming is a rarified skillset with a growing need for experts—in an industry that already struggles with a dearth of talent. Factor in the necessity and benefits of encryption, and it is increasingly common to see cryptographic systems incorrectly implemented by even the most skilled engineers. This is no reflection on engineers' abilities, but no one would want the most brilliant cardiologist in the world performing their brain surgery. Like most important things, it takes expertise and attention to detail to get things right; cryptography's power is a testament to the incredibly granular specificity of correct implementation.

It is stunning how vulnerable even the smallest or simplest human errors render a cryptosystem—from the carelessness of leaving a clear text key sitting on a filesystem somewhere to the oversight of a bad implementation of a buffer. Even the lack of understanding that encryption algorithms are very different from each other can have huge implications; even the best encryption algorithms, such as RSA or Diffie-Hellman, potentially have a set of weak initializations that should never be utilized. But if an organization's chosen cryptographic library does not thoroughly check for these, it is possible for one of these bad keys or configurations to be utilized, rendering the system unsecured.

Vulnerabilities also exist in the supporting functions that feed the cryptography itself. Random number generation is the one that often receives the most focus, since strong encryption using weak random initializations can reveal patterns in keys, undermining the strength of the encryption. There is a whole methodology derived from cryptanalysis to achieve that randomization, since without it, the keys themselves could be weak.

Together, these factors converge to create a situation where improperly executed implementation by those who are not cryptographers creates the appearance of effective encryption while eclipsing side-channel vulnerabilities that can be exploited to a massive extent. Consider it the perfect storm that forms our current cryptography crisis—and a glimpse of the severity of storms to come if left uncorrected.

That's why the scientists in the most sophisticated cryptography organizations build their cryptography to withstand single points of failure. They do their very best, but still plan for the worst.

AGILITY NOW!

But by building in safeguards that allow us to agilely upgrade to the next secure encryption standard, we can not only be prepared to adjust to the problems that emerge today, but also be prepared to take on the challenges of tomorrow.

It is important to understand that this correction must happen at an industry level, but it must also occur at the organizational level, between CISOs and their teams. They will be in a much better position to galvanize and effect that correction, and will also drive the iteration of agile cryptography. As important as the challenges are now, they will only increase in importance as standards and algorithms change. And, yes, pending quantum computing shapes the pace at which we embrace cryptography agility as a new digital reality.

Here's how CISOs and chief technology officers (CTOs) can make a difference.

The first step—both in sequence and importance—must be for every organization to dedicate a team member to understanding the basic structure of the company's cryptography footprint. Although, of course, it is not possible for any but the most powerful companies to have a dedicated team of cryptographers, it is an indicator of cryptography's importance that they all do. Nonetheless, every business still needs an employee who understands which version of OpenSSL is deployed, for instance, and who can ask vendors the correct questions about the encryption and security of new equipment. This role provides a valuable point person for outside consultants as well, who can be efficient and effective resources for better understanding and assessing the strength of a system's cryptography. Without this role in place, the next step becomes far more difficult, if not impossible. And it is already extremely challenging in its own right.

Organizations must conduct an audit of the systems they have in place just to determine where they are actually using encryption. Finding all those systems and compiling the different types of algorithms and libraries used is extremely laborious and painstaking. For most companies, there is encryption everywhere—in hardware and software alike, in current and outdated versions, some functional, some not—with little to no record of what was deployed and when. The issues this creates can make a CISO's head spin.

What libraries and algorithms have been used? Where are the keys stored and how long must they be kept? How are they secured?

How are they accessed for upgrades and updates? These are serious questions with very tangible business impacts and associated risks, and yet many companies have no way to answer them. And, to date, there is no process to automate that audit—though it would be a valuable, and extremely lucrative, contribution. (On your mark; get set; go, innovators.)

Once organizations have a dedicated professional auditing their cryptography, they may have to steel their nerves when they see what is revealed. Often this includes old, broken algorithms; configurations that leave security gaps; weaknesses in software; and an intensifying sprawl of Internet of Things (IoT) devices that contain some degree of encryption but have never had their default passwords changed. Understanding and preparing for the risks and contingencies these situations create is critical to maintaining the security of a network—now, not in the future.

But perhaps the most valuable understanding this process drives is the recognition that the need for agile cryptography is an imperative now—not in a decade or two. One of the most significant challenges facing cryptography today is figuring out how to replace encryption algorithms and manage digital certificates and keys in better and more managed ways without breaking things. Agile cryptography is a relatively new science but an increasingly important one. It takes into consideration that all cryptography will eventually become obsolete, so there needs to be a strategic process in place to manage things such as algorithm migration.

Currently, there's no simple process in place to help you migrate when cryptographic algorithms are obsolete or compromised, nor is there any documentation that explains how to replace your encryption libraries easily. Part of the challenge lies in the way we have implemented encryption.

There is encryption in hardware because it is difficult to open and find the key. But what if the algorithm used in the device is declared weak? What then? Is the nightmare of ripping and replacing equipment really a solution? That is extremely difficult even when an organization knows where it is. There may be an old virtual private networking (VPN) device someplace that a remote team is using to connect to the mothership that is never considered because it's been there for years. That kind of situation is extremely common—and there is no acceptable remedy in place.

QUANTUM RESISTANCE

It is a well-worn maxim among those who deal with crises that the best time to prepare for one is before it is happening. Nothing intensifies damage like allowing issues to fester and grow.

For cryptography, the overemphasis on the speculation of quantum computer availability is allowing many to believe that they have time in the years ahead to address these issues. But that is a process that should already be under way. When organizations get into it, the depth and intensity of the complexity it reveals will likely come as an unpleasant—and seemingly unending—surprise. If this causes some organizations to hold off on assessing their cryptography, they should remind themselves that if it seems challenging now with functioning encryption, imagine attempting the necessary next steps without it.

In other words, cryptographic agility, built in now, addresses both pre-quantum and post-quantum computer risks.

While there are many more advanced uses that have seen very rare implementations—including zero knowledge schemes that can improve authentication, multiparty computation that can bolster the security of stored and used keys, and a variety of homomorphic or functional encryption technologies—the challenge for users of the most commonly deployed cryptography is one that demands immediate, widespread attention. No individual organization can fix it on its own, of course—but every organization must be ready to be part of that solution. Those who do not take action may well realize, long after it is too late, that the arrival of quantum computing will not be the beginning of the cryptography crisis. It will not be the end, either.

ABOUT THE CONTRIBUTOR

Taher Elgamal – CTO, Salesforce

Taher Elgamal is an industry veteran in Internet security. He is the inventor of the Elgamal Digital Signature scheme, which is the basis for Digital Signature Algorithm (DSA). While serving as chief scientist of Netscape Communications, he was the driving force behind SSL. Elgamal was the recipient of the 2009 RSA conference Lifetime achievement award.

Elgamal serves as the CTO, Security for Salesforce. He was the founder and CEO of Securify and was the director of engineering at RSA Security Inc. prior to joining Netscape in 1995, and founding Securify in 1998. Elgamal has served and is serving on many public and private boards. He also served and is serving on the advisory boards of many security and software companies.

Elgamal has MS and PhD degrees in electrical engineering from Stanford University and a BS in electrical engineering from Cairo University.

CRYPTOGRAPHY: THE GOOD, THE BAD, AND THE FUTURE

Dan Boneh, Stanford

Cryptography is an important tool for protecting information in computer systems. It is used to protect data transmitted in computer networks and data stored in long-term storage. It is used for access control and data privacy, and more generally, gives some control over who can read and write what data. Cryptography is absolutely vital for commerce—without it, businesses could not transact online with other businesses and with their customers, or even among themselves. Without cryptography, computer systems would be far less useful than they are today.

Despite its enormous success, cryptography is difficult to deploy correctly in practice. A system handling sensitive information may be user friendly and reliable. Yet if the cryptography is not done correctly, the system could be completely vulnerable to attack. No one will know about the vulnerability until it is exploited. As we will see, seemingly small errors can lead to a complete compromise. Even an error that leaks a small amount of information can be exploited by an attacker and result in a complete break.

Here we explore why cryptography is so hard to get right and ways to address this. We will look at some common mistakes and ways in which cryptography often fails in practice. Generally speaking, failures fall into one of three categories:

- *Mistakes in the design* where a deployed cryptosystem or protocol is not as secure as the designers had hoped. For example, we will look at some issues in the design of a web encryption protocol that led to attacks.
- *Mistakes in the implementation* where the scheme is well designed but the implementation deviates from the design in a way that does not affect regular operation and yet opens the system to attack. A good example is a well-publicized bug called "goto error" in a cryptographic library that exposed some systems to attack.

- *Side-channel attacks* where the system is compromised by an attacker that measures side information, such as the time that the system takes to respond to requests or the amount of power used to compute a response. This information is often sufficient to mount an attack.

In the next three sections, we will look at each of these categories in turn and discuss the ways in which the cryptography community addresses these issues.

DESIGNING CRYPTOSYSTEMS AND PROTOCOLS

Over the past several decades, it has become clear that we cannot design cryptographic protocols by following a simple set of guidelines and hope that the final design is secure. Instead, the field of cryptography has been transformed from an art into a rigorous science where every proposed cryptosystem and protocol must be accompanied by a rigorous security argument.

It is best to illustrate this through an example. Consider public key encryption. Here a user, Alice, generates a pair of keys, one called a public key and the other called a secret key. She keeps the secret key to herself and makes the public key public. Anyone who obtains Alice's public key can send her an encrypted message by running an encryption algorithm that takes as input the public key and the message and outputs a ciphertext. The ciphertext is then sent to Alice, who can decrypt it using her secret key. In particular, Alice runs a decryption algorithm that takes as input her secret key and the ciphertext and outputs the decrypted message. The decryption algorithm may also output a special "reject" symbol to indicate that the received ciphertext was malformed. The triplet of algorithms—key generation, encryption, and decryption—is called a public key cipher.

Before we can construct a public key cipher and argue that it is secure, we need to define what a secure cipher is. This turns out to be much harder than expected and took many years, until a widely accepted definition called *chosen ciphertext security* emerged. We cannot give the full definition here, but it suffices to say that a public key cipher is chosen ciphertext secure if an adversary can learn nothing new about the decryption of a challenge ciphertext ct, even if the adversary can ask Alice to decrypt any ciphertext of its choice other than *ct*.

Now that we know what we are trying to construct, the next question is how to construct a chosen ciphertext secure public key cipher. Over the years, a number of such schemes have been designed and are deployed in real-world systems. An important property of these schemes is that they are accompanied by a theorem that proves the following fact: If there is an efficient chosen ciphertext adversary that breaks the scheme, then there is also an efficient algorithm that solves a certain hard computational problem, such as factoring a large integer or computing a discrete logarithm. Hence, if we are willing to accept that no efficient algorithm can solve the hard problem, then there cannot be a chosen ciphertext attack on the scheme. This type of theorem is called a proof of security for the scheme. It would be better if we could prove chosen ciphertext security unconditionally—that is, without having to assume that a certain problem is hard—but that is currently beyond our reach.

Generally speaking, this is how cryptographic design works. Step 1: Define a security model that describes what adversaries we are trying to defend against. Step 2: Propose a concrete construction. Step 3: Prove that the scheme is secure, in the given security model, assuming certain accepted computational assumptions. Often these steps need to be iterated to ensure that the model is adequate, the construction is practical, and a theorem can be proved.

Over the years, we have learned that these three steps are necessary for a sound cryptographic design. Unfortunately, as we will see in the next section, these steps are only the beginning and are not sufficient by themselves to ensure security.

Bleichenbacher's attack. To conclude this section, let's see an example of an elegant attack that shows how a small information leak can completely compromise a cryptographic protocol. The attack applies to a widely used public key encryption standard called RSA-PKCS1 mode 2. The standard specifies how key generation, encryption, and decryption work. Decryption proceeds in a number of steps. In the first step, the decryptor uses its secret key to apply a process called RSA inversion to the given ciphertext. Next, it checks to see if the resulting data begins with the characters "02" and if not, the decryptor outputs "reject". If so, then the decryptor performs a few more simple steps and outputs the resulting message.

In 1998, Daniel Bleichenbacher showed that this widely used standard is not chosen ciphertext secure and presented a practical attack. To see how this attack works, suppose that the attacker has intercepted a ciphertext ct encrypted under Alice's public key. The attacker wants to decrypt this ciphertext, but he does not have Alice's secret key. As it turns out, it is quite easy for the attacker to create a new ciphertext ct' where the RSA inversion of ct' is twice the RSA inversion of ct. The attacker can now send this new ciphertext ct' to Alice and observe her response. If Alice sends back a message saying that the ciphertext was malformed, the attacker learns that the RSA inversion of ct' does not begin with the characters "02". If she sends back any other error message, then the attacker learns that the RSA inversion of ct' does indeed begin with "02".

How is this useful? This tiny information leak seems insignificant, and yet it can be used to completely decrypt the ciphertext ct. To do so, the attacker creates a sequence of ciphertexts, each one related to ct, but where the RSA inversion is some known multiple of the RSA inversion of ct. It sends each of these ciphertexts to Alice to decrypt and observes her response. After about 4 million queries, the attacker learns the entire decryption of ct. Four million queries may seem like a large number, but if Alice is a web server then 4 million queries can be processed in just a few minutes, as was demonstrated in practice. This is a wonderful example of how a seemingly insignificant information leak can completely compromise a system.

There are a number of ways to address this vulnerability. The recommended approach is to move to an encryption scheme that has been shown to be chosen ciphertext secure. These days systems that need public key encryption use a variant of the ElGamal public key encryption scheme that is known to be chosen ciphertext secure under a standard computational assumption.

IMPLEMENTING CRYPTOGRAPHY

Modeling and proving cryptographic security as discussed in the previous section is a necessary first step, but it is far from sufficient for ensuring security. Even when the cryptosystem or protocol is well designed, it is still possible that implementation bugs will cause the system to be insecure. The following are a few examples that capture common bugs that occur in practice:

Weak Sources of Randomness. Much of cryptography depends on locally generated randomness that is unknown to an attacker. For example, when parties need to generate keys, it is important that those keys are chosen at random from a strong entropy source that the adversary cannot predict. This is much harder than it looks and is often the source of vulnerabilities. Consider a cheap IoT device that needs to communicate securely with a cloud server. When the device is first turned on, it needs to generate a key pair for use in a public key encryption scheme. The trouble is that at that point in time the device does not have a strong pool of entropy. Recent works beautifully show that such devices often end up generating the same key or closely related keys. Because the entropy pool is so small, anyone can recover the private keys of many devices from their public keys.

The only way to defend against this problem is to ensure that devices have sufficient entropy when they need it for cryptographic applications. Fortunately, several modern processors include a hardware random generator that can provide entropy on demand, and this entropy can be used as one of several sources of entropy for cryptographic operations. This is still not available on all low-end processors, but we can hope that in time it will be.

Missed Checks. To defend against data coming from a potentially malicious source, cryptographic systems often include a number of checks that must be applied in order to reject malicious inputs. For example, when decrypting a given ciphertext or verifying a digital signature, one rejects the data if it fails to pass a number of checks (such as checking for "02", as discussed in the previous section). It is a fairly common mistake that some of these checks are dropped or implemented incorrectly, thereby opening up the system to attack. Some examples include the aforementioned "goto error" bug where a number of certificate checks were accidentally skipped, an attack on the RSA-PKCS1 signature scheme where a critical step in signature validation was skipped, and an attack on validating certificate chains where an important step was not implemented. In all these cases, the system operates fine but is completely vulnerable to attack.

Fault Attacks. Suppose a software library implementing integer multiplication has a hidden bug: The library computes the correct product for all inputs, except for a single pair of numbers where it obtains the wrong product. Bugs like this are difficult to detect by testing because the offending input will likely never be encountered during testing. Nevertheless, such a bug can result in a complete exposure of a secret key. Consider a device holding a secret key. Several works show that an attacker can send malicious input to the device to trigger the bug. As a result, the device computes the wrong result, and this wrong result can make it possible for the attacker to extract the secret key from the device.

A Bad Optimization. Developers love to write optimized code, and rightfully so. Optimizing cryptography code, however, can be quite dangerous because the optimizations can lead to vulnerabilities. A well-known example, called the ROCA attack, is a devastating vulnerability in RSA-PKCS1 key generation code that was a direct result of an optimization to the key generation algorithm. It made key generation faster, but the resulting keys were insecure: The private key could be computed given only the public key.

While these bugs make it seem as if the situation is bleak, that is not quite the case. Impressive advances in software verification make it possible to prove that a software implementation matches the cryptographic specification. These verification tools hold the promise of eliminating some of the bugs discussed here, except for the question of weak randomness. The weak randomness problem is much harder to address, although there is progress there, too, thanks to the introduction of new sources of entropy from the embedded hardware.

SIDE-CHANNEL ATTACKS

Even when the cryptography specification is sound and the implementation is bug-free, the system can still be insecure due to a clever type of attack called a side-channel attack. Side channels refer to information leaked by a working system as it executes a cryptographic algorithm. Some example side-channels attacks include, among others:

Timing Attacks. Measure the time that the system takes to run the cryptographic algorithm

Power Attacks. Measure the amount of power used by the system as it executes a cryptographic algorithm

E/M Attacks. Measure the electromagnetic radiation generated by the processor as it executes a crypto algorithm

Log Analysis. Examine the error messages written to a log file

These attacks are extremely effective. For example, in some cases, a timing attack can extract a server's secret key, even if the measurement is not very precise. Similarly, by measuring the system's power consumption, an attacker can sometimes read the bits of the secret key directly from the power chart. A more subtle use of the measured information, called differential power analysis, can be used to extract the key bits even when the measurements are highly noisy.

Defending against side-channel attacks is quite difficult. Many cryptography libraries attempt to defend against timing attacks by making sure that every operation takes a fixed amount of time. Defending against power and E/M attacks is even harder. Many of the defenses either make the device more expensive because of additional hardware requirements or make the system slower because of extra complexity in the software.

It is fair to say that understanding the full power of side-channel attacks, and designing cost-effective defenses, is still a very active area of research.

ADVANCED CRYPTOGRAPHY

So far, we mostly focused on the core of cryptography: Data confidentiality, data integrity, and user authentication. But cryptography can do so much more. This last section briefly discusses more advanced capabilities, some of which can seem like magic. Some are ready for use and are being deployed, whereas others are further out.

Zero-Knowledge Proofs. Let one party, Alice, prove that a certain fact is true without revealing anything else about that fact. Anyone can verify the proof and be convinced. As a simple example, suppose Alice encrypts a number between zero and five under Bob's public key. Let ct be the resulting ciphertext. She wants to prove to Claire that ct is indeed an encryption of a number between zero and five but without telling Claire what the number is. She can do so by giving Claire a zero-knowledge proof that confirms this fact. Claire can verify the proof and be convinced, without learning anything about the decryption of ct, other than it is a number between zero and five. One of the most surprising results in cryptography is that any fact that Alice can prove to Claire, she can also prove to Claire in zero knowledge. This result has far-reaching implications to data privacy; Alice can convince anyone that some data satisfies a certain property without revealing anything else about the data.

Multiparty Computation. Reduces the need for trusted parties. A simple example is a sealed bid auction. Usually bidders submit their votes privately to a trusted third party, an auctioneer, who declares the winner. But how can the bidders trust the auctioneer to keep their bids private and honestly declare the winner? Multiparty computation is a technique that converts any problem that can be solved using a trusted third party into an interactive protocol among the participants that eliminates the trusted party. At the end of the protocol, the participants learn the final outcome, but nothing else is revealed about their initial inputs. In particular, they can run the sealed bid auction as an interactive protocol among the participants. The winner is declared, but nothing else about the bids is disclosed.

Functional Encryption. Shows that decryption is not an all-or-nothing proposition. It is possible to provide someone with a "functional" secret key that reveals certain information about the plaintext and nothing else. As an example, consider a service that filters spam email. If an email for Bob is encrypted under Bob's public key, then the service cannot do its job unless Bob gives it the secret decryption key. The trouble is that the service can then read the entire email in the clear. Bob could instead give the service a functional secret key that computes the "is this spam" predicate and outputs yes or no. The spam filter could use this functional secret key to test whether the decrypted email is spam without learning anything else about the contents of the email. Although functional encryption has some remarkable applications, we do not yet have a general-purpose scheme that is efficient enough to be used in practice. This is still an active area of research.

Post-Quantum Cryptography. Ensures that cryptography continues to be strong for many years to come. Quantum computers use the laws of quantum physics to solve certain problems that are believed to be intractable for classical computers. One such problem is breaking existing public key schemes. This has significant implications for the security of encrypted data; data that is encrypted today using a public key encryption scheme, such as ElGamal encryption, will be decrypted once a large enough quantum computer is built. We do not know when such a quantum computer will be available, if ever, but some expect one to be ready in a few decades. This means that data encrypted today may become exposed at that time, and this worries organizations that deal with highly sensitive long-term data. To address this risk, we can update our public key encryption algorithms so that they remain secure even if the attacker is equipped with a large quantum computer. There are currently a number of known techniques that resist these attacks, as far as we know, and we expect them to be standardized by the National Institute of Standards and Technology (NIST) in the coming years. At that time, organizations that are concerned with long-term confidentiality can double-encrypt their data with both classically secure encryption and post-quantum secure encryption. Hence, quantum computers are only a short-term risk. Once post-quantum cryptography is used widely, they will no longer pose a risk. Cryptography will survive.

CONCLUSIONS

We encourage companies that deploy cryptography in their products to develop sufficient in-house expertise to properly design and validate the schemes they deploy. Many resources are available for learning more about real-world cryptography. Some books include *Introduction to Modern Cryptography* by Jonathan Katz and Yehuda Lindell (Chapman and Hall, 2014), and *A Graduate Course in Applied Cryptography* by Dan Boneh and Victor Shoup (Stanford, 2017).

While cryptography is an important tool, it is important to remember that it is only one aspect of the much larger field of computer security. It is quite possible that a product implements its cryptography correctly and yet the overall system is completely insecure because of a software vulnerability or a design flaw that has nothing to do with cryptography. The computer security problem is much more complex and will be solved only by treating its strategies and solutions with the same precision that is noted as essential for cryptography, but this is a topic for other chapters in this book.

ABOUT THE CONTRIBUTOR

Dan Boneh – Computer Science, Stanford University

Dan Boneh is a professor of computer science at Stanford University, where he heads the applied cryptography group and co-directs the computer security lab. Boneh's research focuses on applications of cryptography to computer security. His work includes cryptosystems with novel properties, web security, cryptography for blockchains, and cryptanalysis. He is the author of over 150 publications in the field and is a recipient of the 2014 ACM prize, the 2013 Godel prize, the RSA award in mathematics, and six best paper awards. In 2016 he was elected to the National Academy of Engineering.

7
ACCESS CONTROL

"A one-size-fits-all approach to access control is no longer sufficient."

Erik Devine,
Riverside Health

"We live in a world we want to trust, but because there is so much at stake, we also need to verify."

George Do,
Equinix

As a parallel and complement to effective segmentation, covered next, access control effectively protects specific datasets in alignment with their value, importance, and risk if breached. Access control has deep roots in our cultural history; those with belongings such as food or tools wanted to limit others' access to their stuff by using doors, cabinets, keys, locks, chains, and many other mechanisms. Access control quickly expanded to include geographic borders and—perhaps even more strongly—borders defined by shared ideology, theology, identity, and beliefs. Access control writ large is in headlines today in terms of mechanisms to control borders, immigration, and citizenship.

The business of Internet security is about granting or denying permission for people to get to assets. Proxies sometimes represent people—software, processes, hardware—but each of those things serves a person's need. Assets can be either data—zeros and ones—or computing—the power to manipulate the zeros and ones. Access control provides a means of ensuring that people, processes, and technology touch only the assets they are supposed to.

In a world of perfect authentication, access control is merely a mechanism for a known, approved, and verified person to access assets through an impenetrable guard. The problem is that authentication is one of the failed foundations of the Internet. That means we can't verify that an individual is "known and approved." Making matters worse is that it is rare to find an "impenetrable guard."

Further, at the core of access control is a pragmatically pessimistic recognition: Access control is fallible. You will be compromised. However, sound strategy does not endorse fatalism. Effective access control makes it as difficult as possible for adversaries to achieve their devious intentions.

Access control has two best friends: Cryptography and segmentation. Their relationship could be viewed as mutually supportive, but in reality, cryptography and segmentation, because they are well understood and implemented security tools, are the crutches of access control.

In the scientific method, you take great care to conform to rules and details of the discipline. The same is true in cybersecurity. Doing access control correctly—with rigor and attention to policy and detail—is the equivalent of performing laboratory tests correctly. Without robust attention to detail, the best-laid strategies won't succeed.

But one new strategy need not replace all strategies that came before it. While many view security with the flawed understanding of zero-sum innovation, where each advance replaces what came before it, access control is directly connected to the concept of border protection.

For organizations safeguarding digital borders today, network protection also comes with a new set of issues: How do we define a need for inclusion in a network whose borders cannot be defined? How are those definitions communicated and enforced, and when does that process of enforcement create more vulnerability than protection?

Access control does not answer these questions, but it does provide a process for answering them. How they are answered is a direct reflection of the internal alignment of the business users and decision makers, and a strong indicator of the overall efficacy of a company's data security. These are the details—the necessary rigor—of the cybersecurity scientific method.

Access control is a strategic security evolution of the protection of belongings and country borders, both in sophistication and degrees of protection, that is a key driver of the best practice that security should enable rather than impede business. With effective access control, organizations can create far more nimble and malleable security protocols, suitable to adapt and scale to address fast-moving threats and opportunities alike.

MANAGING ACCESS IN CHALLENGING ENVIRONMENTS

Erik Devine, Riverside Health

The growing number of users, devices, and applications that are demanding access to network resources is a challenge many IT teams are struggling to manage. The healthcare industry is a perfect example of the rising volume of access control challenges many organizations face, not only because their network environments are so complex, but also because poorly managed access can have serious consequences.

Most healthcare organizations can be treated as two completely different businesses: Administrative and medical. The administrative side is concerned with business processes and financial issues. The medical team is concerned with providing critical health services such as emergency care, surgeries, scans, and X-rays; the administration of controlled pharmaceuticals; and other medical treatments. And both of these groups are strictly controlled by regulations to protect patient privacy.

Managing access in such an environment requires constantly striking a balance between security and privacy and providing potentially life-saving information and services. You can't make access controls too tight, or people may not get the care and resources they need, and you can't make them too loose because you are dealing with sensitive information.

Another complication is addressing the needs of the individuals and groups outside of hospital staff who require access. Many are an essential part of the core business, such as satellite hospitals, affiliated clinics and practices, or billing services. Others, such as labs, professional consultants, and specialized physicians, require access because they provide specialties that are not available in-house. At Riverside, we have more than 300 different external connections to the database that we manage.

Of course, this sort of challenge isn't entirely unique to healthcare. Many organizations today have a variety of users with legitimate needs to access different network resources and data—which is why a one-size-fits-all approach to access control is no longer sufficient.

WHERE DO YOU START?

The most important first step is to determine your organization's most significant risks. If you have highly classified data that demands limited access by authorized users, that's a natural place to start. But implementing access controls across the tiers of the rest of your business is more complicated because so many factors go into determining your highest risks.

Determine User Roles

Access control often starts with determining the roles of your network users and comparing what they have access to with what they should be able to access. You can begin to uncover that by talking with vendors and industry peers. Once you can determine what sort of access a surgeon should have, for example, you can then compare that to what is already in place. This is a critical exercise because you may be exposing the network to unnecessary risk, or you may be limiting innovation and the ability to produce better outcomes.

Conduct Third-Party Audits

A systems audit lets an analyst see what is on your network and who has access to those resources. Such an audit should be conducted regularly because as networks become more interconnected, the roles of many of the devices deployed naturally begin to expand. Often, it is only after a systems audit that you understand how the different systems on your network are interconnected. Mapping those connections and system interactions is critical in helping you identify potential risks when you provide access to resources.

TALKING TO STAKEHOLDERS

The next step to managing access is to clearly understand the needs of your stakeholders. This requires you to speak their language; otherwise, they won't understand you and you won't understand them. As a result, you may end up imposing controls they don't like, which they may respond to by implementing shadow IT. Then suddenly, everything you've worked for is on the back burner because they found a way around your controls. Why even have that fight?

You're better off going slower and getting everything done right than rushing through to get it done quickly—and then realizing that while you "did a good job," you now have so many backdoors and workarounds that you could question why you even went to all that effort in the first place. If you're going to put in the work, you might as well have a good outcome.

In a hospital, for example, the clinical language used by healthcare staff is entirely different from the business language used on the administrative side. Understanding those languages helps establish the right sorts of controls and access privileges. The same is true for HR, finance, sales, marketing, research and development, and every other department of any company.

Part of the trick to listening to what people say they need is being able to step back and decide which of those requests are critical. One of the most significant insights this has given me is that many of the traditional access controls, such as tying a user to a specific segment of the network or to particular resources, don't work in a hospital. For example, healthcare providers like to change shifts or cover each other in different parts of the hospital. In addition, we have temporary doctors and nurses who may come in every so often to practice in their specialty and then leave for months. Unless you have the right sorts of flexible controls in place, you will get a call at 4 a.m., saying, "Doctor X needs access, and he can't get in because he can't remember his password. Oh, and he needs this immediately because he is going into the operating room."

Accommodating these needs starts with understanding what people are trying to do and what resources they are trying to access—and that starts by understanding their workflows in a nontechnical way. Does that take a little longer, which means we can't answer tickets as fast? It does. But it also gives us information that we didn't have before. Once you know what's going on, you can not only fix the problem but if it happens again, you can respond much faster.

Of course, this requires give and take on both sides. That involves educating users about risks and risk management. In the past, when the CIO would try to impose something like two-factor authentication, 20 or 30 physicians would throw their hands in the air and say, "I make a million dollars a year. I don't want to have to have my phone with me all the time to authenticate my access." And far too often, IT's response would be "Okay, we'll turn it off for you," which is *exactly the wrong response.* But with regular communications about risks and regulations, when the CIO says, "This is what we're doing because it's important," users see the value. That is a considerable shift, and it's because we have had a conversation about the costs related to risk.

SECURING IOT ACCESS

The problem of access control goes far beyond just people. If you're like most companies, the volume of devices starting to proliferate inside your environment is growing exponentially. Those all need controlled access as well. In today's hospitals, medical Internet of Things (IoT) includes essential tools such as infusion pumps and monitors, multimillion-dollar MRI systems, and robotic surgical devices on which people's lives depend. Not only do these devices all need access and bandwidth, but many of them come with backdoors that connect to manufacturer support teams for updating and troubleshooting, and they can create significant security challenges.

In addition to dynamic access controls, addressing this challenge requires constant monitoring. We perform a lot of automated behavioral analysis looking for anomalies. While this isn't operating as a full AI, we're certainly on our way. For example, we have tools in place that can automatically alert us to abnormal volumes of traffic, or certain kinds of traffic, or a device that's talking outside of the realm in which it usually communicates. That enables us to focus on what to do with that anomaly, such as block or investigate it, rather than spending our time hunting for the problem in the first place.

The other challenge is connecting access to risk. For example, you may need to ask why a department still has an X-ray machine that runs on Windows NT. And the answer is probably something like, "It costs $15,000 to replace that machine, and we never needed to because it's always worked."

That is when you need to have a conversation about risk and vulnerabilities coupled with an approval process that starts with the question, "What are you trying to do?" The goal isn't to say no, but it may involve saying, "Let's do it, but let's do it another way that's safer." The user still gets their result, but now we not only know what the device is, but we can also control it a little better.

ADDRESSING PRIVILEGE CHANGES

In my world, physicians will get credentialed in something new and then someone on their staff will approach IT with a request for access to a new set of data, devices, and resources. Such a request can trigger a significant amount of verification on our end. For example, we need to verify that this physician has indeed changed her credentials. Then we need to know if she will still need access to the old data resources she had been using. Likewise, a nurse will transition from one floor to another that provides entirely different levels of care, say from radiology to ICU. We need to know if he still needs radiology access as well as ICU access. Is he going to be working in ICU for the next six months and then go back to radiology? And what are the implications when an individual starts accumulating different levels of access? Those are all challenges that must be understood if they are going to be addressed.

What we do is to monitor users to understand their behavior. Is this nurse typically now just operating out of ICU, both ICU and radiology, or just radiology because he never actually moved to ICU? This is something that a lot of doctors and nurses do—they sign up, go through all the training and certification, and then never show up. And then, the question becomes, "What are we supposed to do now? Do we need to disable the account they haven't been on for 30 or 60 days, or do we enable something else?" Those are the questions you have to ask when managing access in a complex and dynamic environment, and it requires collaboration with the various stakeholders.

It's way more complicated than I ever imagined. You can't just put protocols in place, perform behavioral analysis, and then make decisions, because people are trying to do complicated jobs, and they don't think in those terms.

ENHANCING ACCESS CONTROL TO ADDRESS CHANGE

Unfortunately, we have historically placed too much of the burden of access control on the end user. We need to enhance access so users don't have to remember a list of long, complicated passwords. Biometrics, single sign-on, tap-and-go badges, and a host of other tools can help with access, so you can be a little more stringent about controls while giving users a tool that doesn't require them to remember everything. I think every CISO can agree that we'd rather provide an end user with a badge or a fingerprint reader than have them write their passwords down on sticky notes and then paste them all over their computers.

And it's not just the initial access that we need to consider. Access controls have to be able to extend across critical network segments when needed. User access needs change all the time—which means that your access controls and policies cannot be rigid. You have to make sure that people have proper access to the correct data. A single provider in our hospital may have to cross two or three hundred security points that all protect against different things, and this is only going to get more complicated.

The goal of any access control strategy, then, needs to work toward translating human needs into technology to simplify the process so that users and devices can keep up with digital demands. Solutions such as single sign-on, tap-and-go, or biometrics need to not only make sure users are who they say they are, but also ensure they can get into the system as quickly and seamlessly as possible to securely access the resources they require to get their jobs done. In the area I work in, lives may actually depend on that.

ABOUT THE CONTRIBUTOR

Erik Devine – CISO, Riverside Health

Erik Devine has over two decades of experience, excelling in finding new innovations and solutions within information technology and security. He's spent 15 years as an IT and security leader. Devine's current focus is on cultivating an information security culture in healthcare while balancing the clinical and research workflows to help improve patient outcomes and new medical innovation.

Devine is also passionate about developing security frameworks and defensive technologies, and spreading security awareness throughout the enterprise and community.

A SYSTEMATIC APPROACH TO ACCESS CONTROL

George Do, Equinix

In my mind, access control is the number one gating mechanism for achieving the fundamental goal of cybersecurity, which is to keep the bad folks out while letting legitimate users in to do whatever they need to do. It sounds simple, but as it turns out, it's actually very hard to do.

The challenge is that it is difficult to determine the intentions of the users and devices requesting access to network resources. Since cybercriminals and malware work hard not to be identified, access controls allow us to sort legitimate users from bad actors. Historically, we used passwords at access points to do this. They seem like a simple solution to the problem: If you know the password, you are probably a legitimate user and can get in, and if you don't, then you aren't, and you can't.

The problem is that users hate passwords. That's because good passwords are hard to create and even harder to remember. But they're not only bad for users. They are also bad for security because they are very hard to protect. Because passwords are hard to remember, users tend to use workarounds such as birthdays, the names of their pets or children, their college mascots, old addresses, and similar memory devices—which defeats the whole purpose of requiring complex passwords.

Password controls tend to be easy to circumvent because people tend to use the same patterns. Publicly available social media information makes them easy to crack, and if not, they are relatively simple to social engineer or phish out of users. Out of all of your employees, they need only one, which means that determined hackers can typically get their hands on a password pretty quickly, and when they do, they have access to a connected device, and then your network, and from there it's game over.

ACCESS CONTROL IS THE WEAK LINK IN MANY SECURITY STRATEGIES

A quick look at the growing numbers of network break-ins tells you that access control is a security hygiene area that needs more attention. But most organizations overlook it because they believe that their current password scheme is adequate, or that options such as multifactor authentication or biometrics are too expensive, cumbersome, or complicated.

Traditionally, everything in the network was either static or carefully locked down and managed, with a single point of access that needed to be secured. Today, however, we live in a very disruptive world where networks rely on access control more than ever. Virtual devices are constantly spinning up and down, organizations are adding IoT devices to the network in record numbers, web applications are being developed and updated at unprecedented rates, and people are using more and more of their own personal devices for work, connecting them to the network either remotely or locally.

This growing complexity has severe implications for access control. How an organization went about protecting its information assets yesterday is very different from how they need to do that today. Not only are there more devices to authenticate, but where there was once a clear perimeter, it has either been widely distributed or there is no perimeter at all.

Because today's distributed networks are made up of hybrid multi-clouds, highly mobile workers and devices, and converging IT and OT environments, they tend to be constantly in flux. So rather than having a strict perimeter to control access, each network layer typically now has its own login. You log into a network via VPN, log into a network domain, log into cloud services through a user portal, and log into devices, applications, and operating systems. And each of these access points has related weaknesses that criminals can exploit. The result is a hacker's paradise.

In addition to making access to essential resources increasingly complicated, security practitioners have to protect and monitor all of those points of access simultaneously. Complicating the problem further are all of the non-user devices needing access. Virtual machines, web applications, and an ever-expanding set of end-user and IoT devices are overwhelming many networks. And other than a set of IP addresses, most organizations have little idea of what's on their network at any given moment. The challenge is how to wrap a unified access control process, including policies and access points, around such a dynamic environment so that you can consistently protect all entry points, including those that are always changing.

WHERE TO START

If you are a new CISO walking into a situation like this, your first question is likely to be, "Where do I start?" Here are three steps that will help you get started:

1. Don't panic. Regardless of how complex the network you have inherited is, this is a problem that can be sorted out if you break it down into chewable, digestible bites.

2. Determine what and where the crown jewels of the company are. They could be your backend enterprise resource planning (ERP) system, customer relationship management (CRM) system, or the systems that run the data center. Equinix, for example, has over 200 data centers made up of programmable logic controllers (PLCs) and supervisory control and data acquisition (SCADA) and incident command system (ICS) systems. All of those devices are critical to providing uptime for our data centers and customers. Those are our crown jewels, so that was where I focused when I became CISO.

3. Work your way out from the center. Start with the data, services, and technologies that are the most critical to the business—the ones you cannot afford to have go offline. Then you begin to apply things like multifactor authentication combined with very strong encryption and extreme levels of logging and monitoring to that inner core. As you work your way out to your least critical environment (which is usually that untrusted segment of the network where printers and iPads are attached), you can begin to relax those security controls.

SECURE YOUR MOST CRITICAL ASSETS FIRST

Locking down and hardening your most critical assets is a multi-step process. I start by deploying network access control (NAC) on the network segments where those assets reside. If anything new shows up there, I want the NAC solution to alert me right away.

Second, as much as possible, you need to treat that area as a black network. That means that you need to design it so that it talks to anything outside of that network segment only under very strict, and strictly controlled, protocols. That includes locking down the firewall rules protecting that part of the network to the nth degree.

Next, you need to implement uber-auditing. The firewalls, servers, and other devices on that part of the network need to log every activity and authentication or login attempt by anyone or anything, at any time, and anywhere. Those logs then need to be forwarded to a separate system, because if hackers break into the system, the first thing they are going to do is try to erase those logs. That's a lot harder to do if you have stored those records elsewhere. Those logs then need to be fed into a management and analysis system, such as a security information and event management (SIEM) system, to ensure you have constant access to events, event correlation, and easy-to-read analysis.

Of course, that network segment will also typically require management and administration access. That access needs to be configured so that administrative tasks can run without introducing additional risk. This will require encrypted and monitored access from known and highly secured devices as well as multifactor authentication to ensure the identity of a user.

GOOD SECURITY TAKES TIME

These processes are a lot easier to implement if you are setting up a brand-new network. However, when you need to secure a network that's been running for a long time and has a lot of access control issues, the gut reaction of most CISOs is to slam the gate shut. But what you will find out is that locking down access will usually start breaking things, and often, those things are really important. Instead, you need to start by applying a rule set that allows most if not all of the traffic through. But then you log everything: Who's talking to who, and what to what. You then need to analyze each connection, application, and workflow from source to destination, and ask things like "Is that connection legit?" and "What breaks if we block it?"

You will likely need to spend a couple of weeks or more, depending on the size and complexity of the network, monitoring and tracing all traffic threads and connections. Only then can you carefully shut the gate because you first established a baseline and worked through it.

APPLY CONTINUOUS MONITORING

Access control doesn't start and stop at the gateway. It needs to go above and beyond that, and that requires building a profile for each application, workflow, and networking or IoT device. Each profile needs to include baseline information, such as this device or application uses only certain protocols, talks only on specific ports, or talks only to a handful of known sources.

Once that is established, access control means that if there's any deviation from that baseline, the security team should be alerted immediately because it's an anomaly. It doesn't necessarily mean a device or application has been compromised. Maybe a new application or device has been added to the network somewhere else that you hadn't accounted for. But it could also mean that somebody's breaking into that network segment, or even that a user or hacker has made an unauthorized change somewhere else and you are seeing the ripple effect of that compromise. Regardless, any baseline change is critical enough for the security team to be alerted so that they can assess what happened and why.

Of course, given the rapid change occurring in today's networks, even this level of baseline monitoring and assessment may not be enough. If you are working inside a discrete network segment and have to track only what's happening inside that space, that's wonderful. But today, applications and workflows need to move laterally across the network, accessing different devices, data, and other connected resources, including mobile endpoints, hybrid cloud environments, and virtualized devices that come and go. In this situation, access control becomes extremely complex, even for just tracking something as it moves around the extended network.

Even then, however, you can still start with, "Where are my most critical assets? Which part of the network are they on? Which server? Which database? Which data?" Whether your critical assets or resources reside in the cloud, on-premise, on some temporary side server, or even need to move from place to place as requirements change, the strategy is still to overlay a discrete and secure network segment for it that can dynamically span the larger distributed network.

THE CHALLENGE OF SHADOW IT

We live in a world we want to trust, but because there is so much at stake, we also need to verify. We need to maintain an open culture because that drives innovation, so we don't want to block people from the tools and resources they need to help make the business more successful. But what's to stop a user from zipping up a file and sending it to their online account as an email attachment, or uploading a file to an unauthorized cloud storage service? Of course, it's also important to recognize that not everyone looking for ways to circumvent the system is trying to steal data. The fact is, they are usually just trying to get their job done. Unfortunately, they may have also inadvertently exposed the company to unnecessary risk by doing so.

While we need to reduce security sprawl, this is where a tool like a cloud access security broker (CASB), which can discover and secure shadow IT, is essential. When we first deployed this tool in our network a few years ago, we found that a few hundred users were using a questionable mom-and-pop cloud storage provider to store sensitive company documents and other data so that they could be more easily shared or accessed from home. Although we want to allow outbound traffic, we don't want to allow traffic or data to flow to questionable or unsecured sites. A CASB allowed us to identify that issue—one we may have never otherwise discovered—and shut it down.

SUMMING UP

Access control enables organizations to better quantify and manage risk, which leads to a more accurate calculation of ROI—which is the holy grail of security. Unfortunately, access control is also one of the most overlooked tools in a CISO's security toolkit. This is due, in part, to a misunderstanding of its role in a security strategy, and because many people feel that access control is increasingly difficult to set up and maintain, given the dynamic nature of today's networks.

The trick is to not let the growing complexity of today's networks derail your efforts to establish and maintain essential access control policies and procedures. CISOs can do this by breaking down complex issues into manageable chunks. This includes identifying your most critical assets, baselining behaviors, strictly controlling the environment in which they reside, and using modern, flexible tools that can span and adapt to the evolving requirements of digital business.

ABOUT THE CONTRIBUTOR

George Do – CISO, Equinix Inc.

George Do has been working in the information security field for over 20 years, concentrating on a wide range of areas, including development and transformation of global information and cybersecurity programs. He has extensive experience in executive IT governance/risk/compliance (GRC), information security frameworks, system and network security, incident response (IR), system forensics and investigation, intrusion detection and protection, penetration testing, and security firewall technologies. Joining Equinix in 2019, he developed a new global information security program from the ground up to ensure business risks are adequately managed. Before Equinix, Do worked at Exodus, Savvis, CenturyLink, and Tivo in senior security roles, notably as a principal security architect consulting with customers to secure their organizations. He also worked at the National Aeronautics and Space Administration (NASA) to protect government information assets, including implementing firewall and intrusion detection systems, public key infrastructure (PKI), and the development and maturation of an agency-wide incident response capability.

8

SEGMENTATION

"A well-segmented network is an invisible masterpiece of teamwork and collaboration."

Colin Anderson,
Levi Strauss & Co.

"Key benefits to segmentation are cleaner environments, better ease of management, and improved security."

Hussein Syed,
RWJBarnabas Health

Agile macro- and micro-segmentation have replaced boundary defense as the preeminent cybersecurity strategy. Such segmentation places security where it is most needed: around the assets themselves. Segmentation makes it far more difficult to compromise a specific asset and greatly limits the damage of a breach if threat actors manage to succeed.

Looking back, vast, complex, and highly interconnected networks existed long before the digital revolution. Although digital innovators often train their focus forward, there are powerful and valuable lessons to be learned from history's accounts of the rise and fall of even the most ancient systems of power, structure, and connectivity.

At the height of its preeminence, in the mid-second century, the Roman Empire spanned more than 3 million square miles, with a population of more than 60 million in a world of just 300 million people. The empire was connected by 250,000 roads—more than 50,000 of which were paved—transforming Europe with the extraordinary innovations of Rome's engineers. The Roman army covered land and sea, with a fighting force of nearly half a million soldiers and sailors. But as the empire stretched farther and farther past its borders, beyond the western edges of the Rhine and the Danube, and into the lands of the Huns, Franks, Saxons, and Visigoths, its vastness swallowed its powerful army's ability to defend its ever-expanding perimeter. The empire had become too unwieldy to defend itself from intruders.

At the same time, the barbarian tribes began to leverage the Romans' own innovations, especially steel, against the empire to breach the borders and establish stronger, more stable, and more sustainable strongholds deeper and deeper within Roman boundaries. Within 100 years from its height, the Roman Empire had collapsed and the so-called barbarians that could not be conquered stood in the rubble of the city of Rome.

There are parallels to be made between the fall of Rome and the defense of information in an ever-expanding and difficult-to-protect digital civilization. Primary among them is the strategy of boundary defense that dominated the first 50 years of cybersecurity. Organizations placed an imposing physical and virtual barrier around the outer perimeter of their assets and did all the defense there.

An important improvement of that strategy, known by a number of names, including "active cyberdefense"—where threats are both detected and mitigated in cyberspace-relevant time, informed by near-real-time situational awareness—has been dominant for the last decade.

But even with those improvements, boundary defense as a primary security strategy is dead. That's because even when this perimeter-focused security works, it has an inherent structural flaw that exponentially increases risk: Boundary defense is only as strong as its weakest point. Having a "hard crunchy exterior" (good defense at the boundary) and a "soft gooey interior" (weak defenses once inside the network) remains a recipe for disaster. If threat actors somehow manage to breach that one point, there is little to no security beyond it to prevent attackers from broad access to virtually any data of value. Most of the major data breaches of late have been due to insufficient attention to the insider threat (an employee who is untrustworthy) or stealthy persistent threats that make it inside the boundary and, like the barbarians in the Roman Empire, never leave.

Further, perimeter defense is not a viable strategy, because yesterday's monolithic boundary now consists of many dispersed ones—wireless mobile devices and the cloud—that have stretched network borders and made them indefensible. Now those borders barely exist at all.

Fortunately, that has given rise to the far more effective security fundamental of segmentation. Its importance is vividly illustrated in the headlines about many recent major breaches of household-name organizations—all of which were either caused or worsened by a lack of strong segmentation.

With the idea of inevitable breaches at the forefront, segmentation operates from the principle that it is critical to prevent unfettered access to all areas of a network. From there, CISOs are empowered to make the critical assessments of asset value, deploying protection zones and mechanisms that are as varied as the data they contain.

Once an environment is segmented, access control policies can be established that reflect a far more sophisticated and dexterous approach to security. That way, not only is it hard to compromise that segment, but the scope of a potential compromise is limited to that segment alone.

A Strategy for Segmentation

- The primary strategy is to do micro- and macro-segmentation at many different places:
  - With significant agility
  - With sufficient granularity
  - Without overwhelming complexity

- Micro-segmentation and macro-segmentation, done with agility, can:
  - Prevent compromise
  - If compromised, limit the scope
  - Speed the recovery from breaches

Micro-segmentation is perhaps the most diverse and accessible strategy of our day. Even more promising is the fact that agile segmentation represents the first time that security can be viewed as a business enabler rather than a business inhibitor. Specifically, agile segmentation can enable business coalitions that were previously deemed unsafe.

For many years, organizations that were seeking to collaborate were left with two bad choices: open up their networks to each other, enabling rich collaboration but putting all of their data at risk, or not share data, limiting the potential for collaboration. By contrast, agile segmentation improves security and increases collaboration.

Agile segmentation, done at both the macro and micro levels, has become the preeminent cybersecurity strategy of our day.

As a form of access control, effective segmentation also provides a level of strategic agility that is much more in keeping with cybersecurity's mission to enable rather than hinder business.

Though segmentation is far more effective and dexterous than the broad brush of border defense and far more secure than the false comfort of Maginot Line–style defenses, that dexterity demands a more conscientious and considered approach. Whereas in the past grants of access were a high-risk binary decision of yes or no, today's more segmented access control capabilities allow IT teams to embody the role they need to have in a data-driven world—that of business enablers. While this requires a deeper understanding of who must access a network and why, implementing segmented access control catalyzes a more connected and collaborative approach to both data protection and data usage. This requires deeper, even granular, knowledge of specific parts of the business and stakeholders, and the full endorsement of C-suite leadership to determine, set, and enforce access permissions. That may trigger organizational tensions and growing pains.

The process of establishing segmentation is a powerful tool for both security and alignment in a modern business landscape where success, and even viability, hinges on information protection.

Together, well-implemented cryptography, reasonable access control, and secure segmentation can provide a good-enough solution to the problem of the failed foundations of the Internet.

SUCCESSFUL SEGMENTATION ISN'T SEPARATION: IT'S COLLABORATION

Colin Anderson, Levi Strauss & Co.

In cybersecurity, effective segmentation is often what determines whether your company finds itself on the front page of the *Wall Street Journal* or the back page. That's because, for the past several years, the importance of segmentation has been written in headlines.

In front-page incidents involving the compromise of hundreds of millions of consumers' private information and staggering internal and external costs, perhaps what is most shocking is their crude simplicity. It begs the question: How can a phony phishing email or a stolen password lead to millions or billions of dollars in damages and put countless consumers at risk of identity theft and fraud? How can we mitigate that type of risk?

THE ANSWER IS SEGMENTATION

The strategic principle behind segmentation is not new. The goal is to reduce the number of assets an attacker could compromise, minimizing the potential attack footprint. Without proper segmentation, one weak point in a lower-security area allows criminals access to the most vital, mission-critical, and valuable data in a network.

With large enterprises spread across the globe and an intensifying commoditization of cyberattacks, it is a simple fact that you can't keep everybody out. Attackers will get in. But you can choose what these threat actors are able to access and where they can go once they are inside. The ability to limit what they do when they get in makes all the difference in the world.

Without segmentation, your entire network is only as strong as its absolutely weakest point—and once that point is compromised, attackers have the ability to go on quite a walkabout. They can traverse your network, starting at a more public area like a demilitarized zone (DMZ), and quickly move to a highly secured area. Or they can slowly move to that area; attackers are getting much more savvy in the ways they avoid detection, staying off your team's radar—inching their way closer to the areas of your network where you might have your financials, your HR information, and other critical assets.

When organizations choose not to invest in segmentation, or when they get it wrong, it exposes them to much more significant business impact. It may not be an easier conversation, but it would certainly be more prudent to discuss the costs of not segmenting rather than the price of implementing it carefully.

SEGMENTATION CAN BE COSTLY AND DISRUPTIVE

Implementing and executing a segmentation strategy is a series of challenging, complex, and meticulous decisions (or, more frankly, compromises).

It is safe to say that there is no such thing as a low-risk access point anymore. That recognition has given rise to what is known as the *zero-trust model*. You have to specifically *allow* assets and applications to communicate with one another. Rather than putting all your controls on the edge of your network on your firewall, for example, you move those controls into the heart of your network and create policies, restrictions, and segmentation to limit the ability for an attack to jump from one asset to another.

Achieving that zero-trust model with an intensely granular degree of segmentation is a great objective. But there is no easy button that will get you there. The process is difficult, painstaking, and disruptive.

Often that scale of disruption is simply a non-starter—which is where the decisions and compromises begin. Making those decisions wisely and effectively requires the kind of deep knowledge that is nearly impossible without all-in organizational collaboration.

Simply put, segmentation requires a multiple stakeholder approach. To minimize the intense levels of frustration and workflow slowdowns, it requires strong collaboration between your networking team, infrastructure and systems team, and applications team. That's because for segmentation to work, people's ways of working need to change.

If you are initiating efforts that require people to completely rethink and recalibrate the ways they work, you need a strong understanding of how they work now. This includes departments, teams, and functions and internal and external stakeholders, from the C-suite down to entry-level hires. That's not to mention understanding how specific applications and systems behave and how the segmentation will affect them. Who are their partners? What other applications or servers does an application need to talk to? What is the circle of trust that you want to create around a specific application? To do that, you often need to get down to the protocol level, the fine workings of the applications—and that requires a lot of different domains to work together.

Often, the level of success is equal to the level of business pragmatism of the process and the end result it achieves. In short, all stakeholders need to be able to see what is in it for them.

LOOK FOR WIN-WINS

One factor that often goes overlooked, for instance, is external vendor costs—especially for multiple protocol label switching (MPLS). Segmentation can lead to substantial ROI in terms of saving MPLS costs. Global networks rack up astronomical bills to telecommunications service providers. Segmentation can allow you to keep those communications to a small circle of systems, reducing the load on some of the networks' most expensive circuits.

In such instances, not only does segmentation exponentially reduce potential risk, it also reduces a multimillion-dollar telco bill by taking traffic that was traversing a network and keeping it local to those who really need to talk to each other. Not only does this allow a CISO to strategically invest controls and resources around the assets that need it most, it also strengthens a shared sense of purpose and collaboration internally.

Don't discount the importance of this buy-in; without it, segmentation becomes much, much more challenging.

At the heart of segmentation is a process of convergence. It is similar to the convergence you see in companies that adopt a DevOps mentality, where philosophies, processes, practices, and protocols are combined to deliver applications and services at faster rates, with engineers developing as well as supporting the systems that run their applications. Segmentation requires teams to blend skills and wear multiple hats.

Often, infrastructure individuals are most comfortable—and consider themselves most valuable—as subject matter experts. It's their identity. "I am a networking person." "I am a server person." "I am an applications person."

When you start creating software-defined networks of segmentation, those skills must converge into one individual who needs to know a little bit about networking, a little bit about the application he or she is working on, and a little about the systems that are running that application. These skills must converge because they are creating the rules that allow their systems to communicate with other systems.

And if you think that figuring out the granular intricacies of the technology is challenging, wait until you get to the people part. Even with the support of executive leadership, without buy-in and commitment from the bottom up, it is difficult to be successful. Individual engineers will begin dragging their feet, progress will be slow, and it will be a long, uphill struggle.

CISOs who think otherwise or dismiss this must recognize that they cannot do it on their own. A network cannot be segmented by a security team in a vacuum. There must be a strategic approach to converging teams, skillsets, and the individuals who will be supporting the segmented network moving forward.

Consider the human complexity of who needs to be involved in the segmentation process. First and foremost, you need experts in whatever set of applications you are building a network around. If you are using VMware, for example, you need the systems people who understand VMware and know how to create these policies around a set of systems. And if you are using any kind of network hardware—a firewall, a router—you may have to bring in your network people. It depends on how you are going about your segmentation journey. And it most certainly is a journey—and there is some learning that needs to take place about how best to undertake it.

That's why, when it comes to segmentation, step one is start small. Begin in a development or QA environment and learn how you might want to approach segmentation in a broader sense across your network. Find an application where you know the developer or have access to how it behaves so that you can create the right types of policies for that specific application and create a small zone around it.

Once you get the basics under your belt and you understand how the technology you are using works and how the applications behave—the ports and protocols that they need—you must pivot to the design effort. You identify your finance systems; let's suppose you create a segment or zone where your finance systems live and talk with one another and you create a little software-defined network with all of your finance systems, for example, within that specific zone. Then, you tackle the next zone and the next. How do you eat an elephant? One bite at a time. The same is true of segmenting a network.

Some people might want to start with their highest risk assets, with what is most important, and create zones around those assets. Others might be more risk averse and start with lower risk assets—something less mission critical—so they can learn from that and then take on an area that is higher risk.

Remember, though: This is all internal to an organization, which is only a portion of the challenge.

Most companies today have a large and growing ecosystem of partners that help them deliver different business services. We all have these partners, so it is critical to understand what access those partners need and ensure they can access only what is needed. To achieve this requires good access controls, providing the ability to allow someone into your network but only letting them go where they need to go.

For outsourced development partners, for instance, create a virtual desktop environment that allows outside developers to come in across a VPN and then land in a sandbox environment. They will have access to the information and the code they need to work on, but they are in a sandbox they can't get out of. Strong access controls will identify who is coming into the network, and good segmentation will create the guardrails that allow them to get their jobs done efficiently without the ability to poke around and see what else is out there.

And this, perhaps, is the guiding strategic approach to not only segmentation, but cybersecurity overall. Security must be an enabler of the business, not an impediment. To achieve that, security must appear seamless. Segmentation, the very process of creating seams, must be done in a way that feels seamless to the end user. That requires some tough decisions, but let that principle be your guide.

For the customers and stakeholders who access your system to make purchases, drive revenue, or shape profits, it is important for those high levels of segmentation to be invisible. This often requires extra hoops and hurdles from teams that have just undertaken an arduous, challenging development process and made substantial changes to the jobs they do and the way they do them.

This is all the more reason to devote significant focus to the way teams are managed and motivated, from initial design to execution to sustained upkeep of the newly segmented system. A well-segmented network is an invisible masterpiece of teamwork and collaboration. Though it is an increasingly fundamental imperative, that doesn't make the undertaking any easier, so manage the people with as much care and consideration as the technology. People are far more central to its success. Like many fundamentals of cybersecurity in an increasingly volatile and fast-moving digital landscape, segmentation can be challenging on many levels. But as the headlines have proven—and will surely prove again—it's worth it.

ABOUT THE CONTRIBUTOR

Colin Anderson – CISO, Levi Strauss & Co.

At Levi Strauss & Co., Anderson manages an international team responsible for information risk management, regulatory compliance, and IT enterprise risk management for a global organization with $5 billion in annual sales and over 2,700 company-owned and franchise retail locations in 42 countries. Previously, Anderson was the CISO at Safeway, the $40 billion North American grocer. Prior to Safeway he led information security at Commerce One and network engineering for Bank of America Capital Markets, responsible for providing 100 percent availability for their North and South America equity trading floors. Anderson is a frequent speaker on information risk management and compliance topics, and an elected independent non-executive director for the nonprofit retail cybersecurity organization R-CISC.

WHY WE NEED TO SEGMENT NETWORKS

Hussein Syed, RWJBarnabas Health

People tend to resist change, which is why adapting to digital transformation is so painful for some organizations. For decades, networks stayed virtually the same. Everything was one flat network where people plugged in their equipment. Eventually, these networks became too large to manage effectively. Virtual local area networks (VLANs) were then created to address performance issues by breaking the large, monolithic network into smaller, more manageable subnetworks.

There were also very few threats. But as that began to change, security saw VLANs as a way to keep different network elements separated so that devices that handled various levels of sensitive information could coexist on a single network without compromising critical resources or escalating risk.

But now, for the first time in decades, networks are undergoing a radical change. They're moving into the cloud, they need to accommodate a growing number of mobile users and Internet of Things (IoT) devices, and the traditional perimeter is eroding. In such an environment, network segmentation has become even more critical for defending data and resources.

SEGMENTATION DRIVERS

There are three primary drivers of network segmentation.

The first is to *break a network down into smaller, more manageable segments*. Most IT teams are wrestling with managing the scale of today's networks. IT networks and operational technology (OT) networks are converging. They have to distribute resources across remote offices, mobile devices, and multi-cloud environments. Organizations are adding IoT devices to the network at an unprecedented rate.

To complicate matters further, different lines of business within an organization own many of these networked resources. IT may control the computing infrastructure; physical security or facilities management may hold the OT environments; and in settings like healthcare, connected offices and clinics may need to be integrally connected to IT and even OT resources but are owned and managed by an entirely different organization.

Rather than trying to manage all of this complexity as a single network, breaking it down into logical segments means that you can put more granular controls in place. This gives administrators a smaller set of devices and users to monitor so that they can detect and respond to abnormal behavior faster and more easily.

The next driver is to *protect* systems that may not be able to run with the same level of security or controls as others. Some security controls impact the performance or the functionality of specific systems, especially in OT environments. Network segments also help prevent malicious activity, insider threats, and malware from spreading across your network while limiting the amount of damage that can occur because you have a smaller area to contain.

Segmentation also enables different network segments and resources to run the way administrators and users need them to run. For example, in the healthcare sector, where I work, there has been an explosion in the number of medical IoT (MIoT) devices on the network. Some of these devices cost millions of dollars and are incredibly technical. They may require a live backend support connection to the manufacturer to troubleshoot problems in real time. And data collected from these devices frequently needs to be distributed to outside specialists for analysis. While such connections may be necessary, they also introduce risk to the rest of your network. By segmenting them, they still get to leverage the existing infrastructure, and you get to isolate that risk from the rest of the network.

The third big driver is that segmentation creates a *cleaner environment*, especially on larger networks. Segmentation can often produce better performance and throughput for some systems simply because there is less traffic.

UNDERSTANDING DATA FLOW

The most critical information required to implement, manage, and secure a segmented network is how systems communicate, who needs to connect to an application that accesses those systems, and how that access occurs.

Understanding this enables you to establish tiered authentication to authorize how people, devices, and applications can connect to a system. It also allows you to keep your application servers and database servers isolated so that, for example, users never know where the database server sits. They can connect to it only through the applications. This approach enables you to more easily implement database activity monitoring to ensure that no intrusions take place through an application tier, as opposed to direct access to the database.

SECURING LATERAL DATA FLOW

Of course, not all resources want to stay inside a network segment. Print services, applications, and database services often need to run horizontally across different segments. Addressing this challenge in a segmented environment requires understanding the data flow of those resources and identifying what systems they need to communicate with. You also need to know which users or clients need to connect with those systems.

Systems still have to work by communicating with other systems, which means that even though you have isolated them, they also need to be integrated. The beauty of integrated systems is that you don't have to establish protocols manually. If users or devices generate data in one place and your data governance rules are properly defined, then that data can move securely from one system to another for whatever purpose. But if you have not adequately documented that flow of information, you will have a break in communication where somebody can't get to something they need, and suddenly, "do no harm" goes out the door.

Once you understand how data needs to move between resources, you can create a different sort of segmentation fence around them. In some cases, you run systems in extreme isolation so that one system can never communicate with another because there is no need.

In other cases, you establish limited communication based on the profile of an application that allows some applications, ports, or protocols to communicate between systems but not anything else. Risk can then be isolated to a particular set of resources so that you can effectively monitor them.

This need to create horizontal environments is also one of the prime drivers for adopting micro-segmentation. As different clients migrate toward accessing a common data center and other resources, micro-segmentation secures access based on defined profiles, such as what types of communication will be allowed.

MANAGING COMPLEXITY

As networks evolve, they are also becoming increasingly complex. In a hospital, you've got patients and doctors moving in and out of the environment, as well as remote labs and clinics that require access. Many of these users are also highly mobile, adding another layer of complexity. The question then becomes, how do you manage all of that in a segmented environment?

Some of it comes down to authentication and access control. Software-defined networking is another approach that allows administrators to apply controls at a higher level. Again, if you understand your data flow, who or what the client is, and how communication should take place, you can securely provide those resources with controlled access to the system.

For example, if you have an application that accesses or transmits sensitive data, you must understand how clients connect to that application so that you can adequately segment it. Perhaps users connect through a web tier using a browser. You can then add digital and client certificates for better access control. You can define that only computers with a client-side certificate can connect to that system before they can even log into it.

But because that system sits in a different environment, users won't be able even to ping that system because it's completely isolated—which also means that if malware or ransomware gets into the network, it won't be able to connect to that system because it can't see it.

MANAGING A BREACH

Building an effective segmentation strategy requires a lot of documentation of how and where data flows and how applications and systems connect and interact. You have to maintain visibility across your segments. Eventually, some attack is going to burrow through from one segment to another, and good forensics will then be able to trace that attack through network segments. That way, you can quickly understand how many devices it impacted, where the attack originated, and what and where its target was. Having this sort of lateral view is essential to good troubleshooting and security analysis.

You don't just need visibility into each network segment. Unified visibility across all segments is essential. This may require installing tools that collect real-time information, not only about a specific network segment but across all segments. That information then has to be delivered to a configuration management system or security information and event management (SIEM) solution on a regular basis so that it can be analyzed and correlated; then if something happens, you are alerted.

MONITORING NETWORK HEALTH

You need to be able to continuously assess the health of your network as a whole. This means allowing monitoring systems to have access to a network segment but nothing else. Firewall access lists can be used to define that system X can have visibility into a specific network segment to deliver your threat data back and forth, deliver antimalware updates to devices, or send out an alert to your control system about an activity that requires investigation.

You also have to ensure that you are never limited to seeing only slices of the network at a time. Instead, you must be able to see an event in network segment X and immediately correlate it with those problems occurring in network segments Y and Z, which indicate you have a much bigger problem. To do this, you need a way to collect logs from all these sources into one place, correlate them, and tie them to external threat intel to identify a threat. Configuration management database (CMDB) and SIEM tools can play a critical role in establishing and maintaining that sort of visibility.

SEGMENTING A LEGACY NETWORK

Of course, implementing segmentation as part of a new network is relatively simple. The challenge is that that rarely happens. Most of the time, you are applying a segmentation strategy to a legacy network made up of some hybrid collection of new and aging technologies. And in some cases, you end up having to rearchitect everything, which can be challenging, because you also always want to leverage existing technologies where possible. This is where firewall-based segmentation can play an important role. Internal segmentation firewalls can be used to break an extensive network into smaller networks, allowing you to move systems into them slowly. You should start small and run your operations in a monitor-only mode so that you can begin to understand the behavior of the systems and where they might break down. Then you can gradually move toward a more advanced means of segmentation within the environment by understanding or profiling those systems and documenting their data communication patterns.

This takes time and patience because this network is operational. You also need executive and stakeholder buy-in so that you have some idea about how much time or forgiveness you will have when things break or systems stop talking to one another. You should also form a plan to roll back, revisit, and reorganize when something goes sideways before you go back and try again.

ENGAGING KEY STAKEHOLDERS

The key here is to engage stakeholders in the conversation so that they understand the need for segmentation. Educated people make decisions based on information. They must be familiar with emerging threats and the changing threat landscape. They must understand that the organization no longer has the luxury of minutes or hours to detect something because networks, devices, and threats are so much faster.

You also need to collect as much information as possible to improve your decision-making process. Your users and stakeholders and system administrators understand how data needs to flow and how, when, and where their systems communicate. Once you have that information, you can design a segmented environment so that it has the least impact on the user. And you have to remember that it's an iterative exercise to get to the final stage.

This is not a technical problem. Once you understand the people and processes, technology is there to help. And if you get that backward, then you have issues.

KEY TAKEAWAYS

The key benefits to segmentation are cleaner environments, better ease of management, and improved security. From a technology perspective, you can do things faster. If you have the architecture footprint laid out correctly, you can implement solutions more quickly because you don't have to look at how one new thing affects everything else in the network. There are significant advantages to troubleshooting a smaller environment as well. Variables are fewer in segmented environments, and you have better control over them, giving you the ability to implement solutions quickly.

If you're in a highly regulated environment, it is easier to document and ensure regulatory compliance because a segmented environment simplifies meeting your security controls or policies. Segmentation also minimizes the impact of an adverse event in one environment because your other segmented environments can keep functioning, which is essential for any organization looking to compete in today's digital marketplace.

ABOUT THE CONTRIBUTOR

Hussein Syed – Chief Information Security Officer, RWJBarnabas Health

At RWJBarnabas Health, Hussein Syed is responsible for information security and the organization's HIPAA compliance and security governance program. Syed and his team are responsible for information security functions for the healthcare system. The company is New Jersey's largest integrated healthcare delivery system, providing treatment and services to more than 5 million patients each year.

Syed's knowledge and methodologies have developed through years of working in diverse environments utilizing technologies and business processes. His experience culminates in a rich set of credentials for his concentration in information security. He is responsible for Barnabas Health data security, a HIPAA-regulated environment comprising eight sitewide area networks, two data centers, more than 30,000 endpoints, and approximately 800 applications utilized in clinical, business, and research areas.

Syed has more than 22 years of experience in IT, of which 15 years are in information security. He is a member of the New Jersey Chapter of the Healthcare Information Management Systems Society (NJHIMSS) Security and Privacy Task force and serves on security advisory councils for various security companies. He has spoken at Gartner, NJHIMSS, and Trusted Computing Group events and participated in other security-related events.

ADVANCED STRATEGIES:

SOPHISTICATED
CYBERSECURITY
OPERATIONS

THE DIGITAL BIG BANG

Our understanding of our universe, our planet, and ourselves was revolutionized when we deepened and broadened our examination of our surroundings both in the heavens and on Earth. With increased visibility into space, we understood—and continue to better understand—where we came from, where we are now, and where we're going. The same is true on our planet: we're examining and inspecting the complex and small details that are often hidden from our view so that we can better understand their potential for good as well as the ways that they can harm us.

We're also actively planning for failure. In my view, our exploration of space, in the long run, is about preserving the human race when our sun dies and destroys the earth (all stars expand and inevitably die out). With that in mind, space exploration is (in addition to the near-term scientific benefits) ultimately about finding a new planet, around another star, to inhabit after the sun burns away the earth's life, water, and atmosphere. We have already started those incremental and necessary steps by sending astronauts to the moon, robots to other planets, and soon astronauts to Mars. But before we could send anyone to the moon or robots to Mars and beyond, we first had to orbit Earth. So whenever we wonder about the value of pursuing seemingly basic things in space, we need to remember that basic things lead to advanced things.

That's the emphasis of Part IV of this book: looking at the more advanced techniques we need to master based on the firm foundation we've discussed so far.

The power of treating cybersecurity as a science is most clearly revealed when cybersecurity architectures are built around speed and connectivity, and the fundamental strategies of cryptography, access control, and segmentation are in place. With this sturdy and resilient foundation to build upon and the fundamental strategies in place, you can leverage more advanced technologies—including visibility, inspection, and failure recovery—to achieve powerful things that were hoped for but seemingly always on the horizon.

As these increasingly complex and sophisticated technologies emerge, the ramifications are not simply greater benefits. Advanced technologies also give rise to more complex degrees of risk that demand increasingly advanced security techniques and solutions. Without a resilient base of scientifically applied fundamentals, cybersecurity strategies will collapse in the future like poorly designed suspension bridges. Cybersecurity strategies simply will not be able to withstand the weight of fast-moving innovations and the security practices needed to support them.

Achieving visibility on vast, hybrid deployment networks—extended and perforated by greater and greater numbers of mobile access points—is more challenging than ever before. With more points of access comes more opportunity. Criminals try to seize those opportunities with increasingly convincing grift. The malware that allows entry is now routinely hidden in a host of emails, attachments delivered using scams designed to trick users into unwitting installation. One quick click on a hastily read and seemingly innocuous email can trip a compromise that decimates an organization. More complicated and dispersed networks demand more sophisticated and efficient inspection capabilities. In addition, we must be ready to mitigate threats that lurk in the corners and the relentless strafe of malware that cybercriminals refine with meticulous precision. Inspection is the safeguard that allows security teams to preemptively stop attacks. Effective security strategy eliminates independent tactics (where a single security function stands mostly alone) and uses multiple techniques (inspection being one of the key ones) working together.

With the fundamentals in place, the advanced strategies explored in Part IV—visibility, inspection, and failure recovery—form a powerful flank. Together these strategies achieve an extremely effective defense that removes the shadows from which threat actors operate, allowing organizations to quickly detect their presence and then, with tremendous efficiency, undo any damage caused.

Thriving in cyberspace requires being a master of your domain: examining it and being agile enough to adjust when things go wrong.

9
VISIBILITY

"Securing a network is difficult enough, and nearly impossible without appropriate visibility."

Michael Chertoff,
Former Secretary,
Department of
Homeland Security

"Start with the intel. Start with the intel. And then, start with the intel."

Tim Crothers,
Target

"One of the main visibility challenges for the CISO is seeing what changes are coming."

Daniel Hooper,
PIMCO

Visibility operates from a simple principle: You cannot defend what you cannot see—and you certainly cannot effectively protect yourself from attacks and attackers that strike from positions of veritable digital obscurity.

Visibility is integral to cybersecurity but has experienced an intense paradigm shift over the past decade. The number and type of connected devices, and the fluidity with which they come and go, requires a greater emphasis on visibility. The number of devices on your network greatly increases the attack surface. You need to know where and what they are. The variety of devices on your network creates both complexity and opportunity. You would like to know what kinds of tools are at your disposal to defend yourself, and where you might be vulnerable. The mobility and agility of devices, due to wireless and portable computing, makes static and query-based analysis instantly out of date. You need real-time status.

Without visibility, any defense against attack is reduced to luck and happenstance.

You can't defend what you can't see.

As more and more network operators identify the need to enhance detection and response capabilities to improve their network protection, it gives rise to a simple question with many complex answers: What is a network? Multi-cloud deployments and DevOps approaches have dispersed organizations' data, while ever-increasing degrees of mobility create exponentially more points of access. In this context, traditional ways of achieving visibility—reviewing log files or any query-based analysis—are obsolete, unable to scale or achieve the speeds necessary to be effective. Vendors have flooded this vacuum to meet visibility needs. But the result is often less clarity rather than more, as security teams drown in massive volumes of data that often do more to obscure relevant information than to reveal it.

Instead, network operators have had to redefine networks with an approach that is less inside-out—the information that comprises an organization's assets—and much more outside-in—where and how proprietary data can be accessed. Simply put, a network must now be defined as the full sweep of its attack surface. This reimagining has fundamentally changed visibility from the ability to see the full vista of a network to the ability to better understand and detect threats, both in nature and in action. As a result, the effectiveness of visibility increasingly hinges on the type of strategic insight and situational awareness that empowers the speed and reach of today's business.

Now it is impossible to look at everything at all times—because of scale and speed—so the question becomes "What should be looked at and when?" Answering that question clearly can create alignment at all levels of an organization that delivers truly effective and efficient cybersecurity by protecting assets in relation to their value and importance. Such clear prioritization allows for a much more strategic approach to the question of how best to expand and deepen visibility.

As we will see in the chapters that follow, that strategic approach is now critical to achieving effective visibility. With everything from encryption to privacy regulations greatly complicating what can be seen, what is allowed to be seen, and for how long, visibility draws its strength as much from the sophistication of insight as it does from the innovation of tools. It is a security truism that you cannot protect what you can't see—but as the very nature of visibility changes to meet today's security necessities, that trope may be changing as well. A more appropriate guide may be, "You can't see what you don't know to look for."

VISIBILITY: IDENTIFYING PATHOGENS, RISK FACTORS, AND SYMPTOMS OF CYBERATTACKS

Michael Chertoff, Former Secretary,
Department of Homeland Security

Though included as an "advanced" strategy in this volume, visibility on your network is a vital element of any effective cybersecurity and risk management program. It is exceedingly difficult, if not impossible, to detect, prevent, or respond to a cybersecurity incident if you lack a clear picture of your information systems network. In a cyberspace context, as in medicine, a multitude of information of varying types is generally needed to successfully identify, diagnose, treat, or prevent a cyberattack. This can include observation of the following:

- The pathogen (malware, virus, denial-of-service attack, or use of an exploit)
- Risk factors (a fundamental flaw in network or application architecture that makes you susceptible to attack, such as flawed code, an unpatched exploit, or an open port)
- Symptoms (an unexpectedly large amount of data leaving the network, the sudden encryption of large volumes of data, communication with a suspicious server, or degraded network performance)

In short, lacking visibility into the key elements, functions, and activities of the network leaves any enterprise susceptible to a potentially devastating cyberattack. All this information is vital to not only detecting a potential attack, but also responding to and preventing one. While visibility across the entire network and technology stack is important, I would focus on four key areas of visibility that are likely to provide security professionals with the greatest understanding of potential threats lurking on their systems: visibility on devices, visibility on software and code, visibility on network activity, and visibility on access.

Although full visibility on any one of these may not, by itself, be enough for a company to defend against a cyberthreat, visibility across all four will give most enterprises a fighting chance at preventing, detecting, and responding to a cyberattack. Security executives would be well served to work with their technical teams to ensure that their enterprise has visibility into these vital aspects of their networks.

VISIBILITY ON DEVICES

The first type of visibility that an enterprise needs on its network is visibility of devices, which itself requires understanding the underlying network and the dramatic changes that have occurred over the past decade. What was once a relatively simple network with a clearly defined perimeter is now much more fluid, with devices spread across physical locations, software performing many traditional networking functions, and the adoption of the cloud for a variety of applications that once took place on premises. Each and every computer, printer, IP-based phone, mobile device, switch, server, network appliance, smart TV, virtual machine, and countless other Internet of Things (IoT) devices utilize the network to transfer data both within the network itself and to the broader Internet, depending on the network configuration. This can open the network to machines used by attackers to spread malware, steal valuable data, operate botnets, or manage ransomware.

Network visibility into connected devices is therefore necessary for any successful effort to make the network secure. A single compromised device with unfettered access to your network can serve as a point of entry and foothold for attackers, allowing them to spread malicious code and compromise other devices on the network. Such awareness is also a prerequisite to proper network design, allowing an organization to segment mission-critical machines from backup printers, limiting device access to certain network ports and protocols, and monitoring device activity for abnormalities.

Knowing what devices are connected to the network is a good start, but it's not enough. Every school year, schools not only ensure accurate class lists, but also verify students' immunization records. Likewise, you must also know details about the connected device, including its configuration and software versions. Such information allows technology professionals to quickly identify what devices may be vulnerable to exploitation and give them the opportunity to ensure that all devices on the network are running the latest, patched versions of software and firmware. Vulnerabilities in outdated firmware and software are frequent targets for attackers seeking to compromise a network.

VISIBILITY ON CODE

Visibility on code essentially takes visibility on devices one step further, asking not only what version of software or firmware a device is running, but also what is included in that software or firmware. What third-party or open source components are embedded in that software? What versions of those components are in use? What vulnerabilities do those components have, and how can they be addressed? These are important questions, and attackers are increasingly relying on flaws in underlying code bases, long an afterthought for many developers, as the starting point for a broader compromise.

For commercial, off-the-shelf software, this is seemingly simple: The software provider periodically updates its product to address vulnerabilities. Actually, it isn't this simple. Many providers rely on codebases beyond their control, open source or third-party, and may not be working to make sure those components, such as a JavaScript or SQL function, are up to date and have addressed identified vulnerabilities.

The problem gets significantly more complicated for open source, custom, or in-house-developed software, where responsibility for ensuring that all the involved code is up to date becomes both more complicated and the responsibility of a smaller number of people. Many developers are used to simply "pulling" underlying codebases from repositories, most Internet-based, without putting too much thought into whether the code being pulled is up to date or addresses potentially dangerous vulnerabilities. It is also important to keep in mind that most software developers are not security professionals, and understandably, they consider development needs over the security concerns of an organization's CISO. In these circumstances, companies need to work with the following:

- Their providers, to ensure underlying code bases are up to date

- Their programmers, to ensure they are pulling codebases that are safe and up to date
- Their security teams, to conduct audits and scans of their software and code to identify potential threats

This is, understandably, one of the most difficult visibility issues to address. Many enterprises rely on a significant number of custom-built and designed programs that draw on dozens, if not hundreds, of codebases that are either open source or provided by third parties. Abandoning open source code isn't a workable, or even recommended, solution. Enterprises need to take a multipronged approach to address the issue, putting in place development procedures that lend further scrutiny to third-party and open source code, conducting enhanced software composition analysis, and expanding the use of automated testing of code for vulnerabilities across its life cycle. In the development world, this is called development security operations, which is often shortened to DevSecOps.

VISIBILITY ON ACTIVITY

Having clear visibility of activity on the network can provide an enterprise with an extremely useful picture of potential threats, providing the data needed both for early warning of a potential threat and the information needed to quickly and efficiently remediate any issues that arise. Some of this information is collected automatically by any number of technologies or services operating on a corporate network. However, not all services and technologies collect the same data or provide the fidelity needed to prevent, detect, and respond to a potential threat. In an IT context, many technologies and systems default to a minimal level of logging, requiring changes to the base configuration to collect the most valuable data.

Similarly, much of the activity on a corporate network falls outside the scope of a single application or server's basic logging functions. Enterprises should ideally be actively monitoring their network traffic, seeking to identify anomalies and indicators of potential threat or compromise. Encrypted traffic in transit to an unusual server, critical intellectual property data transiting systems dedicated to building services, or an employee's cellphone connecting to a key command-and-control server are examples.

Increasingly valuable are behavioral analytic and machine learning tools that can detect anomalous behavior too subtle for humans to detect. Even if network activity does not violate a rule or seem obviously suspicious, deviations from normal network behavior may be a tip that there is nefarious activity.

Detailed file access logs, user account logs, file history logs, archived network traffic data, and other indicators are also incredibly valuable pieces of information to data breach responders seeking to determine what data may have been compromised and by whom. Enterprises would also be well served to make investments in their security information and event management (SIEM) capabilities, allowing their security staff to better correlate the significant volumes of data an enterprise may have regarding activity on its network with potential threats or suspicious activity. Such capabilities are useful not only in breach response, but in both detection and prevention as well.

VISIBILITY ON IDENTITY AND ACCESS

Visibility on identity and access is in many ways a subset of visibility into activity on your network. The 2018 Verizon Data Breach Report identified the use of compromised credentials as the most reported action leveraged by the attacker in a cybersecurity breach, followed closely by other identity-related compromises, including privilege abuse. User credentials, while associated with a user or person, in reality act in much the same way your car or house key does. Consider hotels as a physical world analogy to cloud services. You get access to your room, but not to the hotel safe or building control systems. Conversely, though that key may be assigned to you, anyone who gets hold of that key can access your room just as easily as you can. To manage access appropriately, you need to start by knowing how many keys are issued to you and make sure that, if your friends want to use the keys, you can ensure they are, in fact, the ones using them.

Visibility on IT authentication attempts is also important. Is the access attempt being made from the assigned user's home or from an obscure town in rural Russia? Are they attempting to access their usual email data or key financial data? These are factors that can help an enterprise determine whether the credentials are, in fact, being used by those they are meant to be used by. Visibility into such information can help an enterprise ensure that only those who are supposed to have access to key information obtain access.

CONCLUSION

Visibility into key technology building blocks is vital to an enterprise's ability to adequately defend its systems. Securing a network is difficult enough—and nearly impossible without appropriate visibility into the devices, code, activities, and access on that network. As in almost any discipline, the more information you have, the easier it is to identify and address a threat.

ABOUT THE CONTRIBUTOR

Michael Chertoff – Former Secretary, Department of Homeland Security

Michael Chertoff leads The Chertoff Group, a global advisory services firm that applies security expertise, technology insights, and policy intelligence to help clients build resilient organizations, gain competitive advantage, and accelerate growth. In this role, he counsels global clients on how to effectively manage cybersecurity risk while incorporating a proper mix of people, process, and technology to achieve their security goals. He serves on the board of directors of several security companies and is a frequent speaker on security and risk management issues. From 2005 to 2009, Chertoff served as Secretary of the US Department of Homeland Security. Earlier in his career, he served as a federal judge on the US Court of Appeals for the Third Circuit and as head of the US Department of Justice's Criminal Division. He is the author of *Exploding Data: Reclaiming Our Cybersecurity in the Digital Age* (Atlantic Monthly Press, 2018).

20/20 INSIGHT: REDEFINING VISIBILITY TO STOP MODERN CYBERCRIME SYNDICATES

Tim Crothers, Target

Of all the cybersecurity fundamentals, it is arguably visibility that has CISOs and their teams racing to keep pace with the rates of innovation in both security and threats alike. And although there is no silver bullet for maintaining that rate of velocity or achieving the optimal levels of visibility, a subtle pivot in perspective can help tremendously. By not limiting ourselves to conventional definitions of visibility, we are able to reimagine what visibility means in a way that is not only much more effective, but also far more efficient and appropriate for modern cybersecurity.

The analogy that many of us have long used is that visibility is like a security camera: We know we have both appropriate and malicious activity on our networks, and visibility is the mechanism we deploy to differentiate between the two. In the late 1990s and early 2000s, this made perfect sense. Our enterprise IT systems tended to have very few and very specific connections to the Internet or other external systems, so visibility capabilities could be concentrated at the perimeters of an organization's environment like guard towers along the front lines.

But as personal devices started to be leveraged heavily, organizations stopped housing IT in their own data centers and moved to cloud services, and product teams started developing containerized applications where multiple disparate business systems could share a single IP address; the very principles and practices of visibility had to change. But just because that needed to happen doesn't necessarily mean it did—or that it changed sufficiently and quickly enough. The mechanisms that we used to achieve visibility up to the mid-2000s simply no longer provide clear visibility within a modern IT infrastructure. And though many organizations have lagged behind on updating their visibility capabilities, the cybercriminals most certainly have not lagged behind in updating their approaches.

Recognizing this reality reveals critical human dynamics that at times get overlooked in cybersecurity discussions and decisions that primarily focus on technology. When we start incorporating a deeper understanding of human behaviors, we find that our abilities to use those technologies—and even which technologies we choose to use—change dramatically.

Our adversaries have always had to evolve their tactics and abilities quickly. They know that security vendors are constantly improving defenses. And because the crimes they commit are the business they are in, they don't have the luxury of utilizing approaches that are years old.

Cybercriminals are like salespeople who work on 100 percent commission. If they don't successfully steal, they don't eat—so they are in a constant, relentless state of attack and iteration. Their focus is trained laser-like on achieving their goal of finding and stealing monetizable information—with no approval processes, project backlogs, quarterly budgets and objectives, or any other business goals to slow them down or distract them from their singular purpose. Whereas enterprise organizations strive to build "learning cultures," successful cybercrime syndicates begin with that as a given.

As a result, organizations that lagged behind or failed to recognize the necessity of maintaining the velocity of innovation found themselves not only behind the curve in terms of the actual technologies that were being deployed in their own networks—but even farther behind the threat actors and the methods they use for attacks.

Unfortunately, many organizations don't even see or consider the ramifications. From 2012, when cloud deployment really took off, to 2014, when more organizations started moving to agile development models, IT underwent a transformation while many security teams maintained an older approach centered on network hosts and application models. This created a sizable gap for adversaries to exploit against them.

As the DevOps approach becomes even more common and more agile, that gap gets even wider. Information security teams that try to use the old model of pulling in all the data to do pattern matching quickly realize that approach won't scale. The amount of data is just too large and moving too rapidly. Rather than searching for a needle in a haystack, they find they are now searching for a needle in thousands of haystacks that are generated dynamically, live for times as brief as 15 minutes, and then are gone.

Perhaps that's a blessing in disguise. Once we recognize old approaches are no longer appropriate, it allows us to get much more creative, innovative, and strategic. By taking a different approach to visibility, we can achieve the best of both worlds. We can enable the greater levels of agility in our businesses while potentially improving the level of our security.

Much of this comes down to where we choose to look—and the understanding that, when it comes to visibility, more isn't the same as better. Better is better. Which is why, to improve visibility, we must first focus on the needs of the attackers.

If we understand what cybercriminals need to succeed, we will know the activities they need to perform. For instance, if the goal is to steal intellectual property, most attackers will start with something like a malicious email. But if they are successful, that is only the beginning for them. Though it is relatively easy to trick a user into clicking on a malicious link that installs malware on their laptop, that user is most likely not going to have direct access to the intellectual property an attacker wants to steal.

An attacker gains access to a vulnerable but often unimportant system, but must traverse the network to get what they are really seeking. This begins a process of privilege escalation and lateral movement. The way most hackers accomplish this is by harvesting locally cached credentials that they can leverage to traverse the environment.

And here is where we see the power of redefining visibility as not simply the ability to see, passively, like a security camera—but rather as a constantly evolving process of developing insights and acting on that deeper understanding.

Knowing what the attackers are after allows us to switch from a position of constant, whack-a-mole defense to a campaign of much more strategic offense. When we understand that they are looking for locally cached credentials, and why, we can then set up a sting. We can run a script in our local hosts that caches fake admin credentials—knowing there is no legitimate business use for harvesting credentials—and wait for them to take the bait. A cybercriminal who has gained access to a network has no way of knowing whether nabbed credentials are valid until they try them, and when they do, they trip a series of alarms and fail-safes that prevent them from going any further.

These are often referred to as deception techniques, but they fall squarely in the type of strategic, intelligence-based visibility that we need today. What is the point of visibility if not the ability to detect threats so we can mitigate damage?

For organizations that are already behind on their visibility techniques, this type of security activity may seem out of reach. But achieving greater actionable insights into what security capabilities they need will help them close that gap more effectively and more efficiently than anything else—and, importantly, at lower cost.

Thankfully, there is a clear first step to achieving this: Start with the intel. Start with the intel. And then, start with the intel. Although most organizations are not in a position to afford a deep bench of former three-letter-agency operatives to gather threat intelligence for them, there is no shortage of knowledge sharing available to companies of all sizes. But because it is a frustrating, counterproductive legal liability for organizations that have been breached to speak publicly about what happened, sharing information often requires one-on-one communication. A simple, mutual nondisclosure agreement will allow organizations to speak much more openly. Also, a host of organizations and peer groups are dedicated to reporting and assessing threat trends. The key here is to look not at details but rather at the patterns being exploited. What are the themes of the threat actors, and subsequently, what are the implications for your organization? Threat actors are people too. As people, they fall into habits and patterns like all of us.

With a knowledge- and intel-driven approach to visibility—knowing where to look and what to look for—the security improvements will be dramatic. For instance, if you are a chain restaurant and you see that a vast cybercrime syndicate like Carbanak/FIN7 is systematically targeting other companies in your industry with phishing emails that install a malicious JavaScript with strong obfuscation and anti-sandboxing capabilities, your visibility into this type of attack will be exponentially better—often at zero external cost. Studying the tactics of cybercriminals who steal to support themselves uncovers patterns that you can use to defend your own organization much more effectively.

Forewarned is also forearmed—because having better threat visibility puts you in a position to build and deploy a wide range of prevention, detection, and response capabilities that are low cost and highly effective. That greater insight will also empower you to more effectively prioritize your security needs: You will have more granular knowledge of the latest techniques hackers are using, the specific types of malware and tools, and how hackers approach an organization targeted for breach. And by sharing knowledge with strategic partners, stakeholders, and competitors alike—because cybercrime against another company in your vertical should never be seen as a competitive advantage—something else begins to emerge that turns cybercriminals' primary attributes against them.

What makes threat actors effective is their tenacity. Because of their grueling, all-or-nothing business model, they must attack relentlessly. But an enormous amount of legwork must occur before every attack—creating the phish, designing the malware specifically for the target, and registering domains for the command-and-control servers, among other prep work. As relentless and inexhaustible as they may seem, attackers are human—and they are repeating the same tasks and operations over and over again. That means they inevitably fall into patterns. The fake names they use to register the domains get reused or start to become similar; the domain name reveals clues about which company they are planning to attack; they fine-tune malware by uploading it to Google's VirusTotal or similar repositories. Rigorous data analytics on previous attacks reveals these patterns. The more organizations share knowledge, the greater the ability they will have to spot these patterns and pivot to a proactive rather than a reactive state.

That type of knowledge sharing and collaboration costs nothing—and it has a halo effect on the situational awareness of an entire team, which is another form of improved visibility. And it is also not confined to external stakeholders.

All organizations should make sure there are no internal silos that create inefficiencies or blind spots. The network visibility framework fabric that a security team builds can be leveraged by the network team for troubleshooting, by the operations team to review performance, and for a range of other uses. Similarly, virtually all organizations have data feeds used by teams like operations or development that can be leveraged by the security teams in different ways but that yield significant insight into how applications and systems are being used. Insight is just another word for visibility.

As advantageous as it is to partner with security teams across verticals and organizations, there are also huge benefits to collaborating with your company's non-security teams. For a business that must be judicious with budgets and allocations, it not only achieves better security results, but is also a much smarter and more efficient use of organizational dollars. Before determining what visibility you need, check first to see what visibility you already have—it may be far more than you realize.

In a technology-driven culture, it is easy to fall into a thought process that sees progress only in massive leaps forward. Those jumps are exciting and gratifying—especially to those who allocate budgets and are looking for solid ROI. But they can quickly lead to diminishing returns—or worse, a false sense of security.

Greater levels of visibility, pursued for their own sake, do not equal more effective security. In fact, too much visibility can make it harder to clearly see the most dangerous threats. Wasting time and effort looking at data that is not relevant only provides criminals with the ability to more effectively hide in plain sight. Incremental, steady increases in visibility are not only fine and commendable—they may also deliver much better security. Even an increase from 1 percent to 5 percent visibility can deliver dramatically better outcomes, if the increase is driven by insight and understanding.

It is a perspective and approach that will only become more fundamental to visibility. The velocity we are now seeing will continue to increase as more IT teams leverage open source technology and new approaches to business systems and infrastructure. And as that rate of change picks up, we know from past evidence that our adversaries will do everything they can to match it. More than anything else, it is threat actors' ability to beat defenders in that race to keep up that creates our greatest risks. The key to stopping them is to understand where they are going and how they plan to get there. Using a new approach to visibility to cut them off before they get there can be a key tool in that race.

ABOUT THE CONTRIBUTOR

Tim Crothers – *VP* of Cyber Security, Target

Tim Crothers is a seasoned security leader with over 20 years of experience building and running information security programs, large and complex incident response and breach investigations, and threat and vulnerability assessments. He has deep experience in cyberthreat intelligence, reverse engineering, computer forensics, intrusion detection, breach prevention, and applying six sigma and lean processes to information security. He is the author or coauthor of 15 books to date, as well as having regular training and speaking engagements at information security conferences.

Currently Crothers is VP of Cyber Security for Target. There he has built and leads the Cyber Fusion Center, where the company is working on using innovative and new techniques and technologies to push the envelope of cybersecurity intel, detection and response, and red teaming.

THE CHALLENGE OF VISIBILITY

Daniel Hooper, PIMCO

The primary challenge faced by most organizations today is not just dealing with the known unknowns, such as threats like WannaCry that target a known vulnerability, but the unknown knowns as well. Seeing who and what is on the network and where data is located is becoming complicated due to the proliferation of technology and the speed of innovation across IT teams and the business.

The pace of technology growth is increasing, AI and machine learning are driving the proliferation and complexity of technology, and it is a constant challenge to keep up with that change. In my four years at PIMCO, for example, our core Oracle database has grown from 80 TB to over 160 TB, and we expect it to top 300 TB in the next six months. At the same time, our analytics people are developing new ways to calculate price projections using machine learning, AI, and tools like MapR and Apache Hadoop.

The proliferation of inputs and outputs driven by these new technologies, workflows, and applications is driving the growth of IT as well as the growth of risk. Organizations developing disparate data centers running on different technologies or new products for niche markets may not think of security at the beginning. The assumption may be that these different environments are walled off, but the reality is that data, traffic, and resources always bleed into the production environment and everything starts mixing.

In such a rapidly evolving environment, getting a handle on what systems are online—business, personal, guest, or customer—is not only difficult, but also only part of the challenge. Visibility isn't only about knowing what's on the network—it's also about what's off the network, such as shadow IT, parallel networks, or mobile devices. The reality is that many stakeholders inside an organization are entirely empowered to operate autonomously. The CIO may not think that they are, but many times all they need is a goal and a corporate credit card to go to Amazon Web Services (AWS) and spin up a service.

VISIBILITY IS ABOUT MORE THAN TECHNOLOGY

One of the main visibility challenges for the CISO is seeing what changes are coming. Achieving that requires more than understanding the goals of the business or the plans of IT. It also requires being plugged into the right areas of the business and getting in touch with the various stakeholders across the organization. This requires developing relationships with all the various team and department leaders to understand their drivers and requirements beyond those being provided by IT. While CIOs are aligned with the focus of their business, they are not as plugged into the needs of individual stakeholders.

Organizations outside of the mainstream business, such as HR, spin up their own off-network systems and services all the time. The reason is that HR's requirements for employee performance management or hiring may not be aligned to the core business of the company, which means that existing IT may not be meeting their unique needs. For example, they may need a job application service to advertise jobs. With so many services available online, they don't need to wait for IT to deliver that. But that also means that they may be amassing candidate information that needs to be protected, especially under regulations such as General Data Protection Regulation (GDPR). These off-the-books resources not only create risk; they create risk you may not even know about.

DEVELOP A RELATIONSHIP WITH KEY STAKEHOLDERS

Developing relationships with corporate management often gives you insight into the sorts of resources they require, as well as their plans for development and resource deployment. This includes participating in steering groups and committees and developing relationships with the heads of functions such as those who evaluate cloud vendors. Once those relationships are in place, you are in a position to suggest they take a pause so that you can see how your security strategy can be integrated into their project before it is selected and deployed.

But even these stakeholders and leaders may not have full insight into the things the individuals on their teams are doing to get their jobs done. You need to develop relationships with the teams that approve expenses as well. They can flag charges for online services and new technologies for you to review. In addition, learning what sorts of parallel or shadow IT is running in your network also means using legal as a central contact to review work contracts with service providers.

All of that data can then be brought together in a vendor management system that helps you see who these vendors are, why they have been engaged, how they are being used, and what information they hold. Proprietary trade information, personally identifiable information (PII) of customers or employees, and marketing and business plans held in unknown places using nonvalidated applications and services may have already exposed your organization to unnecessary risk.

You don't want to learn about these challenges the hard way. The outcome of lack of visibility creates the potential for unpleasant surprises, such as an email from the FBI saying they found your corporate information on the Dark Web, or a call from a company that trolls AWS sites for S3 (Simple Storage Service) information to tell you what they just found.

CARROT AND STICK

Addressing this challenge requires a carrot-and-stick approach. You can stay on top of new technologies and resources by letting management know that sharing information gets them access to IT services that make their job easier (single sign-on, multifactor authentication, federating IDs, Active Directory Services to track logins, technology integration, fast-tracking the approval of new technology or services, and so on).

The stick doesn't need to be too harsh. Start with educating people about why they can't just spin up a new chat program because it's easy. Explain their obligation to protect the information of employees and clients, and that a compromise is everyone's problem. Help them understand why they need to come to the tech team with their requests.

One way to facilitate this is by integrating members of the security team into the various business units. This helps your team gain visibility into what people are procuring and why and can help prevent some nasty surprises. At the same time, cherry-pick leading developers from some of these teams and invite them to sit next to penetration testers in real time so they can see how the applications they are developing or subscribing to can be hacked. Nothing gets developers involved faster than watching someone pick apart their application in real time. The same sort of thing can be done with businesspeople. Familiarizing them with how security impacts the information they are sharing can be very empowering.

UPGRADE YOUR SECURITY TEAM

One thing I have done is hire fewer technical people and instead bring on individuals who can relate to business. While I used to hire red team members and hackers, what I really need now are people with some technical background that I can put in front of department heads who can have a business conversation. For example, I need someone who can explain our efforts to prevent nation-states and business insiders from stealing or hacking our corporate data, not in technical terms but in business language.

This leads to a two-pronged IT team with a centralized and decentralized model:

1. The centralized IT team provides classic security support:
   - Core team for patching, maintenance, hygiene, and so on. No matter how advanced the network becomes, companies are always running some legacy devices combined with compensating controls in order to secure their underlying vulnerabilities.
   - This team is responsible for ensuring that the network continues to meet corporate and regulatory requirements, knowing what devices have been deployed across the environment, continuously monitoring the security posture, and configuring and managing deployed security and related devices.

2. The distributed IT team works with people:
- This requires experts who can coordinate, consolidate, figure out reporting, and respond to events and requests at a business level. They are also tasked with learning what users are doing day to day so they can identify the indicators of a malicious actor.
- They also manage the carrot-and-stick approach. Their job is not to just beat people with policy but also to get them excited about how information security is related to their role.

This interaction between the IT team and various corporate departments needs to go both ways.

WHAT ABOUT SECURITY TECHNOLOGY?

The other half of the security equation is the security you invest in on the back end. It's important to remember that security is not a feature or a product. Security flaws exist because of a fundamental mistake in the product or products you have deployed. Security technology needs to do two things: it needs to compensate for the flaws inherent in a device or system, and it needs to improve visibility.

One of the biggest challenges is the span of visibility you are able to achieve. Single-point-of-view visibility across the entire range of internal networks is more product- and labor-intensive, but it is necessary if you don't want to end up like Equifax.

A perfect case in point was WannaCry. One Friday afternoon in May, we started seeing news reports about a new threat. We checked Wikileaks and other sources (okay, we're nerds, and we like to look at stuff like that), but we didn't yet understand that this was worming malware. Once we did and downloaded the appropriate patches, it actually took us about five days to figure out where all the devices that needed patching were located in our environment.

Our inability to immediately understand what resources were deployed and where they were located highlighted our need to get critical information in a timelier manner. This required investing in and deploying a combination of new tools on all of our desktops and Windows servers. That was the easy part. Implementing a similar solution for Linux servers took much longer. And there still aren't easy solutions for Solaris, Oracle, Hadoop, and similar technologies. In those cases, a solution becomes an expensive combination of compensatory security technologies.

What is clear is that both organizations and vendors need to commit more money to people, time, and products in order to enable faster threat identification and environment queries for missing patches and identify vulnerability behaviors.

THE CHALLENGE OF OVERLAPPING CAPABILITIES

Innovation is sexy. Tracking user behavior using user and entity behavior analytics (UEBA) is hot right now. But we are now starting to see that functionality everywhere. The challenge is not with product consolidation but in the overlapping capabilities of tools.

Likewise, some email gateways have now added inline data loss prevention capabilities to help organizations identify potential insider threats. But other point solutions have built out that technology as well. This is also true for other security technologies that overlap and compete while running on the same machine at the same time. Some even block each other when one runs a PowerShell script, which leads to having to internally white-list technologies you actually own. As these technologies start to step on each other, they can actually confuse the CISO team, requiring more money to license additional capabilities that still don't provide a complete end-to-end solution. This means more spending on education, training, and additional solutions.

ISSUES PREVENTING A COMPLETE SOLUTION

The biggest challenge to deploying a comprehensive security strategy is that it's expensive, in terms of both people and tech. I recently hired someone just to monitor Qualys and then marry data together. Not everyone is willing to spend a couple of hundred thousand dollars a year to do that. An organization could easily say that service isn't actually connected to the network or that we already have compensating controls in place. As a result, some leaders may not see the value of doing it.

The trick is to establish priorities with your team. You start by getting the basics and fundamentals right: Are we scanning or not? Does that include phones and meeting room computers, or only the crown jewels? And where does it stop? A recent breach analysis in the news identified hackers spooling up data on a print server running Windows XP, and then storing it there before exfiltrating it. Unfortunately, the ops team owned that printer, so they weren't checking. There continues to be a need to know who owns which devices, establishing a regular scanning routine and a protocol for knowing who to call if an issue arises.

Of course, that's easier said than done. It is notoriously difficult to ensure that you are always scanning the right stuff or that all of the devices you own and have deployed are being regularly inventoried and analyzed. It is also critical that you maintain any sort of program and related tools you initiate, unless they are replaced by a better or more comprehensive solution. Recently, after a big effort to secure our mobile devices, we took our foot off the gas. A recent scan shows that we now have numerous noncompliant devices. This is easy to do, even in your own team. Simply turn your attention to something on fire and leave something else smoldering in the background, and you can find yourself fighting wildfires on multiple fronts at the same time.

ACHIEVING AN OPTIMAL BALANCE

Visibility, and its related issues of identity and access management, is a big investment area. Unfortunately, threat management solutions frequently outweigh it. That is why one of the most critical jobs a CISO has is to balance the spend between people, technologies, and contractors—such as management consultants, professional services, and penetration testing. If the proper tools and controls are in place, however, a lot of hygiene can be very cost-effectively offshored because those functions are repeatable and easy to measure. This allows you to adjust the resource model for people and technology, allowing you to reassign limited people resources to higher-order activities, and adjust technologies as they converge, or as new critical tools emerge that can be more easily incorporated into your existing security strategy.

ABOUT THE CONTRIBUTOR

Daniel Hooper – Global Information Security Officer, PIMCO

Daniel Hooper is an experienced information security professional currently responsible for overall strategy and direction of the program designed to identify, assess, and manage information security risk at PIMCO. In 2014, he expanded the role from technical improvements to working closely with global teams to manage regulatory expectations, communicate to clients, and fund boards.

Previously Hooper worked for Deloitte, Loop Technology, Infoshield, e-Secure, NETELLER, and IBM. At Deloitte, he relocated from the Australian practice to America, where he led the ground-up establishment of an enterprise information security function, developed a high-level IT security strategy, established an IT risk management program for a large global financial services client, enhanced an existing IT risk and control self-assessment methodology to align with the existing corporate operational risk management program, and participated in an organizationwide current state assessment of IT control posture to identify key focus areas relating to IT risk and security.

10

INSPECTION

Inspection is the safeguard that allows security teams to preemptively stop attacks by finding the lurking "known unknowns": The network breaches attempted or already achieved that you know are out there but don't know where. The Scientific Age was born when the technical elite of the day admitted that they didn't know as much as they should, challenged unproven assumptions, and actively looked to fill in the gaps in their knowledge. That concept transitioned from scientific methodology into national strategy when then–US President Reagan said succinctly, "Trust, but verify." Whereas Reagan referred to using rigor—special sensors and multisourced analytics—to find things that weren't intended by our adversaries to be discoverable and ensure general adherence to weapons treaties, the same strategy and methodology should be used by any serious practitioner of cybersecurity. Rigor in inspection of potentially malicious cyber content—whether disguised in attachments to emails or hiding within legitimate traffic—is key to cybersecurity strategy.

Criminals have always used duplicity, manipulation, and subterfuge to gain access via phishing emails armed with malware-laden attachments. Now, though, they are increasingly using polymorphic malware—malicious email attachments that have never been seen in their current form, changed to avoid detection. That means that our standard detection techniques—which look for known patterns—may miss this malware.

Instead, deeper inspection of those attachments has become a key tool for countering polymorphic malware. Specifically, suspicious attachments are examined in contained areas known as sandboxes, where their behavior is analyzed. Sandboxing has proven to be an excellent recourse for neutralizing attempted breaches before they occur. The most sophisticated sandboxes block the delivery of malicious attachments that they have inspected and found to be malicious, and also generate indicators to distribute to other nodes on the network to detect and block similar malicious emails. By evaluating email attachments for maliciousness—executing them in a safe, contained environment, and then inspecting them for evidence of maliciousness—security operators can flush out and prevent those malicious attachments from reaching their intended target. The most sophisticated sandboxes also generate indicators that they send to other nodes on the network to warn them of, and tell them exactly how to block, the malicious emails.

But though the potential harm of email attachments is on most people's minds, adversaries have upped their game and are presenting an arguably greater challenge. Increasingly, threat actors are augmenting their penetration efforts by leveraging a network's own defenses against it, leveraging one of cybersecurity's most powerful tools, encryption, to hide their activity. When encryption was not as widely used as it is today, network security operators evaluated inbound and outboard network traffic using advanced analytics, looking for signs of covert command-and-control activity and stolen intellectual property. The idea was, trust but verify: Assume your defenses are in place but look for unexpected activity all the same.

Encrypted networks inadvertently provide threat actors with the cover they need to launch and maintain covert command-and-control of malicious nodes within the network. With network encryption (Secure Sockets Layer, or SSL), those inspection analytics are nearly useless because the bits are scrambled into meaningless strings. Although encryption protects the confidentiality and integrity of legitimate users and facilitates the sharing of information among such users, encryption also hides the activity of malicious users and creates pathways for them to share their malicious crafts. The resulting risk cannot be overstated. Without the ability to inspect, ubiquitous encryption forces network security operators to "fly blind," making the network immeasurably less secure.

And in an era when it is seemingly acceptable by some to be a rogue "insider activist"—leaking private, financial, proprietary, and even out-of-context-embarrassing company data—the importance of inspection is out of sight (bad pun intended).

How do we address this problem? We can't give network operators two bad choices:

- Using SSL to decrypt everything but not being able to scan for malicious activity, or
- Turning off SSL by default to enable the necessary visibility for the network owner, giving up the benefit of using encryption to hide from adversaries

Neither option is viable. But too often, SSL inspection is being turned off because much of the cybersecurity industry has failed to acknowledge one of cyberspace's two core elements—speed (the other is connectivity). In most cases, cybersecurity architects have built content inspection capabilities that have laid the burden of inspection on overburdened CPUs and slowed communications to an unacceptable crawl.

This is where science can serve us: By creating an inspection capability that embraces the key founding fundamental of speed. Since inspection of content is an essential cybersecurity strategy, computer scientists and engineers can and must create speed-optimized methods to achieve it.

Malicious actors hide. They hide behind encryption, and they hide within otherwise legitimate functions. It's important to realize that they're hiding on your information systems—which they have no right to do. Aggressive inspection of content is a responsibility that must be executed with diligence to protect the confidentiality, integrity, and availability needs of legitimate users.

As the techniques of nation-states, cybercriminals, and rogue employees proliferate, and they attempt to hide in email attachments and the noise of regular encrypted traffic, inspection remains a central tool to detect carefully concealed covert activity. Today, the cybersecurity strategy of inspection—and all the tactical tools it comprises—has become increasingly important and increasingly difficult to implement. But just because it's hard doesn't mean it's not worth doing.

IN AND OUT OF THE SHADOWS:
THE VISIBILITY THAT INSPECTION ENABLES IS NOT CONFINED TO TECHNOLOGY ALONE

Ed Amoroso, TAG Cyber

Any discussion of the security principle of inspection must begin with the understanding that inspection implies visibility. Not only does this make inspection closely synonymous with the overarching mission and purpose of cybersecurity, it also aligns with its evolution from reference monitor to an intensely complex security fundamental.

In the beginning, cybersecurity was exponentially more straightforward than it is today. Simply put, users would request access to a resource, and some form of "security" determined whether they were authorized to have that access. If they were authorized, it let them in. If they were not authorized, it kept them out.

As far as we have come in the decades since, that's still the essential concept of information protection. And if everything worked perfectly, there would be no need for inspection—as a practice in general, and in the immeasurable complexities that have emerged to contend with imperfections in a world increasingly connected by digital technology.

The emergence of those complexities began almost immediately. In the 1980s, those of us who worked in the burgeoning field of cybersecurity noticed that the binary security decision of "access granted or access denied" had a tendency to deliver a couple additional results that weren't optimal: One was that users who were not authorized would be allowed access. The other was that people who were authorized would be denied. We all consulted the user manual and confirmed conclusively that this was not the way it was supposed to work.

As a result, innovation was catalyzed. Inspection was created.

In a fast-moving and constantly iterating discipline, it is easy to fall into a simplistic narrative that depicts everything as an exponential advancement of what came before it. The truth is more complicated and less linear. The progression of inspection, especially, reveals the deep interconnection between cybersecurity best practices and the structural flaws it has addressed from very early on.

The brilliant and prescient cybersecurity pioneer Dorothy Denning drove numerous game-changing innovations—intuitively anticipating emerging threats by those she dubbed "cyberspace scofflaws." She presented "A Lattice Model of Secure Information Flow" in 1975, a model still in use today. In the mid-1980s, while at SRI International, she developed a model for intrusion detection that collected audit trail information to spot anomalies indicative of threat—still the foundation of modern security systems. To this day, most cybersecurity systems include a frontend functional component that ingests information to determine some desired attributes. Inspecting structured data is often more straightforward than inspecting unstructured data, but both are essential in most enterprise environments.

The process of innovation that unfolded in the years since—rapid, progressive, and increasingly complex—has expanded from that simple, yes-or-no access approval, to the collection of data through log files, to what we have today. The difference between then and now is similar to the difference between the rubber band–powered propeller of a balsa wood toy glider and a Boeing 777 GE90 jet engine. It has progressed in every possible way you could imagine.

The seamless and continuous nature of cybersecurity innovations—all deeply interconnected—often makes it difficult to pinpoint specific milestones and turning points. But we may well be in the midst of one that will be regarded as a fundamental shift.

As the efficiency and abilities of artificial intelligence have rapidly improved, we have seen machine learning match up nicely with cybersecurity goals in general, and inspection in particular. Just as visibility is central to security, inspection is fundamental to machine learning.

That's because effective machine learning hinges on collecting myriad samples of something, all with variables that are slightly different, and then teaching a system to account for the differences. If we input 1,000 different pictures of kittens and then input a picture of a cat it has never seen before, machine learning allows the system to deduce, "This is consistent with the information that has been ingested; it's a cat."

In the same way, we can now program a system to recognize a virus by inspecting and ingesting samples and harnessing the power of machine learning: "This is a virus and it sits in a file called 'malware. exe.' It has these properties." AI can recognize that if `malware1.exe` has these properties, then those same properties contained in a file called `malware2.exe`, `1malware.exe`, or even `zebrasam.malware.exe` likely also indicate malware.

Thanks to advances driven by Geoffrey Hinton, and his ground-breaking work in artificial neural networks at the University of Toronto, detecting and correctly assessing variants based on a wide range of inspected samples enables the ability to make determinations based on AI. This is a massive leap forward from the old way of doing it—applying security at an endpoint that parsed information against a massive list of every possible filename and location cache for a piece of malware.

AI is not a security silver bullet, though. Running these algorithms requires an enormous amount of computing power, which is why many companies process samples in the cloud, to be rendered back based on machine learning. As much as AI has advanced—and will continue to grow in power and sophistication—it still begins with the initial ingestion and inspection process.

Ultimately, most machine learning involves a human being feeding data into the inspection engine—so it is still susceptible to the hurdles that are intrinsic to inspection. Some are rooted in the technology of the tools. And, in keeping with another thread that runs through the history of cybersecurity, some are inextricably entwined with the natural human shortcomings of individual users and organizations.

From a technological perspective, the primary challenge to proper inspection is that direct observation is not always possible, due to vantage point issues or obfuscation via encryption or masking. An example involves the increased use of HTTPS across the Internet, which reduces the collection surface for inspecting network packets. A complementary challenge to inspection is that indirect observation requires authorized information flow through intermediaries. An example involves reviewing event logs to determine the properties of some target system; this might not be allowed under local access policies.

Further complicating the challenge, and making inspection expo-nentially more difficult, is inspection's relationship to another security fundamental.

Despite claims often made to the contrary, cryptography compli-cates inspection—period. In fact, the textbook goal of cryptography is to reduce the inspection surface to those who have been prop-erly authorized to know the decryption process and secrets. At a minimum, this introduces the burden to obtain this information in advance of any inspection; at a maximum, it might make inspection impossible. An example is the bump-in-the-wire processing that many security teams desire for their networks. In such cases where encryption is employed, key-managed decryption is required at that inspection point for any useful information to be ingested.

As challenging as the technology aspects of inspection are, though, they may pale when compared to the many interpersonal issues that often arise. The first is the clarity it requires at the outset, which demands a detailed taxonomy. Who is doing the inspect-ing—the manufacturer or builder inspecting what has been built; a program that inspects its own behavior; or the more common case of a piece of inspection equipment, like a network tap or packet sniffer, that is collecting information about something external? What is being inspected—is the data structured or unstructured, at rest or moving rapidly? Is it clear, encrypted, masked, or obfuscated? Just these basic factors—singularly, much less in all the variables and permutations of their possible combinations—can create enormous complexities that must be established and then navigated.

And then the human factor comes in, making everything much more complicated.

There is no getting around the fact that inspection is a form of sur-veillance. And just like other forms of surveillance, how it is deployed raises enormous questions, concerns, and unease. How those doing the inspecting answer questions about its deployment is an incred-ible factor in its efficacy—often in ways they do not anticipate.

Those concerns increase as inspection moves outward. External inspection has sizable and obvious challenges, of course. It is easy enough for a security team to determine whether internal users are employing two-factor authentication—go into the identity and access management system and pull the logs. But vendors, sup-pliers, and other third parties are not going to allow that, making indirect inspection a difficult and high-stakes trust exercise where an organization must take a third party's word that they are complying with security protocols. A quick glance at many headline-generating breaches reveals how ineffective this can be. And at the enterprise level, the vendors have vendors who also have vendors, creating a daisy chain of risk that becomes increasingly difficult to inspect.

Security teams often understand these dynamics. Less widely recognized are the human factors that complicate inspection practices internally. Substitute the term "employee surveillance," though, and the degree of complexity gets a bit clearer. If the inspection is at the traffic level, for instance, there is little risk because few are affected by logging IP addresses and locations of traffic to a site. The deeper the inspection looks, the more issues arise.

But even putting snoopware that inspects every keystroke on the PC of every employee has substantial variables. If the employees are working at a call center, answering calls to address a set range of customer service, sales, or other issues, it is quite possible that nobody will care.

But in the vast majority of businesses, where people use their PCs to do creative work, writing, research, presentations, or anything else that involves independent thinking, poorly considered or executed inspection techniques can create real problems and a much less secure network.

The first thing employees in this type of work environment do when they become aware of IT running snoopware is to get a Gmail or Dropbox account to hide any aspect of their activity that they want to keep private. This can be anything from searching Google or killing time on social media, to sending a personal email, to applying for another job on LinkedIn. They get into the habit of splitting activity between work and personal PCs, which is already normalized by the erosion of work-life boundaries and bring your own device (BYOD). Either for secrecy or efficiency, proprietary information begins hemorrhaging out of an organization via personal accounts or even memory sticks, with no trail of crumbs or even indicators that it is happening.

The result is an incredibly vulnerable shadow IT infrastructure that creates a vast network of unknown unknowns and a deeply ingrained pattern of data usage that makes protecting a network nearly impossible. A whole second compute environment that is out of inspection's reach begins to grow. If there is anybody who thinks that is not how it works, welcome to planet Earth.

The way to avoid this is to make sure the inspection and surveillance you do is at the operating system's kernel API system call layer. What this means must be clearly and transparently explained to employees, who often believe that inspection means the IT team will be reading an email to their mom or their spouse—rather than searching for signs of advanced persistent threats. It's a misunderstanding that has roots in a human truth.

Inspection, like all forms of security, is contextual. People feel one way about the thought of security tools in their homes or offices and quite another way about a surveillance camera on a subway platform at 2 a.m. IT teams must explain—and importantly, deploy—inspection tools and techniques in ways that leverage this aspect of human nature.

Employees should be helped and encouraged to understand that most breaches are impossible for them to detect—and that inspection tools will exonerate them when malware is exfiltrating data via their PCs. This entails a fundamental repositioning of inspection as something that protects employees rather than a surveillance technique that encroaches on their privacy.

Organizations that can't make a clear and compelling case for the transparent use of inspection risk losing control of all their data—which will become shadowed and unreachable by even the most powerful and sophisticated innovations in AI and machine learning. Inspection is a fundamental and powerful tool to mitigate the increasing security risks we face. But no matter how powerful it becomes at detecting and identifying technological risks, we must never allow it to blind us to the human risks it can also create. Remember, to inspect implies greater visibility. That visibility should not—and does not need to—be confined simply to the networks it protects, or even the employees themselves. It should also create greater insight into the behaviors and reactions its deployment can catalyze. Like cybersecurity itself, the most effective inspection techniques start with the identification of a problem—and provide a solution that mitigates rather than exacerbates it.

ABOUT THE CONTRIBUTOR

Ed Amoroso – Chief Executive Officer, TAG Cyber LLC

Ed Amoroso heads TAG Cyber, a global cybersecurity advisory, training, consulting, and media services company supporting hundreds of companies across the world. He recently retired from AT&T after 31 years of service, beginning in UNIX security R&D at Bell Labs and culminating as senior vice president and chief security officer of AT&T from 2004 to 2016.

Amoroso is the author of six books on cybersecurity and dozens of major research and technical papers and articles in peer-reviewed and major publications. His work has been highlighted on CNN and in *The New York Times* and the *Wall Street Journal*.

He holds a BS in physics from Dickinson College and MS and PhD degrees in computer science from the Stevens Institute of Technology, and is a graduate of the Columbia Business School. He holds 10 patents in the area of cybersecurity and media technology and has served as a member of the board of directors for M&T Bank, as well as on the NSA Advisory Board (NSAAB). He has worked with four presidential administrations on national security, critical infrastructure protection, and cybersecurity policy.

THE FUNDAMENTAL IMPORTANCE OF INSPECTION

Michael Johnson, Capital One

In science, theories are supported by facts gathered over time. That is, it's not good enough to *assert* that something is true; you have to *provide evidence* that it is. The scientific method has served us well in virtually every aspect of our lives.

Such an approach is fundamental to cybersecurity as well. It is one thing to have correctly architected your environment with proper network segmentation, least-privileged access controls, secrets management, strong endpoint management, multifactor authentication, and encryption. You must also assume that people will inevitably make mistakes, thereby falling prey to the tricks of an attacker, and that cyberadversaries will attempt to hide in the noise of the network or otherwise try to take advantage of the complexity of today's architectures, systems, and processes.

We can make these assumptions because, since the beginning of time, criminals have lived in the shadows while the tools of their trade were often hidden in plain sight. Malicious cyberactors are no different. For example, in cyberspace malicious code is often hidden inside email attachments. And increasingly, adversaries leverage the network's own features—encryption to hide their activity, or even native system commands like Windows PowerShell—to obscure their activities and evade detection.

DEFINING INSPECTION

Inspection is a counter-strategy designed to detect and identify threats within a network to provide a timely means for containment. Those threats can include an adversary or unauthorized user, artifacts of malfeasance (unauthorized access or unauthorized assets, whether hardware or software), or unauthorized activities occurring within the environment as an indicator of a potential compromise.

Inspection is a fundamental aspect of any cybersecurity strategy. Institutions regularly inspect content as it flows in and out of (or less frequently, across) the network, looking for evidence of covert command-and-control activities, stolen assets such as money and intellectual property, and malicious insiders.

However, there are two substantive challenges to implementing a comprehensive inspection strategy. The first is the reactive nature of looking for signs of an adversary already in the environment. By the time you identify a malicious actor, significant damage may have already been done. Second is the inevitable network performance degradation associated with real-time inspection of every bit of information crossing the environment. These limitations can be addressed through the adoption of technologies and techniques that improve performance and close the gap between breach and detection.

INSPECTION TECHNIQUES

Inspection can be implemented using a variety of technologies, techniques, and strategies. Cybersecurity controls and active cybersecurity capabilities are designed to counter the range of cyberthreats an organization may face, as well as to identify any adversaries that may be in our systems:

- *Cybersecurity controls* provide safeguards and countermeasures to avoid, counteract, or minimize the loss of data or network availability due to exploits acting on a corresponding vulnerability. Most cybersecurity controls involve the active inspection of content.

  There are a number of phases to cybersecurity controls that must be implemented as part of an effective strategy. They include

  · Preventive controls, which prevent an adversary or unauthorized user from gaining access to infrastructure or data.

  · Detective controls, which identify threats within the environment, providing a timely means for the containment of a threat. These threats can include an adversary, unauthorized user, unauthorized access, or unauthorized assets (hardware and/or software)

in the environment as an indicator of a potential compromise.

- Compensating or mitigating controls, which are designed to ensure the intent of the system design or original controls when those original controls cannot be used due to limitations of the environment.

- Auditing controls, which ensure that safeguarding requirements or "guardrails" are established and operating as intended within normal limits.

- Monitoring controls, which provide an early means of knowing when other controls are out of compliance before an adversary has the opportunity to exploit the environment.

- *Active cybersecurity inspection capabilities* are used to identify adversaries that may have already infiltrated our systems. We use these capabilities to look for adversaries within our systems using the following four strategies:

1. Hunt: Iteratively searching through networks and datasets to detect threats that evade existing controls and automated tools

2. Deception: Understanding the tactics, techniques, and procedures (TTPs) of adversaries and then misleading and influencing their actions to our advantage through honeypots and other forms of deception technology

3. Counterintelligence: Focused attention on the organization's high-value assets, specifically looking for TTPs of known adversaries

4. Forensics: Gathering and preserving evidence from a compromise to understand an adversary's use of vulnerabilities, thereby ensuring that any approach used successfully once is never successful again

CONTENT INSPECTION

The deep inspection of content further extends the traditional inspection strategy of looking for telltale signs of an intruder or malicious assets. It involves capturing data packets from applications, transactions, or workflows in transit across a network and analyzing their content for patterns of malicious behavior and sensitive data.

Content inspection falls into two broad categories: Static analysis and dynamic analysis. Static analysis includes identifying indicators of compromise, whereas dynamic analysis is performed at multiple levels of detail, such as instruction tracing or execution side effects observed in sandboxes ("detonation chambers").

New tools and techniques have had a strong impact on the inspection of content and data:

- *Machine learning* that leverages both static analysis and dynamic analysis yields the best results by identifying additional statistics about the code and content being analyzed. Research out of the US Department of Energy national laboratories has shown that machine learning using both static and dynamic analysis performs better than using either alone and can often detect zero-day malware more effectively than signature-based antivirus tools (see https://arxiv.org/pdf/1404.2462.pdf). Machine learning approaches can not only detect threats before signatures are released, but also address signatures that have been pruned from traditional antivirus tools over time to keep the size of their signature sets from becoming too unwieldy.
- *Sandboxes,* or "detonation chambers," should be part of any serious cybersecurity architecture. They became an important tool a few years ago for detecting malicious content hidden inside files or applications attached to emails, downloaded from the web, or introduced by content or devices introduced from the outside, such as infected thumb drives. By evaluating such attachments for maliciousness—executing them in a safe, contained environment and then inspecting them for evidence of maliciousness—security operators can flush out and prevent those malicious attachments from reaching their intended target.

THE CHALLENGE OF ENCRYPTION

Nearly three-quarters of all network traffic is now encrypted, most of it using SSL. As a result, many of the traditional analytics tools in use have become nearly useless because the bits that need to be uncovered are hidden from inspection. While almost everyone believes that more encryption means more security, SSL encryption presents a trade-off that is causing network operators to go blind.

The other problem related to inspecting encrypted traffic is that, especially given the demands of today's digital business environment, most of today's solutions are too slow. Slow solutions force the network operator to choose between slowing down their customers' communications or failing to perform the due diligence of keeping those communications (and others) safe by not inspecting some or all encrypted traffic.

Cybersecurity vendors are the primary culprits here. Too many cybersecurity solutions fail to honor the organizing principle of the Internet: Speed. Security without speed is a losing proposition. Users want security to be frictionless, and when forced to make a decision, organizations will almost always choose performance over protection.

THE FUTURE OF INSPECTION

The future of inspection relies on the development of critical assets and strategies. These include increased development and adoption of machine learning focused on both static and dynamic analysis, the safe sharing of cybersecurity information across organizational boundaries, and countering threats by eliminating the opportunity for an adversary to use fields or flows in ways that were not intended.

Of those three, *information sharing* faces the most significant challenges. In 2015, the US Department of Homeland Security funded research focused on safe information sharing across organizational boundaries as a means of more easily and quickly identifying anomalous behavior within an environment. It does us no good to analyze packets if we don't know if what we are seeing is unique to us or is part of a similar attack that is spread across many organizations.

To achieve this, however, we must design ways to more effectively leverage the "network effect" of seeing across many organizations while protecting proprietary information. Unfortunately, one of the biggest barriers is that many organizations perceive an inherent risk in sharing (including the importance of protecting intellectual property), and so they do not share. And while there are companies are trying to develop databases of indicators and threats, new stringent EU rules on privacy where network traffic is being defined as PII makes creating and adopting sharing models particularly challenging. However, in some very fundamental ways, we are all in this together. As a result, cybersecurity should not be seen as simply a competitive advantage, but also as a community service, and information sharing makes everyone safer.

Using the network itself as a means for *countering threats* also shows real promise. Adversaries use hidden data for covert communications, including embedded malware, signaling, and command-and-control strategies. Research at the US Department of Energy (DoE) national laboratories published in 2002, focused on countering insider threats by rewriting or otherwise changing network packets in a way that would maintain the integrity of the overt message while destroying any opportunity for adding malicious or hidden content (see www.cs.colostate.edu/~christos/papers/ihw2002.pdf). The research defined minimal requisite fidelity (MRF) as the degree of signal fidelity that is acceptable to end users but destructive to covert or hidden content. The potential of this approach is profound. Would you rather analyze each packet or flow, which is slow and reactive, or simply eliminate the opportunity for an adversary to use fields or flows in ways that were not intended?

CONCLUSION

Inspection is a fundamental requirement for any cybersecurity strategy. Competing in today's digital marketplace, however, requires speed and adaptability that traditional inspection strategies can impact. At the same time, new technologies, including machine learning and sandboxing, are being impacted by the growing volume of encrypted network traffic. Addressing these challenges requires several strategies.

To start, information sharing allows security teams to focus on specific challenges, thereby more efficiently identifying threats. Next, it is essential that organizations not rely exclusively on cybersecurity solutions to solve their problems. Engineering as many issues out of the network as possible is an essential first step. This includes looking at techniques such as MRF that simply prevent malicious content from being attached to data flows. And finally, organizations need to replace existing security tools that are not able to inspect encrypted traffic at the speed of business.

These and similar inspection strategies will require organizations to participate in the larger security environment to ensure the secure sharing of intelligence and the development of new tools to address cybersecurity events before they occur, and to pressure security vendors to develop tools capable of operating in today's high-performance marketplace.

ABOUT THE CONTRIBUTOR

Michael Johnson – CISO, Capital One

Michael Johnson is senior vice president, chief information security officer for Capital One Financial Corporation, where he leads and manages cyberspace, information security, cybersecurity operations, and security technology innovation. Johnson partners closely across all of the diversified banking company's business lines on cybersecurity risk management, cloud security engineering, operations, and architecture and standards. He previously served as the chief information officer for the US Department of Energy, where he led and managed cybersecurity, cyberspace enterprise integration, enterprise information resources management, cyberspace supply chain risk management, headquarters information technology operations, and privacy. Previously Johnson served in key cyberspace-focused executive roles in the US Government and Intelligence Community at the Office of the Director of National Intelligence, the Department of Homeland Security, and the White House Executive Office of the President.

11
FAILURE RECOVERY

"Dealing with a catastrophic event ultimately depends on keeping your bearing."

Thad Allen,
Booz Allen Hamilton

"Ultimately, an effective response to a cybersecurity event comes down to the culture of the company."

Simon Lambe,
Royal Mail

When we accept that breaches are inevitable, it raises a logical question: "What then?" and directs us toward the answer we need: "Failure recovery."

Many organizations are stuck in a cycle of

- Being surprised by a compromise
- "Cleaning up on aisle 9"
- Spending more on cleanup than they could have (or should have) spent on prevention

Since compromise is indeed an impending reality for everyone, failure recovery is one of the most critical aspects of an effective cybersecurity strategy. After learning the hard way, some prominent CISOs will be quite forthright in assuring you that "cleanup on aisle 9" is a deeply unsatisfying tactical response to a serious data breach—especially if that clean up causes an entire network to be down for days.

As speed accelerates the rate of digital business, a poorly implemented or poorly conceived failure recovery plan can often unleash an even greater level of loss than the breach itself. Not only must an organization contend with the extraordinary costs of the breach and the need to re-secure a network, but they must do it while in the freefall of post-crisis negative sentiment, loss in sales and consumer confidence, and with a hobbled, even inoperable, network. Even the most seasoned cybersecurity experts and their teams find this an extraordinarily challenging set of conditions. Just as you can leverage speed and integration to automate the hardening of your networks and their overall defenses, you can also automate their resiliency under failure conditions.

As is often said, the best time to prepare for a crisis is before it happens, and the key to gauging that level of preparation is to consistently evaluate a network's quality of resiliency. With a comprehensive segmentation strategy in place, we can harness high degrees of automation and integration to actively harden and defend our networks and maintain that standard of resiliency. This is a strong step toward staying "left of boom"—having a network that is uncompromised and doing everything in its power to stay that way by constantly evolving its security at an appropriate rate. In the event of an organization finding itself "right of boom," automation can make it possible to regenerate from a known, secure copy to get the network up and running safely and efficiently. This eliminates the adversary's ability to leverage the power of relentless persistence during an attack and allows a business to have core services up and running immediately.

Like any serious strategic reality, failure recovery requires comprehensive preplanning, as well as consistent audit and upkeep of the plan itself. But as we will see in this chapter, the benefits of improved event monitoring, strengthened regeneration resources, and greater adaptability to evolving threats are not confined to failure recovery. They also drive considerable increases in security that dramatically reduce the odds, and frequency, of a breach from which to recover.

But when attacks succeed, the advanced techniques of failure recovery are what allow an organization to get to "right of boom" and start repairs as quickly as possible. As powerful as it is pragmatic, failure recovery addresses the statistical near certainties of breach and mitigates damage with efficient resiliency and regeneration. Although all these techniques demand sound deployment of the previous fundamentals, they are now just as critical to cybersecurity—as we will see in the chapters that follow.

Just as we measure quality of service, we need to measure *quality of resilience* and make adjustments in cyber-relevant time if that risk gets too high. For the inevitable time we do find ourselves "right of boom," we need to be able to get up and operating in a known secure state within minutes, not days.

PREPARATION, RESPONSE, AND RECOVERY

Thad Allen, Booz Allen Hamilton

I'd like to begin by expanding on insights that I gained from noted journalist Tom Friedman at a joint speaking event several years ago:

No matter what problem you're dealing with, three forces are converging that are making the world more complex.

TECHNOLOGY

The first force is technology—using the broadest possible definition—from bio to nano to quantum. Technological advances are accelerating so rapidly that they defeat existing legal frameworks and international agreements. Standard ways of doing things aren't fast enough to keep pace with technology. The result is that technical, legal, and governing structures become misaligned, resulting in challenges like those the FBI had to face in unlocking a smartphone after the San Bernardino shootings.

The Internet and the widespread use of social media have also enabled people to inject themselves into complex situations where there had previously been barriers to entry. When a government used to deploy an army to fight, you would find out whether they had won or lost only when dispatches were sent from military leaders. But when the armed forces came ashore in Mogadishu in 1992, CNN filmed it live. That was a precedent-setting event. The new reality is that more and more people and devices you don't control are going to be operating in your physical or cyberspace environment, increasing both risk and complexity.

Most risk aggravators, like complexity itself, create problems that are not possible for a single entity, whether an individual, company, or government agency, to solve. Instead, solutions to complicated problems have to be co-produced—not only across horizontal and vertical boundaries, but across external boundaries as well, such as between the government and the private sector, across international borders, or between business competitors.

ENVIRONMENTAL CHANGE

The second force is environmental change. A greater intersection exists between the built world and the natural environment than ever before, resulting in events of greater frequency, gravity, complexity, and consequence. High population density and structures in low-lying coastal areas are common examples. However, until access was gained to regions of central Africa for development and exploitation of resources, the Ebola virus was restricted to an isolated colony of fruit bats. When the built and the natural environments interact, not only do we create new lines of communication, but we also create new risks and unexpected problems.

GLOBALIZATION

The third force I call Globalization with a capital "G." I'm not talking about the globalization of economics and trade. I'm referring to the globalization of everything. Today, everybody has access to information about everything, including inaccurate information. Right now, responsibility for the truth and validity of what we read on the Internet rests entirely with the reader. Because people don't have the time, training, or inclination to fact-check their information, they tend to retrench into like-minded tribes built around polarized views where nobody is willing to bend or compromise.

The combination of these three forces creates new risk aggravators, and individuals, companies, and even governments simply aren't prepared to deal with that level of complexity. This failure to confront complexity as a risk aggravator and prepare for it in advance means we end up applying old paradigms, old doctrines, and old tactics, techniques, and procedures (TTPs) that fail to meet the challenge.

The examples in the natural world are numerous, whether Hurricane Katrina, the Haitian earthquake, the BP oil spill, global droughts and wildfires, or the tornado in Joplin, Missouri. The same problem exists in cyberspace, evidenced by the growing number of organizations that fail to respond adequately, both internally and externally, to a significant cybersecurity breach.

UNITY OF EFFORT

Addressing these challenges begins by understanding the patterns of these sorts of events and then deciding which parts of the problem belong to which individuals. And because there can be so many different parties involved—and you need them all to address the complexity of today's challenges—the next most critical thing you can do is ensure that these individuals are all committed to unity of effort. Once an event occurs, this team of individuals must be able to quickly produce a problem statement. They need to make sure they understand, despite the complexity of the situation, what the problem really is and the scope of the issues they're trying to solve. That sounds pretty elementary, but it can be a lot harder than you may think.

I have been involved with various types of exercises and "war games" that attempt to address complex situations in advance of an occurrence. Although it is impossible to predict an exact event, the process of thinking through any complex problem improves the insight and skill of leaders. In one scenario, CISOs were challenged to take the place of company officers in a cybersecurity event. Most began by trying to understand the nature and scope of the attack, along with its consequences and impact, and then attempting to solve the technical problem. But then we would introduce challenges about business continuity and sustainability that they hadn't considered. How does this event relate to your supply chain? What are your contingency procedures if communications such as email, text, or even digital voice are unavailable? How do you deal with your external stakeholders, especially if you're a publicly traded company? Most participants left with a new understanding of the breadth of challenges that come from dealing with a major cybersecurity event.

In my experience, just like these CISOs, very few firms have thought through how to handle such events. They may think they have their crisis response nailed, but the convergence of all these challenges in a short span of time can be unexpectedly overwhelming, especially if you haven't considered all the ways it can affect your organization. Part of the problem is that organizations just aren't designed to address these sorts of challenges in their daily operations. If you look at how a firm functions, you see separate lines of effort, with individual teams focused on their own pieces of the organization and only a tiny handful of people orchestrating things at a very high, and sometimes superficial, level. What they aren't organized to do is deal with a catastrophic event that's an existential threat to the entire firm.

The tendency is to get hung up on attribution. If you have six military personnel standing in a cornfield trying to go somewhere and all of a sudden a shot rings out and one of the soldiers drops, what's the first thing you want to know? It's where that shot came from. But in a cybersecurity event, you may never know. And even if you eventually find out, it's going to take a lot longer than the decision window you have in which to act. But organizations inevitably spend a lot of valuable time and resources up front trying to solve that problem rather than addressing many of the bigger challenges that require their immediate attention.

The problem becomes even more complicated in larger organizations. When there is a lack of attribution, teams tend to assume it may be their problem, and they begin to react independently. In the case of one of the world's largest organizations, the US federal government, United States Cyber Command is going to assume a major event is a defense issue. The NSA and CIA are going to assume it's a national security problem. The FBI is going to assume it's a law-enforcement issue, and they've got to start preserving evidence and establishing a chain of custody. Similarly, Homeland Security will be involved because the threat could involve critical infrastructure. Absent a single entity to integrate and coordinate the national response, jurisdictional battles, cross-communications, and redundant efforts are likely.

Every agency tends to do what they believe is in the best interest of the country and their assigned mission. Private sector firms are no different. Unfortunately, that approach does not create natural integration, unity of effort, a proper assessment of the complexity of the problem, or the optimum way forward—until somebody gets those people together and organizes them. Understanding the problem correctly, creating unity of effort across the organization, prioritizing efforts, and responding to a dozen other challenges all become significant challenges, and many organizations and leaders fail out of the gate because they haven't been trained to think that way.

Response and Preparation

There are generally two response levels to an event. From a technical perspective, a lot has to happen in a very short amount of time. That's followed by a long-term recovery plan that includes assessing the extent of the damage and making sure that everybody's doing the right sorts of things so forensic analysis can occur. That is all well documented elsewhere.

But the other level requires people to be immediately looking at things like supply chain, brand, communications, and shareholder credibility. That also requires a lot of preplanning. I've seen some events where, though the technical response may have been executed by the book, the rest of the response was so ineffective that it seriously undermined the organization's ability to recover, especially regarding public perception. You need a plan in place that parses out functional lines of effort, and everybody has to be on board.

You also need to make two levels of preparation. The first is to perform risk assessments to identify potential risks to your organization, such as a data breach that results in criminals selling your customers' personal information on the Dark Web. You then need to prioritize and use the Pareto principle on those risks. The Pareto principle states that roughly 80 percent of the effects of an event come from 20 percent of the causes. So if you're in Kansas, you don't worry about an earthquake, and if you're in San Francisco, you don't worry about a tornado. You then structure a response doctrine for the most likely incidents, make plans, and practice executing them. And every time you have a test, a tabletop, or a war game, you try to break your system—because you want to break it before somebody else figures out how to do it.

The other level of preparation addresses the black swan of an unexpected event. To do that, you have to put a basic set of principles in place that everybody in your organization understands. That way, when you face a hard problem, everyone already knows that there are some things you have to do and there are some things you should not do. But what you don't want to do is declare, "That's a really hard problem," and then, as I used to say in the Coast Guard, put it in the "too hard to" locker. Even the most unexpected challenges have elements that can be broken down and considered ahead of time in generic functions and then assigned to people or entities in your organization.

CENTRAL RESPONSE TEAM

Creating a central response team that meets regularly is the key to the successful response to an event. And the most important characteristic of that team, besides individual expertise, is diversity of viewpoints. Your response team needs to resemble a jazz band rather than an orchestra, using individuals who can improvise. I call them "the dogs that hunt." That ability comes from emotional intelligence, which includes the capacity to be brutally honest and frank about what you're good at, what you're not good at, and what makes you angry. That last one is especially important, because when you lose your temper, you give control to somebody else, and the results can undermine all your other efforts. That sort of honest assessment is critical during the planning and preparation stages. Small decisions can suddenly become extremely important. For example, who will be the company spokesperson? Does the CEO go on camera? You have to be able to decide if that person is truly qualified to be the face of the firm, because most of the time, it's someone else. That can be a delicate discussion, so it needs to occur well in advance, and it can happen only when honest conversations are allowed to happen.

Dealing with a catastrophic event ultimately depends on keeping your bearing. Ships at sea locate their position by relying on the intersection between multiple points of data. If you can establish one range and bearing to a point of land, you know you're somewhere on that line—which may not be that helpful. Once you can establish another bearing to another point of land, however, you've got a high degree of confidence that you're probably where those two lines intersect. But if you have three lines that cross at a single point, that's called a "good fix" in maritime parlance.

This principle applies to crisis management. The most important thing you can do is get a good fix on the problem. Only then can you plan the way forward. However, you get that only through proper planning and building and relying on an emotionally intelligent team with strong diversity and an ability and willingness to speak their mind. When they all agree on a solution, you know you're on to a way forward.

ABOUT THE CONTRIBUTOR

Thad Allen - Senior Executive Advisor, Booz Allen Hamilton

Thad Allen is the former senior executive vice president in the firm's Departments of Justice and Homeland Security business. Allen is known for his expertise in bringing together government and non-government entities to address major challenges in a "whole of government" approach designed to achieve a unity of effort.

In 2010, President Obama selected Allen to serve as the national incident commander for the unified response to the Deepwater Horizon oil spill in the Gulf of Mexico. Working closely with the US Environmental Protection Agency, the Department of Homeland Security, the Departments of Defense, Interior, Commerce, Health and Human Services, state and local entities, and BP, Allen worked to bring unity to the response operations.

Prior to his assignment as the Coast Guard's 23rd commandant, Allen served as Coast Guard chief of staff. In 2005, he was designated principal federal official for the US government's response and recovery operations in the aftermath of Hurricanes Katrina and Rita throughout the Gulf Coast region.

Other Coast Guard assignments include Commander, Atlantic Area, where in 2001, Allen led the area forces following the September 11 attacks.

CYBER EVENT RECOVERY

Simon Lambe, Royal Mail

The media has been incredibly useful in making people aware of security compromises. Just a few years ago, people kept their cybersecurity events to themselves. You knew about them only through contacts within the industry, but that was very much under the Chatham House rule so you didn't talk about them widely. ["When a meeting, or part thereof, is held under the Chatham House Rule, participants are free to use the information received, but neither the identity nor the affiliation of the speaker(s), nor that of any other participant, may be revealed," Chatham House, The Royal Institute of International Affairs.] But now, media and company public responses reinforce the fact that security events are not just a probability but an eventuality. And that changes how we should think and talk about these events when they occur.

Part of the way to approach the challenge of a cybersecurity event is about changing your mindset. In a world where so many events are happening, a system compromise of some sort is inevitable, and so I question whether we should even define a security event as a failure. In many ways, it's a failure only if you haven't been able to minimize the effect, or you didn't recover as quickly as you needed to and to the appropriate level. You do that by preparing from day one so that when a security event does happen, you can catch it in time, minimize the impact, recover gracefully, and then learn from it for the next event.

PREPARING FOR A CYBER EVENT

The growing awareness of successful attacks and system breaches is having an impact on senior management. In many organizations, the instinct when a cybersecurity event occurs is to panic—which is why it is critical to help your executive staff understand that security events happen all the time. My security team does a lot of work preparing company leaders with tables of exercises or workshops. This starts by getting necessary stakeholders together to simulate a variety of events that your organization is likely to experience.

For the first few workshops, you won't have all the answers, or may not even have all the right people sitting around the table. But the goal is to walk out of those first couple of sessions understanding the critical gaps in key stakeholders, processes, and protocols that you need to recognize.

Role-playing is key. For example, I may assign a security team member to create emails that look like attempts to extract information or steal financial data. We then use those as tables of exercise to bring a bit more real life to the situation rather than discussing threats in the abstract. That's important because, while people may be nervous and apprehensive when an event occurs, I don't want them to be scared, which can lead to decision paralysis and blame. Going through a drill many times before an actual event can help prevent that from happening.

The next critical component in preparation is making sure you've got all your communications teams aligned. You need to ensure the right messages are ready to go out, and that you have a plan in place to control some identifying spokespeople beforehand. You need to know what they will say and determine what sort of image the leadership team wants to project to employees, customers, and the media. Engaging with outside advisers before an event occurs is also a good idea.

POST-EVENT PLANNING

Finally, you need to understand how to return your business to stable operations as quickly as possible. Things like post-event forensic analysis can sometimes hamper your speed to recovery, so you should anticipate those requirements. Investigators will often tell you not to touch an affected device or system because they need to perform forensic analysis. Although that concern is understandable, the reality is that they need to be pretty quick off the mark to collect any relevant information—which requires having the right technical capabilities, forensics tools, and forensics people already in place.

At the same time, you should have already considered the forensics process as part of your recovery strategy so that you can return impacted systems and services to normal and enable the business to function. That's what effective security management is all about; it's addressing an event in a way that gets you back to normal as quickly and as safely as possible. Proper planning may include such things as storing data and backups offsite and building redundancy into critical systems. These and similar strategies go a long way toward reducing the time to recovery.

From a professional security point of view, the trickiest part of preparing for security events is quantifying risk. I always avoid talking about threats or threat response in absolutes. Instead, I say "in my opinion," or "to the best of my knowledge, we think..." so that I can keep the lines of communication open about what we see, especially as information and intelligence fluctuate. It's also essential that stakeholders regularly hear you identify some new event or data point and explain that it is something the organization needs to consider. This regular communication helps establish the understanding that managing security events is merely part of routine security operations. Then, when a situation changes significantly, you can get straight on the phone to all relevant stakeholders to inform them that you have escalated a security event without causing panic.

Unfortunately, a lot of security professionals, for whatever reason, tend to hit the big red panic button right away any time an event occurs. Not only does that approach cause a lot of noise, but it also produces threat fatigue. So when a significant event finally does happen, one where you actually have to invoke your significant plans, you come across as crying wolf because you have been setting off the alarms twice a week.

BEING PREPARED: EVENT MONITORING

Reducing the time between incident discovery and recovery is a critical element in event preparation. Achieving this requires comprehensive asset management and active event monitoring, and there are two aspects to this that every CISO should know.

The first is being able to identify the events you are looking for and separating them from the background noise of other events. Doing this requires identifying critical business processes and assets and knowing what sets of security controls you have in place, what data and resources are most vital, and how you're going to monitor all of this. Once you have established that, any time you plan to implement a new technical solution you start by asking, "What's going to be my event monitoring strategy around this?" Unfortunately, far too many security teams don't even know what resources are connected to the network, let alone being able to prioritize them, which is where asset management plays a crucial role.

The second essential component of event monitoring, which is also a struggle for most organizations, is establishing a credible activity baseline to discover anomalous behaviors. It's critical that you know what "good" network activity looks like so that you can then spot any anomalies outside of good.

For larger organizations, effective event monitoring requires establishing a security operations center where you can combine local intelligence with data from fresh intelligence feeds to identify indicators of compromise. Having the right information helps you be as quick off the mark as possible. But you have to get the balance right. Too much information isn't necessarily a good thing.

As an example, the WannaCry event started at about 3:30 or 4:00 on a Friday afternoon. Within a few hours we had our first set of indicators of compromise in place, so we knew what events to look for. In this case, it was particular types of email addresses with specific types of attachments. By the end of the weekend, however, because everybody in the industry had gotten excited about the attack, we had over 100 indicators of compromise with which to work. Which meant my team was investigating more false positives because the quality of the data had been reduced significantly due to the amount of information being made available.

ADAPTING TO EVOLVING NETWORKS

Another challenge a lot of organizations face is that for a long time their networks were relatively static and predictable. IT teams based their security around placing a firewall at the perimeter in what I call the raw egg approach. The shell, your security perimeter, was nice and firm and strong. All you had to do was monitor and control what passed through that perimeter; however, once you cracked the shell the inside was gooey and unprotected.

But just over the last several years, that perimeter has dissolved at a rapid rate due to things like highly mobile devices, the Internet of Things (IoT), and the cloud. Today, you need to take a more datacentric approach to security rather than depending on the traditional perimeter. From a pragmatic point of view, that means establishing the right levels of control based on the risk that certain data poses to the organization. If you've got somebody storing their restaurant menus in the cloud, and loads of people have access to that data, I'm not going to be particularly excited about that. However, if I've got somebody storing a large number of records with customer data in that same cloud environment, that's going to get the belts-and-suspenders approach to ensure I have the right level of controls in place, not only from a prevention point of view but also for detection and remediation.

REMEDIATION RESOURCES

One of the most significant obstacles organizations face when recovering from a cybersecurity event is not only making sure that their teams can adjust from their regular jobs to the job of recovery, but that there are enough resources available to do the job quickly and efficiently. We realigned our security team two years ago to have a dedicated instant management function. The role of this team is first-line triage. They not only deal with events that have been triggered, but also go around looking for events before they become a more significant problem. I have also tasked them with making sure we're prepared and ready to go in case of a significant event. This preparation includes building a relationship with a third-party security operations center not only to help us deal with discovered threats, but also to improve our ability to detect threats before they become a significant challenge.

We have also set up a number of partners that we are ready to call upon should we have an event that requires additional support. However, while third parties can be very good at providing subject matter expertise on specific topics, at the end of the day our internal people best understand our company, how it functions, what our most critical systems are, which stakeholders need to be informed, and so on, which is why I recommend a hybrid model.

BE PREPARED FOR THE UNEXPECTED

You can't solve a major security breach while it's happening. You have to prepare. But even then, one of the biggest challenges is that things don't always go according to plan. Breaches occur through unexpected vectors, attacks target unknown weaknesses, and things behave in unexpected ways. You need to be flexible and adaptable when something happens that you hadn't considered.

We have created a documented human security incident management plan that captures who is responsible for what, has established our lines of communication, and has identified third parties that can provide support. However, I'm not too keen on creating an equivalent technical security instant response plan, because they can become far too rigid. Instead, you need to have the right framework and communications mechanisms in place, with the right threat intelligence. Then you need a bunch of competent, strong subject matter experts who can come together to deal with all the unexpected elements of an event that you couldn't possibly anticipate.

CONCLUSION

Ultimately, an effective response to a cybersecurity event comes down to the culture of the company. We need to avoid the word failure when it comes to information security, because these events are going to occur. They happen to everybody no matter how hard they try, whether it's a small event or a really big one. What's important is how you prepare for these events and how quickly you can successfully recover from them.

ABOUT THE CONTRIBUTOR

Simon Lambe – Head of Information Security, Royal Mail UK

Simon Lambe recently moved from his role as enterprise information security officer for EDF Energy to lead information security for the Royal Mail service of the United Kingdom. Prior to EDF Energy, Lambe was the head of IT security at AXA UK and held a variety of roles at Dyson, including global head of IT security, global head of infrastructure and service delivery, and director of IT and technical services for Dyson US. Lambe has a passion for viewing information security not as a "black box" but as open and transparent as possible. His strategy of focusing information security teams on being service oriented has been welcomed by all the companies he has worked for.

HIGHER-ORDER DIMENSIONS: WHERE HUMAN FACTORS CAN ECLIPSE COMPUTING WIZARDRY

THE DIGITAL BIG BANG

While the cosmic big bang and subsequent evolution of life provoke unanswerable questions about the creator, creation, and the origin and purpose of the universe, we know exactly how the Internet was created, by whom, and for what purpose. The science of the digital big bang and the cybersecurity fundamentals cannot ignore the role and needs of its creator and operator: humans. From the dawn of humankind to the age of enlightenment, through the industrial revolution, the digital revolution, and the pending age of cyber-physical convergence, the higher orders of human knowledge and invention have shaped the trajectory of human existence. Nonetheless, we see that the power of innovation is never entirely free from the gravitational pull of our human nature.

That human nature includes unstable "free radicals" in our cyber-security petri dish that consistently prevent this primordial soup from evolving into a thriving organism. In addition to the technical elements discussed so far, we must acknowledge the fundamental roles of human frailty, privacy, and complexity. People get tired. They make mistakes. They are poorly trained. People will continue to undermine the security of our systems, so we must actively and intelligently use machines to compensate for human limitations. Additionally, it's a false choice between security and privacy. Until we embrace the fact that it's not security *or* privacy but both, sustainable higher-order cybersecurity will not thrive.

As we have progressed to the final section of our exploration of the science of cybersecurity, the cosmic and digital big bang parallels have also revealed truisms about humanity's extraordinary ability to adapt and innovate—and the push-and-pull between the positive and negative ramifications of those innovations. A defining attribute of our species is our unresolvable contradictions. We are intensely social, drawing together to form highly interconnected societies and systems. We also can be shockingly antagonistic and prone to conflict. Our finest minds have worked tirelessly for the benefits of humanity, but some of their work has been harnessed for greed and exploitation.

This is certainly true of the digital universe. From the outset we have seen a technology powered by—and greatly empowering—collaboration also become a tool for criminal activity and even war. Cybersecurity can be a means to mitigate the fault lines and structural flaws that have allowed our spectacular digital technologies to also deliver tremendous harm.

Increasingly, those technologies extend beyond simply processing ones and zeros among computers. A cyber-physical convergence is taking place, where things that we touch, things that we wear—and even things that we are—are becoming part of cyberspace (think building automation, Internet of Things [IoT] fitness trackers, and medical implants).

That convergence leads to questions:

- Will that increased connectivity, functionality, and data—particularly relatively early in the era of IoT, machine learning, and artificial intelligence—increase or decrease our overall state of happiness and productivity?
- In cybersecurity terms, will these incredible scientific achievements allow us, once and for all, to perform a system update to patch the design flaws in the DNA of the Internet that threat actors have exploited since the advent of digital connectivity?

Let's hope so. But hope is not a strategy, and certainly not a science. We will see in the following chapters how these technologies will most likely contribute to security challenges as well as solve them.

Humans will fail machines consistently; there's not much that can be done about that. Machines will fail humans consistently if machines expect perfection, and there's a lot to be done about that.

12
COMPLEXITY MANAGEMENT

> "You're no longer just managing IT and security; you're managing complexity."
>
> *Michael Daniel,*
> *Cyber Threat Alliance*

> "If your security policies can't accommodate evolving business needs, people will find ways to work around them."
>
> *Jay Gonzales,*
> *Samsung*

Copernicus and Galileo came up with special models to explain each point of light in our solar system, greatly simplifying previous models. That simple model of a complex system opened the door to exploring and solving the true unknowns of space. Scientists of the day no longer wasted time pursuing extremely complex explanations of the motions of the network of planets and stars they were watching. The same is true for cybersecurity: We must remove the complexity associated with managing cybersecurity. Then we can focus on discovering and mastering higher-order problems such as freeing up humans to pursue more advanced thinking and leveraging integrated machines to automatically defend against sophisticated tools.

The critical and escalating necessity of complexity management is being driven by the convergence of three separate and increasingly powerful forces. The first is the increasing volume of devices and data, which provides cover for cybercriminals and gives them more things to exploit. The second is the sprawling increase in scale of today's networks, as well as the elimination of clear borders and access points. The third is the human fallibility of IT teams stretched to the point of exhaustion from the relentless sprint of protecting information.

Today's IT teams must defend and contend with vast and volatile networks that are cloud-based and accessible from anywhere, comprising IoT and human points of access. These networks also are in a state of near constant flux from DevOps approaches that scramble to keep pace with the velocity of business. Factor in the complications of securing internal and external vendor relationships and strategic partnerships, the commodification of threat as an industry, and the emergence of sweeping regulations that both complicate and contradict existing data security practices. The result is a highly diverse and dispersed threat vector that threatens to drag CISOs and their teams into a perpetual Groundhog-Zero Day that prevents a progressive, methodical approach to security.

Many organizations fall into the trap of fighting complicated threats by mirroring the enemy: Fighting complexity with complexity. That's a bad idea, like trying to smother a wildfire with lots of pine needles. Instead, organizations must recognize that the solution to complexity is integration, alignment, and simplicity. That is an ongoing process that requires vigilance and clarity from start to finish—of both strategy and execution.

We are already well beyond the point where the intense complexities of connectivity can be managed at speed and scale by humans alone. Complexity management, already driven to near incomprehensible levels, will need the power of machine learning to be effective. Yet what level of complication will be driven by the evolution of AI? What will manage the complexities created by the technologies that manage complexity? Particularly as AI technologies become increasingly mandatory for contending with today's network complexity, it is critical for organizations to ensure that solutions don't morph into added layers of the problem.

Complexity is the enemy of security.

Because of the fundamental challenges of volume and velocity, that solutions-becoming-problems paradigm is more common than many IT teams realize. When these teams begin to catalog and map their networks, many find themselves in the digital equivalent of a hoarder's home—with duplicative third-party solutions and services, all governed by different technologies and policies. These are challenging enough to navigate on an average day. But when intensified by a security incident, they make deploying a security response much more difficult.

Fortunately, we are in a moment when a growing sense of importance and urgency about mastering complexity management creates an opportunity to get our hoarding houses in order. That order results in both flexibility and dexterity. Organizations can choose security tools based on the specific nature of the threat they're most likely to face and then align those tools with the actual resources of the security team. The result is a security profile that is far more efficient and much more strategically poised to deliver the most effective response to a breach. The approach also creates a much lighter and more appropriate technology footprint. As we will see in the contributions in this chapter, this simpler, travel-lighter approach also focuses an IT team on the specific risks they are most likely to encounter, allowing for much tighter integration of IT with the business itself. As we will see, for all the external factors that complicate cybersecurity, managing complexity is an inside job. When done correctly, the result is less complexity and more opportunity for cybersecurity success.

SHIFT YOUR MINDSET TO MANAGE COMPLEXITY

Michael Daniel, Cyber Threat Alliance

Although it's never been easy for a company to manage its IT, the changes happening today can seem particularly bewildering. In a relatively short period of time, we've moved from a world of wired desktops to a world of connected everything, where any device can be made to connect to the Internet, usually wirelessly. A corporate network still includes traditional IT devices, such as company-owned desktops and laptops, but at the very least it has grown to include tablets and smartphones that don't belong to the company. And in many corporate environments, the network has expanded even further, incorporating devices that right now we call the Internet of Things (IoT), but which pretty soon we'll just call the Internet. This expanded network will include everything from cars to refrigerators to light bulbs to cameras, and on the business side, inventory management tools and device sensors to any kind of device you can imagine.

Maintaining cybersecurity with wired desktops was already hard, but the emergence of this hyper-connected network is making it even more challenging. In particular, this expanded environment poses a new challenge because these devices are all different from each other. They run different types of software, they have different types of protocols and varying degrees of protection, and yet they're all connected. Not only has the potential attack surface grown considerably in terms of volume, but the variability and heterogeneity of that attack surface have also increased.

At the same time, your organization is probably growing ever more dependent on this plethora of devices. A disruption that used to be a minor annoyance could now be potentially catastrophic. The need to manage this environment carefully and rigorously is increasing rather than decreasing. Yet the traditional "technology-first" or "castle-and-moat" approaches to cybersecurity, which arguably didn't work or just barely sufficed in the wired desktop world, are rapidly becoming patently obsolete in the new IoT world.

In trying to tackle this challenge, many organizations have focused on finding purely technical solutions. They hope for a single technological tool that will solve the challenge and make the problem go away. But just as with managing any of the other complex aspects of a business or an organization, one tool is simply not going to do the job. It requires integrating approaches from a number of different disciplines in order to get at the problem and moving out of the mindset that because this problem is being generated by the IT environment, the solution has to therefore come from IT. In other words, as a CIO or a CISO, you're no longer just managing IT and security; you're managing complexity.

GETTING STARTED

So how do you manage this complexity? The first step is to explicitly align your business objectives and your cybersecurity operations. Since cybersecurity is not an end unto itself, you need to make sure that your cybersecurity activities facilitate and support your company's business activities, not inhibit them, and that your investments help contain complexity, not increase it. They also have to make sense from a business perspective. You have to understand why you're actually pursuing a particular cybersecurity project, not just because it's a new, bright, shiny object or the latest buzzword making the rounds at cybersecurity conferences. Although this point may seem obvious, all too often there is a disconnect between the business side and security side of an organization. When a disconnect occurs, the different sides of the organization end up pulling in different directions instead of working together.

The second step is changing your mindset about the problem and convincing the rest of your organization to go along with this new approach. In the old way of thinking, cybersecurity involved keeping intruders out of your network through technology. If your organization is trapped in this mindset, you're playing a game that you can never win. Instead, you need to think of cybersecurity as a long-term risk that you have to manage and the goal as enabling your organization to operate while preventing intruders from achieving their objectives. Looked at from this angle, the problem shifts, and you can apply a wider variety of tools in multiple ways to manage your cyber complexity.

KEY CHALLENGES

Once you have aligned your cybersecurity objectives with business operations and started changing the mindset of your organization, you will begin to encounter a series of new challenges. But while difficult, these challenges are not insurmountable, and solutions already exist for most of them.

The first challenge is how to organize your work in this new mindset. It's great to talk about risk management, but how do you do that? The most effective answer is to adopt a risk management framework. Several frameworks exist; a good example is the Framework for Improving Critical Infrastructure Cybersecurity promulgated by the National Institute of Standards and Technology. This framework is not a how-to guide for installing firewalls, nor is it limited to managing risk for critical infrastructure. Instead, it provides you with an organized, logical way to think about how you've got your digital environment arrayed, the steps you are going to take, and how to communicate about them in terms that senior management will understand. It also enables you to define more clearly the risk trade-offs that senior managers across the organization are going to need to make.

The second challenge is a lack of communication across the organization. A lot of times, the people working the business lines don't understand why the security people want to do certain things. Likewise on the security side, the security team simply doesn't understand why the marketing or R&D group, for example, doesn't just implement what seem to be very obvious and sensible cybersecurity measures. To overcome this challenge, you need to ensure you've got a good grasp of the goals and objectives of the various pieces of the organization. You've got to understand what their viewpoints are and why their business operations are laid out the way they are. If you can start with understanding and articulating their needs, you can foster communication and discussions about risk, which usually enables everyone to arrive at a much more sensible way forward in terms of mitigating and managing identified risk.

The most critical function for a CISO is not selecting which blinky box to use. The most effective CISOs make sure everybody's on the same page with regard to objectives, risks, and the risk management framework. They facilitate conversations between business lines so that business objectives and security risk are managed correctly. If, for example, somebody is developing a new capability that needs to be deployed in an environment that isn't locked down yet, then the cybersecurity people—if they understand the business need—can work with those people to make sure that the environment is structured properly and an appropriate sandbox is in place so they don't expose the overall organization to increased risk while still being able to achieve their business objectives.

My experience has been that when one group of people is doing what seems to another group to be completely irresponsible, it's usually because they don't understand the environment the other is working in, or their objectives. If you can line those up, there's usually a much smaller gap to bridge than people realize. However, if that miscommunication and misunderstanding persists, then you get bigger problems—your complexity just increases. In these circumstances, individuals or business groups often begin building their own shadow IT and increase your risk without you even realizing it. They may come up with workarounds that bypass critical security measures because they believe the procedures are interfering with business objectives.

If the CISO and cybersecurity policies don't acknowledge and take into account how people actually have to work, people will just figure out ways to work around them. That's why establishing and maintaining the lines of communication between the CISO and the other lines of business is so important. Only with open, regular communication and the right mindset can you improve the cyber-security of your organization.

MANAGING COMPLEXITY

Of course, once you have addressed the human element of the challenge—getting everybody on board and ensuring they all see that they have a common objective and a common need for security—you're still left with different environments and requirements that often need separate security management approaches. Business IT systems, operational technology (OT) systems, and your cloud environment create different demands, and any connected IoT devices pose their own problems. You've also probably got a highly mobile workforce, with applications and consumers that want instant access to data.

Ultimately, this complexity means that you cannot think of all possible requirements, configurations, or threats ahead of time. That's where your cybersecurity risk management framework comes into play again. The Cybersecurity framework mentioned earlier, for example, provides you with a way to choose the right tools for the risks you face. It enables you to select and implement specific kinds of procedures, business rules, and technologies based on your actual risk, and employ the best practices specific to your network structure, such as identity and credentialing. A risk management framework also drives you to understand your information environment, why you have the data you do, what you use it for, and how long you should keep it.

These data, information, and process questions are extremely important. For example, as a cybersecurity guy, I frequently tell organizations that the best kind of data is the data you don't have, because I don't have to protect it. You should really think hard about the kind of data that you're storing and why you are storing it. That understanding brings you back to those human connections you have created with your various business operation teams, because sometimes, the thing that actually does the most good is not another piece of technology, but a business process solution. By adjusting business processes where possible and setting up the right policies, you can focus your efforts on the technology where it actually provides you the greatest return on your investment and isn't just another blinky box in the stack.

The reason this is critical is because you want to ensure that you're not just making incremental changes to your current cybersecurity posture but looking holistically at your entire network security solution and strategy. When a new problem emerges—say a new IoT or mobile device is added to the network and there is no security solution in place that fully deals with it—a lot of organizations go out and buy a new technology solution that does deal with it. However, they rarely look at how that new security solution for mobile devices integrates with their other existing technology. What you end up with is this kind of strata effect, where you just create layer upon layer upon layer of security, and you don't know how it all interacts. You don't know where you've got seams, where you have overlaps, and where you have gaps. That's what the bad actors exploit: The seams and the overlaps and the gaps created with all of the various cybersecurity tools in place. So instead of solving the problem, the new solution has actually just increased your complexity. This problem is much bigger and more pervasive, especially with larger organizations, than most people realize.

As you implement and update your risk management framework, you need to periodically perform a zero-based review of your entire security stack. This task is not easy. It requires you to examine your solutions, see how one solution plugs into others already in place, and determine if and how you can tie all these things together. The other part of the task is not only to see what new solutions you might need, but also to see if there is something you can get rid of. Can you replace a tool with a business process? Have business operations or information requirements changed in a way that allows for some different approaches? You should also take this opportunity to engage with the financial side of the organization and make sure you know how much the company is paying for all these tools and services. You need to decide whether a new tool is a completely necessary new layer that truly adds to your existing suite of tools, or if there is some functionality that you can let go of, that you no longer need, that you can retire out of your organization, that will help free up the resources to focus on that new capability, new device, new app, or whatever it is. Using this approach will help you manage the complexity that new solutions bring—and ensure that you remain focused on enabling the business to achieve its objectives.

You also need to know your limitations when approaching these sorts of complex activities and make sure that you're seeking outside counsel and advice when you need additional expertise. Given the complexity of today's technology and best practices, no organization has all of the expertise it needs in house. This is why high-performing organizations also know when to bring in outside experts. But in the end, you cannot transfer the risk or the decisions to outsiders. A company's leadership always retains the ultimate responsibility.

MANAGING RAPID CHANGE

Of course, complexity can also increase on the business side of the organization. Many organizations are undergoing rapid digital transformation, fully embracing the shift away from analog processes and paper storage. However, as that shift occurs it opens up whole new risks and creates new complexity. For example, while in the past it may have been impossible to steal every personnel record or research file because the intruders would have needed a semi, now they can steal all of that information rapidly without anyone even knowing.

The CISO's job is not to stop this shift. However, it is the CISO's job to ensure that a discussion occurs at senior management levels about how these changes will affect the organization's IT complexity and its risks. Everyone needs to understand that though there is a benefit to driving change rapidly, there's also a potential cost in complexity and risk that needs to be factored into the decisions that senior management is making. To weight these issues properly, your organization needs to understand how much risk they are willing to take on. Business transformation pacing often gets driven by the desire to achieve benefits without considering the downsides (other than people's resistance to change). However, if you approach the problem with complexity management in mind, you can guide digital transformation in a way that enables your organization to capture the benefits while appropriately containing the risks.

If you don't manage your digital transformation efforts well, the results can cause real harm, because as things get more complicated, they become the new normal. And then you move to the next level of complication. Meanwhile, your IT team just gets stretched thinner and thinner during the process, especially if you haven't made sure that everybody's aligned so that you can adjust business goals without having to compound the complexity on the IT end. That's when the complexity can spiral out of control.

INCIDENT RESPONSE

Finally, effective complexity management includes having a good incident response plan developed, one that you practice regularly. No matter how good you get at detecting, preventing, and containing complex cyberthreats, at some point you're going to deal with an actual incident. And you need to have the right protocols in place to deal with that unexpected event.

Because today's environments are so complex, you will never think of every potential eventuality or outcome ahead of time. It may seem counterintuitive, but in that sort of environment, the planning process becomes even more important. It can help you make sure you already have the capacity and capability to respond to the unexpected. Almost assuredly, when an actual incident occurs, it will not happen according to the plan. But that's where the planning process kicks in—as Dwight Eisenhower famously said, "The plan is nothing. Planning is everything." Moreover, planning provides a methodical way to engage everyone who has a role in executing the plan from the beginning—thinking through what the entire response will look like, determining required capabilities, and establishing an understanding for roles and responsibilities. It's not that you will simply be able to execute your incident response, but if you've gone through the planning process properly, that process will also enable you to be adaptable and flexible in your response capabilities. This requires forming a collaborative planning team, understanding your resources, mapping out roles and responsibilities, role-playing, and having the right people in place so that when that security event finally occurs, everyone knows their job and lines of command in order to avoid panic and resources being frozen in place.

I can't emphasize this last point enough. In an increasingly complex environment, having flexibility and a broad enough skillset available so that you can modify plans on the fly as things go sideways, especially in places where you didn't expect, is one of the most critical tools in your arsenal and may be the most difficult to attain. Achieving this state is the sort of benchmark that separates excellent CISOs from merely good ones.

CONCLUSION

Managing complexity is...well, complex. It requires technical, business, and human skills, coupled with adaptive and flexible thinking. It's hard, and sometimes that complexity will get away from you for a bit. However, with the right mindset and toolset, you can manage your organization's cybersecurity complexity. And that's a good thing, because today's world isn't giving you a choice in the matter.

ABOUT THE CONTRIBUTOR

Michael Daniel – President and CEO, Cyber Threat Alliance (CTA)

Michael Daniel leads the Cyber Threat Alliance (CTA) team and oversees the organization's operations. Prior to joining the CTA in February 2017, Daniel served from June 2012 to January 2017 as Special Assistant to President Obama and Cybersecurity Coordinator on the National Security Council Staff. In this role, Daniel led the development of national cybersecurity strategy and policy, and ensured that the US government effectively partnered with the private sector, nongovernmental organizations, and other nations.

SEVEN STEPS TO REDUCING COMPLEXITY

Jay Gonzales, Samsung

One of the biggest challenges organizations face is managing the layers of complexity they are implementing as part of their digital transformation efforts. The network is undergoing radical transformation: Workflows, software, and infrastructure are moving to virtualized and multicloud environments and next-generation branch offices. Bring your own device (BYOD) and IoT devices are inundating networks. More and more users require access to critical resources through a growing and continually changing set of applications, while agile development is changing the rate at which those applications are released and updated. And at the same time, the role of the CISO is changing from one of a technologist to that of a business adviser.

That's just the start. Samsung has the usual administration, sales, and marketing teams that we need to protect. But we are also a reasonably large R&D organization with multiple labs doing research, development, or testing and evaluation, each with its own unique and continually changing network and resource requirements. To complicate things further, many of these teams need to share network resources. So securing our environment involves continuously identifying the scope of what's being done on the network, determining whether new resources and technologies have to be integrated into—or isolated from—the rest of the network, and then implementing appropriate controls to ensure that essential business functions are never compromised.

Our challenge isn't unique. The question a growing number of CISOs are asking themselves is, "How do I begin framing this complexity with the resources I have available?" To answer that question, here are seven things I recommend:

1. REDUCE EXISTING COMPLEXITY

In the past, whenever network changes occurred, companies would find and deploy very specific security solutions to address very specific problems. This means that many organizations are now dealing with a complex security environment made up of dozens of different vendor technologies, each with its own processes and management consoles.

Today, however, most security teams no longer have the resources to add more solutions, which means they have to be much more strategic about the security tools they implement. My approach is to either figure out how to squeeze more functionality out of the tools I have in place, or if I am considering a new device, ensure that it not only does something my other tools can't do, but that it can also replace some of the devices I already have.

Reducing complexity also requires having an accurate inventory of the tools you already own. To do this, we stopped buying technology for about eight months to figure out what devices were in place and what gaps we needed to address. We now maintain this baseline through regular internal and external assessments to ensure we are always aware of where we sit from a cybersecurity perspective.

2. ADJUST YOUR POLICIES

Once you have identified all of your network's components and devices, the next step is to put a process in place that lets you address specific requests for exceptions to policy. If your security policy is prescriptive, it will be more challenging to manage exceptions. And if your policy can't accommodate evolving business needs, people will find ways to work around them.

Establish policies that enable the constant macro/micro conversations that today's networks require to keep everything tied together and moving forward. When someone needs to do something outside of the rules and resources specific to their team, you should be able to respond with "How can we help you?"

This industry is seeing a real paradigm shift from prescriptive to interactive security policies, with CISOs now thinking more in terms of broad goals and objectives rather than specific rules. As a result, when you establish a rule that everyone must put a lock on their front door, you don't need to tell them exactly what kind of lock, where to put it, how high it should be, or who should have a key. You just need to set the expectation that they need to lock the door, and as long as the door is locked, you should be good with it.

3. APPLY SEGMENTATION

Most networks were originally designed with a strong perimeter security strategy. Security teams would then deploy an inline security device in front of critical resources, such as demilitarization zones (DMZs), server farms, and data centers. The rest of the internal network was flat and was either largely unprotected or filled with security devices that needed to be managed and configured. Those approaches either increased risk or consumed overhead.

Today, establishing internal security controls for things like IoT devices or research labs no longer requires implementing new firewalls. Instead, segmentation and micro-segmentation provide rich protections without impacting visibility. Internal segmentation can be used to dynamically isolate devices and functional network zones on demand, while micro-segmentation can secure workloads that move into the cloud or move east and west within an environment such as a data center. Because segmentation can be managed centrally, it can go a long way toward reducing the complexity caused by extensive security device deployment.

4. IMPLEMENT NAC

Once you understand what's on your network and have simplified your policies and implemented segmentation to isolate network zones and resources, the next job is keeping track of ongoing changes, including identifying any devices being added to the network. Even within network segments, you need to know what devices are being added and how they should be categorized.

Network access control (NAC) ensures that when somebody brings a new device or system online, you know what sort of device it is and for what purpose it is going to be used. And if you don't know what the device is, or if the NAC system has flagged it as not meeting policy, then it gets quarantined until it has been identified or somebody goes through the process of getting it patched or updated. This approach helps maintain the fluidity that networks require without adding additional cost or complexity burdens to the security staff.

5. EMPLOY AUTOMATION

Dynamic access control is just one piece of the larger notion of automation. Many of the human resources in most security teams are dedicated to mundane tasks such as managing and updating device configurations, onboarding devices, reading logs, or applying patches—which is why the next critical step in reducing complexity is to automate as many of these processes as possible.

If you can automate menial tasks, like being able to run a script to pull a log for a specific incident, that means you can assign the person who used to do that job to something more critical. The biggest challenge to implementing automation, however, occurs when people don't know the process, the process isn't mature, or people simply don't follow the process.

6. MANAGE PEOPLE

Solving the challenge of establishing and enforcing process requires interacting with the other teams and divisions within your company. In many organizations, the most important job of the CISO is not overseeing security technology and the technical team but establishing peer relationships with other groups so that challenges can be addressed up front rather than waiting for them to turn into bigger problems.

One reason why this approach is critical is that in many organizations, the security team doesn't have direct oversight of network operations. To deal with this challenge, security teams have either simply imposed security rules or walked over to IT and said, "Hey, this is happening. What changed? When did it get approved?"

But that's a pretty inefficient process, especially when both attacks and transactions today occur at digital speeds. What's needed is to get out in front of these challenges by building relationships with the heads of your business units. The truth is that each team has its own needs, requirements, and challenges, and you need to understand them before you try to add something on top of what they already can't do, or to something with which they're already struggling.

To stay out ahead of these challenges, I have regular meetings with lab heads where I ask things like "What's changed?" Then I can explain what we're trying to do and ask, "How is this going to impact you?"

This sort of interaction is essential. When you don't communicate with your various business leaders and department heads, you end up trying to manage something that you know nothing about—as opposed to going out and collecting information, building relationships, and saying, "We want to help you, but you need to help us." If you don't know what they're doing and you implement a new protocol, it could impact them in a way that wasn't intended, and you will end up dealing with the consequences.

That's also when users start seeing you as a disabler rather than an enabler. In many organizations, that means that as soon as the security team shows up, they assume you have already made a decision, and they wonder why they are even having a meeting. They begin looking for ways to work around the restrictions you have in place.

When I first got here, it was always "Uh oh, here comes Jay. He's going to say no. We might as well not even try." But after showing that I truly wanted to help them succeed, their attitude changed to "Hey, I have this idea. Can we do it this way? I know this security policy says these things, but we need to be able to do these other things despite the policy." This is why I believe that the most crucial aspect of managing complexity is managing critical relationships within the business.

But talking alone isn't sufficient. Without a clear understanding of everyone's requirements and objectives, conversations can quickly become "This isn't working. Please fix it." Unfortunately, "please fix it" doesn't provide any scope of work for my team because I don't know what's wrong. Those relationships need to be enhanced by defining your requirements. It's easier to manage interactions between teams when everyone has their requirements documented so that you can quickly identify problems and the scope of the effort required to fix them.

7. MANAGE CULTURAL COMPLEXITY

One interesting challenge in managing complexity sometimes occurs in international or global organizations where a cultural disconnect exists between the local and the overseas teams. In those cases, some of the complexity may merely be the result of internal politics and culture.

For example, one security team may be very compliance-focused and compliance-driven. Their expectations may include using a checklist and asking, "Are you doing these things, yes or no?" and then grading a team or a business unit with "You failed because you're not doing A, B, and X." A team from another culture may see compliance as merely the place where you start and that they need to add a whole lot on top of that.

Addressing these challenges requires having open conversations, facilitated through buy-in from local leadership. The goal in these exchanges is to help other teams understand what your cybersecurity goals are, what your local culture expects your cybersecurity team to be doing, and how their efforts serve the business. The goal is to help them see that if the results are the same, meaning the organization is secured, the process for how each team achieves those objectives should be secondary.

This is a long way of saying that some of the complexity you may have to deal with is not always technology-focused. It's more along the lines of getting everyone, up through executive management, to understand precisely what your team is there for, what's expected of them, what they're doing to meet both the local and corporate security needs, and what tools and authority they need to be successful.

CONCLUSION: SECURITY CAN NEVER BE A BOTTLENECK

Ultimately, the goal of security is not to merely protect the business, but to enable it to move forward. To make that happen, security cannot afford to become a bottleneck for the things that need to get done.

The most significant challenges are first, identifying every group with a vested interest in how the network operates, and second, identifying things that are happening that you didn't know about, and finally, identifying user groups that have found a way to get things to work inside the environment, especially when that involves circumventing devices, policies, or protocols. This is actually a good thing because you then not only understand what those groups need to do their jobs and where your security strategy has become a bottleneck, but perhaps most importantly, where the gaps in your security implementation exist.

If you find a team that has figured out how to work around the system, you need to learn from them. The last thing you want to do, especially when something is already up and running—and running as desired—is to cut them off. Instead, learn why they need to do what they are doing and find a way to enable it that doesn't circumvent security. That may require getting them to move to a more controlled environment, or it may simply involve isolating them from everyone else.

Ultimately, reducing and managing complexity starts with asking, "What do you want to do?" "What do you need to do?" and "What tools do you need to get this to work better?" And for those teams that already have a workaround in place, a good question might be "How did you get this working without telling anyone what you needed?" That might tell you more about your security strategy than anything else you do.

ABOUT THE CONTRIBUTOR

**Jay Gonzales, – Chief Information Security Officer,
Samsung Semiconductor, Inc.**

Jay Gonzales has spent the last 18 years working in cybersecurity. His background and experience are primarily in the government sector, where he spent 13 years as an active-duty Marine specializing in information assurance and computer network defense (IA/CND) and another three years with the Naval Criminal Investigative Service (NCIS). Prior to his current role, Gonzales was a risk manager within the HP Global Cyber Security Team.

Gonzales had several roles within the government civil service. He began as an NCIS Cyber Security Liaison assigned directly to the Department of the Navy CIO, providing regular cyberthreat intelligence briefings and updating department-level cybersecurity policies for the Navy and Marine Corps. He also provided direct support in the development of the Department of Defense Critical Infrastructure Protection policies and planning. In addition, Gonzales was a Ministerial Advisor to the Afghan Ministry of Interior Affairs, developing an IT Education and Training program for the Afghan National Police Force in Kabul.

13

PRIVACY

> "If you collect it, you must protect it."
>
> *Kevin Miller,*
> *MGM Resorts International*

> "Stronger privacy policies lead to safer organizations, better protected customers and greater business success."
>
> *Peter Keenan,*
> *Global Financial Services Firm*

Privacy has fomented passionate policy debates, protests, and some of the most sweeping and severe regulations ever placed on digital organizations. While many cite the European Union's General Data Protection Regulations (GDPR) as a year-zero milestone, the truth is that privacy issues have always been fundamental to functional societies.

In the same way, protection of privacy must be an integral component of all cybersecurity efforts.

Just as security techniques and protocols that don't account for the fundamental element of speed are simply turned off or abandoned, leaving a network completely unprotected, lack of privacy catalyzes a similar reaction. If users feel privacy is at risk, they find simple workarounds that create a vast, and far more vulnerable, shadow IT infrastructure comprising devices and systems that most IT teams can't even see, much less protect. If you are going to do cybersecurity at speed and scale, then you also need to do privacy risk detection and mitigation at speed and scale.

As we move forward, how will our digital innovations impact one of the most fundamental aspects of modern life—our desire for and right to privacy and autonomy as individuals? As the post-GDPR era unfolds in an attempt to protect the individual from our collective embrace of digital innovation, we see that even privacy is subject to the human shortcomings of contradiction and overcomplication.

It is ironic that, to effectively protect an information system that rises from a binary code of ones and zeros, we too often convey black or white choices between security and privacy. Successfully securing our networks depends on finding the right balance between these two forces.

When security experts abdicate the need for this balance—often in favor of practices they assume will create stronger security for their organizations—they generally achieve the opposite effect. While some IT teams are quick to blame end users, the responsibility is theirs and can be directly attributed to the missteps that demand users comply with an untenable and unsustainable false choice.

For both ethical and pragmatic reasons, security experts must never force people to choose between security and privacy. Security with no privacy is often no security at all—and immeasurably more dangerous to an organization than the reasonable concessions and compromises that ensure privacy.

But beyond that simple cause and effect, there are many more reasons to place privacy concerns at the center of all security efforts. A balanced approach to privacy informs and empowers a wide array of security techniques—from the levels of encryption to the techniques of inspection, authentication, and visibility, to name just a few. Cybersecurity solutions that protect privacy are more powerful and sophisticated.

It is no coincidence that the perception that privacy rights were being trampled by powerful digital companies resulted in the rise of GDPR and other regulations that place incredible complications on all those security fundamentals. Those regulations have created massive challenges—and even baffling contradictions—that IT teams around the world must now contend with every day.

What is also clear is that an overcompensating reaction that over-values privacy often creates even more risk and may even expose much more sensitive personal information to cybercriminals who are more than happy to exploit reduced visibility to perpetrate information theft.

DON'T PANIC! SECURITY PROS MUST LEARN TO EMBRACE THE NEW ERA OF PRIVACY

Kevin Miller, MGM Resorts International

As security professionals work feverishly to protect the ever-expanding technology landscape that drives digital business, dramatic changes in society and law that fundamentally shift their responsibilities can appear, as if out of nowhere. But there is no need for panic. If security professionals embrace these changes, the results can be very positive.

We've become accustomed to headlines about massive organizations ravaged by data breaches. These compromises not only affect tens of millions of customers, but also impact the bottom line with huge fines, legal fees, and costs for security upgrades. And, more importantly, these breaches result in permanent brand damage and a loss of customer confidence. From this, cybersecurity has newly emerged as a key business risk. Executive leaders and board members now regularly demand updates from a previously overlooked and underfunded security department cloistered within IT.

It's been easy for the big headlines and management's urgent cyber concerns to overshadow a looming international privacy law. But as one business replaced another on the front page, a new era of privacy was dawning in Europe, the world's largest market with 500 million residents and the world's largest trading block, which accounts for 16 percent of world imports and exports.

In May 2018, the European Union's General Data Protection Regulation (GDPR) came into force. The law replaced the Data Protection Directive from 1995, which required all 28 member states to pass their own data protection laws. This resulted in a mishmash of regulations often at odds with one another. The GDPR is meant to "harmonize" the data privacy laws across Europe.

The law's 99 Articles and 173 Recitals codify the rights of individuals and the responsibilities of businesses that offer goods and services in the European Union (EU). Individuals are now guaranteed the right to know what information is collected about them and how it will be used, the right to access and correct that information, the right to delete the information (aka "the right to be forgotten"), and even the right to object to certain types of processing. What rights an individual has depends on why the information was collected in the first place (called a "lawful basis for processing"). GDPR's exceptions are narrow, specific, and few. They include law enforcement and national security matters, scientific analysis, and data used strictly for personal or household activity.

The scope of this complex and far-reaching law is intentionally massive. It applies to every organization, from a nonprofit to a scrappy start-up to a global enterprise, that offers goods or services in the EU, irrespective of any payment. The law applies even if an organization simply "envisages offering services" (for example, has a website that targets EU residents and accepts payment in euros). And the GDPR applies throughout the supply chain. Personal information shared with third parties (such as suppliers and vendors) subjects them to the requirements, too.

Accountability is one of the main features of the GDPR and represents a significant shift in mindset for those who must comply with the law. While not a new concept, the accountability principle in Article 24 of the GDPR requires organizations not only to implement "appropriate technical and organizational measures," but also to "demonstrate" compliance with the regulation. There are 39 Articles in the GDPR that require evidence of compliance, a completely new task for many corporate security teams.

For the first time, this regulation has real teeth in the form of a powerful enforcement scheme. For months leading up to the GDPR enforcement date, headlines warned of fines for violations as high as 20 million euro or 4 percent of global annual revenue (whichever is larger). It was widely expected that the huge fines would be levied only for flagrant violations, but penalties that large could easily sink a company without vast resources.

Thankfully, the European data protection authorities provided some calming perspective. The Chairwoman of the Article 29 Working Party (which represents each of the EU member state authorities tasked with enforcing GDPR) called the enforcement date "a starting point" and a "milestone for a way that we'll start to work together." They have consistently emphasized engagement and transparency over deadlines and fines. But still, a billion-dollar company could face fines of $40 million—definitely enough to raise concerns in boardrooms around the world. From the perspective of a security professional, hopefully it will help influence business leaders to reconsider the priority of their data protection efforts.

While the reach and ramifications of GDPR are truly massive, many questions will be answered only through enforcement and litigation. One thing is very clear: What is considered personal data has expanded. The GDPR defines personal information very broadly as "any information relating to an identified or identifiable natural person." Although there is no definitive list of information that constitutes personal data under the regulation, the GDPR provides some clarity: "[A]n identifiable natural person is one who can be identified, directly or indirectly, in particular by reference to an identifier such as a name, an identification number, location data, an online identifier or to one or more factors specific to the physical, physiological, genetic, mental, economic, cultural or social identity of that natural person." For a business that gathers even a modest amount of information about their customers, that's a lot of information to protect!

In the GDPR era, organizations must know what information they gather and why—something much easier said than done. Information that was previously considered so benign as to be included on a business card is now covered data—a name, postal address, email, telephone number, and a photograph on an employee badge. Even a small company maintains information not just from customers, but also from current and prospective employees, contractors, suppliers, vendors, dealers, and more. Every process that involves personal data must be considered when complying with the GDPR.

To many modern digital businesses, data is considered the company's most valuable asset. But now, data may also be considered a liability and even a risk. If you collect it, you must protect it—from the moment it is gathered, to how it is transferred and stored, to how it is used and shared, to how it is archived and eventually destroyed. Complying with the GDPR is not an IT problem that can be solved by purchasing a new tool. The law's requirements will drive extensive change to processes that don't even touch technology.

To make compliance even more complex, satisfying the GDPR's requirements involves two distinctly different but equally difficult issues: Privacy and data security.

For residents of the EU, the most visible result of the GDPR will be around privacy. To start, many organizations have had to rewrite their privacy policies to meet the law's requirements. For example, a privacy policy must now include specific information about what personal information is collected and why, what information is shared and with whom, and how individuals can exercise their rights. The law is even adamant that the policy be understandable (no legalese) and easy to read. Plenty of skeptics doubt that lawyers are up to the task!

Wherever data is gathered, an organization must be transparent about how they plan to use the data—what the law calls a "fair processing notice." The GDPR is especially specific about information gathered based on the consent of the individual, with a requirement that it be "freely given, specific, informed and explicit." A preselected "I agree" check box is no longer acceptable under the GDPR. The result is that companies must reexamine each process that accepts personal information and ensure the correct notices are in place. For many, this is a monumental task.

Not only must a company be open about how they plan to use the data, but they must also ensure the data isn't used for any other purpose for as long as they keep that data. This is called the "purpose limitation" principle, and the implications for corporate IT systems can be huge. Not only must the data be protected, but also the original purpose of the data must be maintained, somehow, throughout its life cycle. To be sure, many legacy IT systems are not built to keep metadata like this, let alone act upon it.

Under the GDPR, individuals have certain rights to their data, and each organization must be able to satisfy requests for free within 30 days. These requests are called data subject access requests (DSARs). Though easy to understand in theory, deleting data to satisfy a right to be forgotten request, for example, is anything but easy. A company may have hundreds of applications connecting to thousands of databases containing many millions of records of personal information. They can't simply delete data about an individual without putting the entire system at risk of failure. And to make things even more difficult, though an individual may want to be removed from direct marketing lists, they likely still want the company to honor the warranty for the product they purchased years ago.

What does a company do, for example, when they receive a request for information from Katherine Miller? They certainly don't want to send information to the wrong person. A search over the company's databases (marketing, payroll, customers, loyalty clubs, customer service, and so on) may result in tens or hundreds of possible matches—such as Katie Miller and K. Miller. Don't forget about information collected about Katherine before she married. Some records may have postal addresses from years ago, some with current or past phone numbers, and a host of email addresses. Some larger companies expect to get nearly 250 requests per month. What constitutes a "thorough" search? How long will it take to perform the search? And importantly, how many people will be required to conduct these searches? These are far from trivial questions.

Privacy aside, the challenges faced by many organizations to secure the data can be just as daunting. While security-minded organizations have been protecting personal data for years, there are significant hurdles to those new to the GDPR. For example, the law permits the transfer, processing, and storage of data outside the EU (called a *cross-border data transfer*) only when the destination is deemed to have an "adequate" level of protection. To the EU, the data protection laws in the United States are not considered adequate. Although there are several methods (such as binding corporate rules or US/EU Privacy Shield) for a company to comply with this rule, it's anything but trivial for global companies to comply. In the era of cloud computing, it's not easy and often not possible to choose where specific data is stored. This will be an ongoing struggle.

Of course, if you don't keep data, you don't need to secure it. Long considered a best practice by security professionals, the GDPR calls out data minimization specifically to lighten the compliance burden. Only the data that's absolutely necessary to accomplish the task should be collected and processed. Any nonessential data should not be collected, and if it was, it should be deleted. Encryption and storage limitations are also important concepts in the law. Encryption has been around forever, and basically everything that can be encrypted should be. Storage limitations means simply "retention and destruction." There are many reasons a company may need or want to keep data. Governments, for example, often require tax information to be kept for years. But data that is no longer needed should be deleted. A well-defined data retention and destruction policy is very helpful, and procedures that implement the policy are essential.

The GDPR also encourages several data handling techniques that can make the security team's job easier. The process of *anonymization* is nothing new. But unfortunately, it's only practical in some limited situations because it involves eliminating all data that can uniquely identify an individual. If you really anonymize the data, much of the value disappears—to the business, to consumers, and so on. Let's face it; people value personalized experiences like targeted advertising, as long as it's not creepy.

One step down from anonymization is so-called *pseudonymization*, an incredibly awkward word to pronounce. This is where the personally identifiable information is kept separate from other data but linked in a way so that individuals can be reidentified. This is a relatively new and clever concept that will take time to incorporate into business applications.

The GDPR is even affecting the very structure of many security, legal, and business risk teams. The law has elevated privacy within organizations to a level where some organizations that process large amounts of personal data are required to hire another senior leader called a data protection officer (DPO). This is a new role designed to independently oversee the data protection strategy of a company and serve as a liaison to the local GDPR supervisory authorities. As many as 75,000 DPOs are expected to be hired globally.

So far, we've seen how the GDPR will fundamentally change how privacy and data protection are regulated in the EU and, by extension, around the world. And we've seen how the new law will impact large and small companies who do business there. What remains is to discuss how this will actually be accomplished in the field. How will the GDPR affect the CISO role? What will the compliance journey be like for an average company? Is GDPR compliance really achievable?

In many companies, the CISO role is a relatively new IT position, often reporting to the CIO. Many first-generation CISOs came from an IT background and are heavily technical. Yet this is changing.

Trends like global privacy and the growing digitization of traditional business is pushing the CISO to become a "business" leader. Many CISOs now report to the General Counsel, the COO, CEO, or even directly to the board of directors' Audit Committee.

There is good reason for this change. CISOs who are tasked with GDPR compliance may find themselves working more with human resources, legal, sales, and marketing than with IT. That's not to say that IT doesn't play a central role. It certainly does! But many IT organizations are modernizing their data security standards anyway as they adopt best practices in development and operations. Adoption of cloud technology for mission-critical traditionally on-premise applications like enterprise resource planning (ERP) are forcing a higher level of security scrutiny anyway.

What's lacking in many organizations is a meaningful understanding of the data that is consumed and processed by the business. What information does HR gather from new employees? Is Marketing properly recording consent for direct marketing? Is the corporate email system being used to send and receive unencrypted personal information with vendors? Is the corporate retention and destruction policy being followed? What EU data is being transferred and stored in the United States? Does the organization really satisfy the requirements of US/EU Privacy Shield?

The CISO may well be the one to ask these questions and help the organization find answers. It's easy to feel overwhelmed, but the best way to move forward is with a step-by-step, methodical approach. And you'll need to get very good at documentation!

So where do we begin?

The first job is to map the data flows. Sit with the business teams and whiteboard their processes. Ask open-ended questions so that you can fully understand the business requirements. These maps help everyone understand all the details around a data flow: Who supplies the information, what data is gathered, where it is stored, how it is used, where it is shared, who has access to the information along the way, and eventually what happens to the data. Heavily regulated businesses may already have this information, but many companies do not.

Once you have the flow maps, or at least the important ones, you must determine your "basis for lawful processing." A CISO may be able to make an informed guess at this, but the question of lawful bases is best left to Legal. The legal basis answers the question, "What gives your organization the legal right to gather this information?" It's important to know this early because you will need to design your controls to accommodate the rights of individuals who depend heavily on this decision. You may also need to "classify" the data as it enters your system, which can influence your selection of controls in later steps. Keep in mind that the GDPR puts a lot of rules around information gathered based on consent of the individual. It's best to use consent rarely (for example, in direct marketing).

Next, perform a *gap analysis* on each workflow. Don't get mired in the details. Instead, do a high-level analysis of each workflow and evaluate each step in the process. You may decide to encrypt data in transit, without being concerned about how that will be accomplished. At this point, you're documenting what's both required (by the GDPR and other regulations) and desired (to implement best practices). If you're unfamiliar with the details of the GDPR, consult with your legal team or an outside specialist. There are a lot of requirements in this complex law. There is no shame in asking for help.

With your gap analysis in hand, you can now access the risk of the workflow and prioritize. Not all workflows are the same. They typically vary by the volume and sensitivity of the information. Especially sensitive workflows include information about minor children or information relating to race or ethnic origin, religious affiliation, sexual orientation, trade union membership, and so on. Larger companies may have hundreds of workflows, so prioritization is key and keeps you from feeling overwhelmed. Document the risk ownership and risk acceptance at this stage. It's not the job of the CISO to assume risk on behalf of the business. Risk belongs to the information owners, and this step is a great opportunity to make this risk visible.

Now you are finally ready for the fun part for most technologists: Designing and building controls. Start with small, simple workflows to hone your skills, and then tackle the more complex ones. You'll often need to engage subject matter experts in the various technologies along each step of the workflow. Tackle each item identified during the gap analysis. If a step gathers information on an unencrypted web form, you may need to deploy HTTPS. To protect information "at rest," you may need to encrypt an Amazon S3 bucket.

If personal data normally sits on a NetBIOS share indefinitely, create a process to implement your retention and destruction policy. Rinse and repeat! This is where you're flexing your security muscles and really making a difference in the security posture of your organization.

Some changes will be trivial whereas others will spawn a project and take months to complete. As procedures change, you'll need to coordinate training and update documentation. Eventually, you'll be able to hand off the new procedure to the business. But your work doesn't end there! To stay compliant, make sure you create a tickler system to regularly reevaluate each workflow. A good governance, risk, and compliance (GRC) or Information Technology Infrastructure Library (ITIL) tool is a way to automate this.

Although all this work may seem mountainous, it is doable. But you're going to need to adapt and retool. Security teams are typically made up of technologists. And while privacy often requires technology to implement the necessary controls, understanding how to accomplish this takes a business partner mindset. It is a collaborative process that can be painstaking, and it requires a great deal of patience and communications. The most difficult aspect of GDPR compliance is not legal or technical; it is interpersonal. IT teams need to develop skills they have never used or needed before.

The best possible circumstance is when everyone in a company understands the imperative, the risks, and the costs of not complying with this new privacy law. There will, inevitably, be pushback, especially if the GDPR is seen as a nuisance that can be dodged or ignored. But consumers have every right to demand that businesses respect, value, and protect their personal information, and the risks we all face from careless data management are all too real.

At the very outset of any compliance project, the most important thing a CISO must do is sell the requirements to the CEO—as well as the CIO, COO, General Counsel, and the Board of Directors. Business leadership must understand what is at stake and have a realistic understanding of what it will take to get it done. There is no way around the fact that compliance, in both process and execution, is expensive. Traditional information security tools are designed to secure systems, not information. To succeed, IT will need an entirely different set of tools to safeguard privacy. Not only does that require finances, but it also requires something even more precious in the rapid pace of today's business: Time.

That's no reason to put off the hard work and heavy lifting of privacy compliance, though. Things aren't getting any slower, and this type of legislation is not going anywhere. As GDPR-type laws spread around the world, citizens of more countries will surely begin to demand protection of their personal information. Legislators are not going to start from scratch. They may take the GDPR, make some modifications, and put a different name at the top. As we see with the Network Security Law of the People's Republic of China ("Cybersecurity Law" or "CSL"), which shares many of the GDPR's tenets, that does not mean complying with one will mean compliance with all. Each new law will reflect the privacy expectations of the local population, which will be largely cultural.

All the more reason to build and establish secure and compliant processes and systems now and to jettison the dead weight of unnecessary personal data! As the penalties for violations get harsher and regulators get more accustomed to levying them, some organizations may find that personal data has even higher value than they knew, just not in the way they thought. The new era of privacy is here, and there is no turning back. Embrace it and get busy!

ABOUT THE CONTRIBUTOR

Kevin Miller – VP of Privacy, MGM Resorts International

Kevin Miller (CIPP/E, CISSP, CRISC) is vice president of privacy at MGM Resorts International, a global entertainment company, in Las Vegas, Nevada. He has been a contributing author to several books on Juniper and Cisco technology. His privacy background includes the development of a GDPR compliance program when he worked as CISO at Herman Miller, an international office furniture manufacturer. Miller has an extensive background in network architecture and engineering, and holds a bachelor of science degree in computer science from the College of Charleston, South Carolina.

STRICTER PRIVACY REGULATIONS ARE DRIVING THE CONVERSATIONS— AND INNOVATIONS—WE NEED

Peter Keenan, Global Financial Services Firm

The timeframe between the adoption and the enforcement date of the European Union's General Data Protection Regulations (GDPR) inspired many information security experts to talk about "a new era of privacy." But in the financial services industry, where nearly 30 percent of all employees are focused on maintaining compliance to everything from the anti–money laundering laws of the Bank Secrecy Act to the policies set by the Organisation for Economic Co-operation and Development (OECD), we have long understood that privacy protection is not only central to effective security but also integral to earning customers' trust and driving business wins.

There is no denying that the strength and severity of the GDPR represent a fundamental shift in the way personal information is viewed and handled by businesses everywhere. Nor can we deny that the discussions driven by the GDPR are critically important and, indeed, necessary for advancement. But during the massive debate that led up to its codification into law—not to mention the incredible changes in data protection that companies all over the world had to make to be in compliance—a specific narrative seemed to take hold.

The storyline was simple: Powerful businesses and organizations in the private sector were trampling the principles of privacy protection. Therefore, they needed to be kept in check by strict regulations to protect personal information. Although this was seen by some as a direct message to West Coast tech and social media companies, the GDPR's impact is actually much broader. It is true that the path the GDPR has set down is an important one, but it does not necessarily represent a Year Zero for digital privacy principles.

Historically, the concept of "least privilege" has been the guiding principle when designing information security programs. At its most basic level, least privilege means that only the people who need to see a piece of information can see it. By any reasonable standard, this is the very definition of privacy. It is also embodied by the CIA Triad model of information protection: Confidentiality, integrity, and availability. Confidentiality restricts access to information, integrity assures the accuracy of the information, and availability promotes the ability of authorized people to access that information. It is a model that well predates GDPR adoption.

That's not to say the GDPR is duplicative or unnecessary—far from it.

More recently, the ease with which companies can stray from core principles of privacy and security has been widely publicized. Although determining whether information policies align with corporate values is beyond the scope of most IT teams, much of information security involves risk management, and thus, the ability to communicate risks. As a result, we have seen that not only are strong privacy regulations effective tools to protect consumers, but they also protect organizations, often from themselves.

An illustrative example of this practice is Facebook, an organization that has been chosen in deference to its vast reach within the US population and to highlight the privacy concerns that have arisen in the context of the increasing value of personal information. Facebook's basic business model is widely well understood. It has been adopted across a variety of social media platforms, as well as different industries. Facebook takes data that people give them voluntarily and then sells or monetizes that information in various ways.

Though it is increasingly rare, there are some people who are not aware of such practices when they sign up for a social media service. Why? The answer is simple: Because nobody reads the end user license agreement (EULA). They simply click to accept.

And how could they do otherwise? EULAs contain thousands of words of tortured legalese that do anything *but* clarify. In 2012, it was determined that it would take the average person 76 full eight-hour workdays to read the EULAs of all the services they sign up for in a year. Everyone just clicks the button to accept the terms. Nowadays, we hardly think twice about doing so.

But place this ingrained behavior of mindless box-clicking into the context of the increasing value of personal data. Together, the conditioned behavior of consumers and the value of their data create a powerful gravitational pull for organizations—who are bound by a duty to increase profits for stakeholders—to see the situation as an incredible revenue-generating opportunity.

Consider the amount of deeply personal information your bank has about you. It includes everything from the amount of money in your accounts to your credit card transactions, online purchases, health information, marital status, and oftentimes even your location. Your bank activity can reveal aspects of your life at an incredibly granular level of detail.

By inserting merely two lines of text into the EULA that nobody reads, it would be completely legal for that financial institution to monetize all of the aforementioned information. Multiply that by millions of customers, and the potential profits are extraordinary. Some financial institutions could profit more from the data they possess than they do from a core function, such as interest rates. And it is all, essentially, found money.

It is not just banks, of course. The same holds true for phone companies, cable providers, and Internet service providers (ISPs), to name only a few who could profit. Today, across industries, there are very large and very powerful companies that absorb vast amounts of personal data in the course of providing their primary services. Privacy regulations like the GDPR remove the ability to monetize this information. In essence, this protects organizations from themselves by minimizing the tension created by their temptation or obligation to drive all possible profits.

Many organizations have come to realize that they must additionally protect themselves from themselves in a more literal sense. As an increasing number of organizations have grown into a global footprint, and as networks have expanded to the cloud, there has rightly been much attention devoted to protecting the expanding attack surface exposed to outsiders. However, that growing network also encompasses far greater numbers of *insiders* with legitimate access to a network. Protecting vast amounts of increasingly valuable personal information from a rapidly expanding population of employees, contractors, and vendors is an issue that has attracted less attention. Yet it is something organizations must figure out in order to have an effective security strategy.

When looking at the headline-generating privacy breaches of the past five years, 30 percent or more can be traced back to insiders. If you include incidents where an attacker was using the compromised credentials of an insider, the numbers might then be more than 70 percent.

In the financial services industry, companies outsource customer service to call centers around the world and, in the process, grant access to massive amounts of data to thousands of people the company will never know or directly employ. If the temptation to sell that data is strong at the C-level, imagine its pull for someone working at a call center in a developing country.

As we have seen in numerous high-profile cases, there is a large black market for stolen data, with criminals paying just pennies per record. Nonrepudiation, the ability to link an individual to an action, is an issue fraught with complexity when it is applied to online contexts, thanks to the initial design of the Internet. A person in a country with no extradition treaties could quite feasibly spend every waking hour attempting to commit fraud, with very little chance of getting caught and almost no chance of prosecution.

Regardless of whether an undetected breach of private information is launched internally or externally, it is still a symptom of a problem that is both grand in scale and profound in its implications. As networks expand, along with access points and people who genuinely need access, it is increasingly difficult for CISOs to adhere to the key tenet of information security: You must know your environment.

Here is where the financial services industry can provide insight in how to move forward. It also represents an opportunity to harness the power of rapidly innovating technologies and increasingly serious privacy regulations to create greater security. In this respect, especially, there is one area of financial services that is way ahead of the curve.

Ten years ago, credit card companies figured out what many other industries and verticals are only learning to do now. They became able to rapidly identify when a card had been stolen and immediately cut it off. This was made possible with highly sophisticated techniques for anomaly detection, from point anomalies, which detect individual outliers of normal credit card usage; to contextual anomalies, which factor in other relevant information to gauge activity; to collective anomalies, which review instances that individually may not have attracted attention but may collectively signal anomalies by their co-occurrence.

The motivation behind this intense focus is, of course, financial. Merchants in the United States lose about $190 billion to credit card fraud each year. Reducing that number by just one or two percentage points translates into saving billions of dollars. As the fields of machine learning and artificial intelligence innovate and improve, the ability to detect anomalies will also improve. Hopefully, machine learning will soon find greater application in the protection of personal information and other privacy issues.

While the tenet of "know your environment" is generally taken to mean knowing your hardware and software, it must now include knowing what information is on your network at any given moment. As privacy regulations grow, it will be increasingly important for companies to know what data they hold. If you don't have critical information identified and categorized, the chances of effectively securing it are essentially random. Deploying AI to achieve effective information categorization will become increasingly necessary.

This is another reason to be thankful for GDPR and OECD regulations: As enablers of business. Although these regulations have required massive internal changes and often run counter (or at least contradictory) to existing anti–money laundering laws, they have been incredibly effective at elevating security issues to the C-level. A high level of executive and boardroom attention drives more effective information security policies and allocations throughout the entire organization.

Increased executive attention will not only enable more effective deployment of data classification through AI and other technologies, but will also position information security where it needs to be: At the center of all business decisions and initiatives. Too many organizations develop tools and business processes, and then scramble to retroactively design security protocols around them. As more companies use agile DevOps production strategies, security will become a consideration at every point in the development pipeline.

As the central role of security becomes more of an accepted truism in the daily reality of doing business, there will be progressively less space between IT and information security. The result of this convergent evolution will be to introduce sound privacy practices that may be new and may seem cumbersome to some industries, but these practices have long been the accepted principles we live by in financial services.

In many ways, these privacy principles have been defined by OECD regulations. They comprise strict guidelines for collection limitations, including the relevance of data collected and the specific purpose for its collection, the individual's right to know if their data has been collected, and the need for transparency and accountability. Though there are contradictions in the GDPR, such as its lack of specificity regarding the role of system backups, or the need to retain information to comply with anti–money laundering laws, the spirit of the regulations is aligned.

There is no denying that the GDPR, which represents only the beginning of private regulations, has triggered a seismic change in the way some companies must handle personal information. Yet perhaps those who are protesting the loudest are the organizations that most need to change.

Hopefully, through the process of compliance, they will come to understand that greater privacy regulations lead to more effective information security, practices, and techniques. Ultimately, they may come to share our vision in the financial services industry: That stronger privacy policies lead to safer organizations, better protected customers, and greater business success.

ABOUT THE CONTRIBUTOR

Peter Keenan – CISO, Global Financial Services Firm

Peter Keenan is responsible for the global information security strategy and program at one of the world's preeminent financial advisory and asset management firms, with operations in dozens of countries. Prior to this role, Keenan was with Citigroup's global information security team. His most recent role at Citi was as head of information risk governance. In this role he led the team that is responsible for developing and maintaining information security policy globally. Prior to his five-year tenure with Citi, Keenan had 19 years of experience in information security and technology. This included six years as a director with PricewaterhouseCoopers's Threat and Vulnerability Management advisory practice. He also spent over a decade managing his own consultancy that specialized in designing, building, and operating secure high-availability data centers and networks around the world for military, intelligence, and commercial clients.

14
HUMAN FRAILTY

"We can't stop people from making mistakes. We need technology solutions in place to compensate."

Kevin Kealy,
Ingram Micro

"We fail to design for the human and instead we design around the human."

Theresa Payton,
Fortalice

You might think that a book whose premise is "Start treating cybersecurity like a science" wouldn't have room for a discussion about the so-called "soft stuff": The human brain, the three pounds of flesh and blood that serve as the "wetware" behind all the thoughts in this book and recorded history. But it is not software or hardware that's gotten us this far.

Too often, though, in cybersecurity, the soft stuff is the hard stuff. As we have seen over the course of this book, there is no way to entirely remove human frailty from technology innovations. Human weakness is embedded like a strand of DNA in everything we do and achieve. In the parlance of our times, there is not an app for that.

More than anything else, human fallibility is the truth and fuel that powers cybercrime. No matter how sophisticated our cybersecurity efforts, there will always be some aspect of our human frailty that can be exploited. But perhaps that fact is what also powers our relentless drive to innovate and improve our conditions. As Shakespeare wrote in *Julius Caesar*, "The fault, dear Brutus, is not in our stars/But in ourselves." To which I would add that in the science of cybersecurity, what is true of our faults is also true of our solutions.

We often discover after deployment that human frailty—from simple human exhaustion and carelessness to more mercurial patterns of cognitive bias, selection bias, pseudo-certainty, and pareidolia—is an intrinsic weakness of a system. It speaks to the extraordinary velocity of innovation—in just 50 years, our digital, technological advances have surpassed the abilities of the human brain from which they stem.

Our three-pound brain is incredibly powerful and agile. Its 85+ billion neurons boast an electric charge of about six billion volts. Over time, our brain has evolved to respond to situations humans have faced. That's the problem: Our brain is optimized over the millions of years of our existence, yet cybersecurity was born less than 50 years ago.

Humans are not designed to handle things beyond a certain complexity level. When the capacity of our neurological rev limiter and the limits of our human frailty are challenged by the complexities of the digital world, and cybersecurity in particular, the results are some of the most challenging and persistent security vulnerabilities. Thus, cybersecurity routinely suffers because of the bad decision making or poor cognition of human operators.

But that is why computers were invented: To deal with the levels of complexity and scale that humans can't. That is also why we have so relentlessly and vigilantly devoted ourselves to the refinement and proliferation of this capability: To achieve innovations and efficiencies at speeds and scales that would be impossible by human effort alone. So we should not be surprised that we've gotten to the point that the weakest link in the cybersecurity chain is often not the hardware or the software, but the wetware: The 75-percent water, three-pound organ we call our brain.

Human fallibility will continue to be the ghost in the cybersecurity machine, creating security risks. Yet if security leaders can recognize and handle human frailties, they will be much better able to contain the risks.

In the case of cybersecurity, there are core aspects of digital security whose sheer vastness and velocity demand machine learning.

We also can and should use machines to help compensate for human fallibility by looking for weaknesses in human decision making or actions.

Let's have machines serve man, rather than man serve machines.

Digital and human information processing—divergent but both deeply essential—must be clearly and strategically disambiguated to avoid a chaos of contradiction. As we hurtle further into an era that will be defined and dominated by the convergence of cyberspace and physical conveniences (think IoT, automation, real-time analytics, AI), we must recognize human frailty not simply as a security weakness to accept, but also as something to both compensate for and leverage. By allowing ourselves to focus unflinchingly on exactly what the human mind can and cannot do, we will more clearly recognize that there are tasks that are best suited for the higher-order intuition and creative understanding of human thought.

The true potential of AI and machine learning is most vividly revealed not by what it can do, but rather by what it cannot do. By understanding when to apply the power of human thinking and when to apply the power of advanced automation, we are poised for a massive leap forward in the defense of information and toward a more aligned and efficient world where instead of demanding our constant service, the machines we have created serve our needs.

OVERCOMING HUMAN FRAILTY: PEOPLE AND THE POWER OF OBLIGATION

Kevin Kealy, Ingram Micro

Overcoming human frailty is a clever way to describe 80 percent of a CISO's job. A security team needs to be focused on protecting the entire organization holistically, which means more than just taking a technology approach to problems. You can always apply technology solutions to a problem, but it only takes the least capable person in the room to ruin them for you, so you must also take a human approach. At the end of the day, my job is to work with folks to achieve the best result for the company. Ultimately, that's what's important. If I'm not partnering with people, I'm not doing as good a job as a CISO as I should be.

In my experience, education is one of the most cost-effective ways to secure your organization. I believe that people will generally do the right thing if appropriately educated. But even then, you still have to deal with human frailty.

At my company, we provide regular phishing training. We have one individual who has not only resolutely clicked on all of the last six of our phishing tests but has also provided credentials for every single one of them. This continues to happen in spite of the fact that after each of these events, this user is directed to, and watches, a remedial training video that details how to spot a phishing attack. It then outlines the possible bad consequences. And yet, on one of these tests, this individual clicked on the phishing link over 30 times because it wasn't responding in a way that was expected.

The assumption this user is making is that if something arrives on a computer, it should automatically be trusted. This goes right to the heart of the issue of human frailty. We've all seen this before. Most organizations have people who assume that security is someone else's problem. The message I include in my corporate security training is that security isn't a problem; it's an opportunity. Security is everybody's job. And that's what our training focuses on.

THE NEED FOR A TECHNOLOGY SOLUTION

The reality is that you can't stop people making mistakes. That's just human nature. Between 7 and 11 percent of people regularly fail our phishing campaigns. And of those, a significant number even hand over their credentials. We need technology solutions in place to compensate for these issues. In the case of phishing, we implemented multifactor authentication and set it so there's no other way to log in from outside the firewall, which means we now get alerts when people have provided their credentials to an external attacker.

There are two primary goals for any technology solution. First, you want to engineer as much weakness out of your environment as you can, and then, where possible, remove the human from the security process. And that's not just on the end-user side of things. Human frailty also extends into IT, where people are managing configurations, reading logs, and correlating events.

The goal is to boil a massive volume of data down to as small a quantity of information as possible and then present it in an actionable format to skilled operators. When a computer reboots, it can send dozens of pages into your logging system. There's little point in having someone staring at those log files, since they simply scroll past way too quickly for anyone to discern actionable information. And if you're doing patching, which requires a lot of rebooting, you may have thousands of pages of logs telling you that servers have rebooted. Assigning a human to keep up with that data will never work. But a machine learning algorithm can say, "Hang on a minute. I'm expecting some of these reboots, but I'm not expecting multiple reboots of the same machine. This one has rebooted three times, and that may be a problem." Right there, you have added value.

So clearly, relying on AI to sift through vast quantities of repetitive data is valuable. But once the AI has done its job, you still need a human to take a look at what might be actionable. That's because AI is not yet very good with context. And without context, data has little value. An action that could be completely normal in one context can be terrible in another, and you really don't want an AI system to confuse the two. For example, a network sniffer tool called Wireshark is a standard part of most techie toolkits. On a technician's workstation or laptop, Wireshark isn't a problem. But if you find Wireshark on a server containing credit card data, that could be a really big problem. It's the context that makes the difference.

So security often comes down to a judgment call. Automation can reduce the noise so we can concentrate on what's important. But anytime AI can't make a clear judgment call between good and bad, it needs to be flagged for a human, because context is still much easier for a human to evaluate.

THE NEED FOR PEOPLE SKILLS

That's the technical side, but a CISO has to deal with many issues that require people skills rather than technical skills. In too many companies, the security organization is known as the place where business goes to die, or the "Office of the CE-No." In our organization, we are known as a go-to place. And that can be a tricky thing to achieve.

My overriding directive to my staff is to never, ever say "no" to a request. Instead, you always start the conversation with, "yes, if." Such as, "yes, you can do something really, really, really stupid if we put you in a room where you're only going to get your own blood on yourself." You have to allow the business to proceed, but in a way that manages risk.

That starts by building relationships so that people see the security department as a place they can go for help. Of course, my job is to keep the business safe. But if people avoid us, then it's going to be much easier for them to hurt themselves. I have to be approachable by establishing a reputation for helping people achieve their goals. For a security team, that often requires changing the organizational mindset.

The first thing to remember is, if something looks stupid to us, it's probably because we don't understand what that person is trying to achieve. The security organization needs to pivot its perspective and look through the requester's lens, because what they want to do invariably seems sensible to them. They just don't understand the nuances of why they shouldn't do that thing in that particular way. Coaching my staff to answer every question with, "yes, if," forces my team into a frame of thinking that says, if the customer is asking for this, they must want to do this for some reason that we don't yet understand.

Problems like shadow IT are not the result of people trying to misbehave, but people feeling like they can't come to us to solve their problem, so they do it on their own. In their experience, either IT is going to say "no," or it's just going to take too long. And the reality is that they can just buy a service with a credit card in a couple of minutes. So creating a helpful and engaged environment can help resolve that sort of self-inflicted challenge within an organization. When people see security as approachable and helpful, they have less motivation to resort to shadow IT or to do their own thing.

However, some people will choose shadow IT anyway, which is why we must be vigilant. But even then, you still need to understand that people sometimes do the wrong thing for all the right reasons. This is why I've pre-negotiated with cloud providers to make sure that if anybody from our company ever purchases their cloud services, those services must meet a minimum configuration standard, and we get alerted. Then, if someone wants to go running, that's fine, because we know they can't hurt themselves because we've already confiscated the scissors.

Our goal isn't to limit what people do. Instead, we merely want to try to guide their behavior into the proper swim lane. Out front, we need people to see us as collaborative, helpful, and consultative. But behind the scenes, we're as untrusting and paranoid as every security organization has always been. But we don't let outsiders see that too much, because it makes us look shifty and untrustworthy. Mistrust breeds mistrust. So we make it clear that we trust everybody, but we also verify.

A lot of people who have moved into the role of CISO may not understand the human part of the job, but it is the most important part. If people see you as helpful and consultative, chances are good that they will trust you when you tell them that they shouldn't do something. They understand that you're not trying to limit what they do. You just want to help them do it in a more successful way. They'll actually believe you and take the trouble to try to please you, because you've been so helpful to them.

THE POWER OF OBLIGATION

Humans are interesting creatures. We are ruled by obligation. Whenever you go to a car showroom, you'll notice that the salesperson always offers you water or coffee. Always. That's because we're hardwired to consider a gift as a form of obligation. So subconsciously, if someone gives us a gift, we feel it necessary to reciprocate. And what the salesperson is going to do is try to talk you into reciprocating by buying a car.

This can be easily translated to the role of a CISO. If you've collaborated with somebody and given them a successful business outcome, very often they will consider themselves obligated. So when someone from security comes by later and says, "Hey, I really need your help with this," they're much more likely to say, "Sure."

There's a great Creole word I like to use. It's "lagniappe." It means going the extra mile, or that little something extra. If you buy a dozen donuts, and they throw another one in the box for you as the baker's dozen, that's the lagniappe. So whenever we're doing anything in security, I try to add in a lagniappe.

If I have to take something away, such as people's access to Gmail from the office, I'll give them back a single sign-on portal so that when they come on to Office 365, they won't even want their old Gmail anymore because everything is so smooth. Maybe I have to add multifactor authentication for anyone logging in from outside. But when they get there, they've got a single sign-on portal, so they don't have to remember passwords for their expenses or the HR system or whatever anymore.

I always try to add back value as a lagniappe. It's one of my favorite words because it means that little unexpected something extra that makes people say, "Oh, that was nice."

Of course, understanding threat trends and the latest security technologies is an incredibly important part of the job. But the people part of the job is critical, and far too often overlooked. People always remember their last interaction with you more than they remember the rest of it. If their most recent interaction was pleasant and helpful, or they feel like an honorary member of the security team, that's how they remember you. And it makes doing your job of protecting the business so much easier.

ABOUT THE CONTRIBUTOR

Kevin Kealy – CISO, Ingram Micro

The self-described "Prince of security weirdness," Kevin Kealy claims mass pollution of Google and says that he's not the vet or the police captain, does not sing "Danny Boy," and is definitely not the dead guy. He holds a master's degree in information security from the University of London.

He has one book in print, with another on the way. He speaks often—some might say too often—on the subjects of security and technology and is a sought-after pundit on these and other topics.

Kealy has worked in the Internet field for many years, with side trips into voice-over IP (VoIP), ethical hacking, network architecture, and audit mitigation. With two patents for developments in VoIP security, he seems unable to concentrate on anything for too long unless it's security related. He's co-authored several books on topics related to the Internet, forensics, and the admissibility of digital evidence.

Working in both customer-facing and development roles, Kealy worked at AT&T Labs for 16 years. He was the CISO of a Fortune 500 payments company, a major fitness chain, and a major outdoor retailer, and the interim CSO or CIO of several other companies. He is currently the CISO of Ingram Micro.

OVERCOMING HUMAN FRAILTY BY DESIGN

Theresa Payton, Fortalice

Whether it's poor network design, a misconfigured device, a flaw in an application, or someone simply clicking on a bad link or email attachment, humans are often—by design—the weakest link in any network. Here is a terrible and heartbreaking headline that demonstrates the cost of our continued failure to address human error proactively: "Email Mistake Costs Chicago School Employee a Job." On June 15, 2018, a Chicago Public Schools employee lost their job after the employee sent an email to a large distribution, by accident, which included a link to a confidential spreadsheet exposing the personal information of 3,700 students and families. If the IT community had been doing its job, that mistake never would have happened.

For decades, the security problem has been growing larger, and there are many contributing factors. An important consideration is that cybercrime can be incredibly lucrative, so the number of people who rely on cybercrime to provide for themselves and their families is on the rise. State-sponsored threats are also growing, and they're not just targeting the US government; they're also targeting businesses and even individual citizens. Once you layer innovative new technology on an aging infrastructure, you are dealing with a real, complex security challenge. This is not the time for us to rely on humans as our last line of defense.

Even though we've known this for decades, security today continues to be fundamentally broken, and nearly everything we have done is actually making it harder to successfully avoid being compromised. When we first started using the Internet, for example, all that was required of us was a memorable username and a password, and we made that super simple as well so we could remember it. Which is why so many people use their pet's name, or their school mascot, or the year they graduated, or their family nickname for their password. And nobody ever told us that we needed to safeguard the email address that we were using. No one said, "Don't just hand that out to anybody" or "Don't sign up for all those free coupons."

Humans give out their email addresses, and the next thing you know, they're getting taken in by Nigerian princes with no heirs, or they've won the Bermuda lottery. But this shouldn't be a surprise. Scam artists have been taking advantage of the human frailty of trust since the dawn of time. But we have done nothing to fix this problem except to say, "You know what? Your passwords should be harder for people to guess," which by the way, also means they're also harder for you to remember. Oh, and don't recycle your passwords. Also, be more creative with your usernames, and oh, by the way, your email address is now tied to everything from social media to your bank account. The problem just keeps getting worse.

Why do we keep placing the responsibility for solving our security problems on the user?

It's time for us to say, "Okay, the humans are the weakest link." We click on links, we get an email with a cute panda as an attachment and we click on it, or someone gives us a thumb drive and we plug it right in. We accidentally distribute confidential data we shouldn't to lots of people. We already know this.

So, why was that Chicago Public School employee allowed to send out a link to confidential data in the first place? We already know that sort of data shouldn't leave an organization. Why didn't the email system simply say, "You have PII in this spreadsheet, and you're sending it externally? That's a big no," or "Are you really sure you want to send this?" Of course, the IT industry would tell the Chicago Public School system, *we have a solution to this problem. It's called data loss prevention. Let us customize that solution for you for multiple times your annual budget.*

This isn't only about the weaknesses exhibited by end users. Our IT teams have the exact same problem. For example, humans are expected to read and correlate hundreds of log files and find a problem, which is like looking for a needle in a haystack of needles, with predictable results. Human frailty has been proven over and over again to be one of our most serious security threats, and it's not going away.

Businesses and consumers are actually driving this bad behavior. When I graduated from graduate school at the University of Virginia, we were all about efficient code, error-free code, and sending errors to different places so that we didn't have these open-ended events. It was all about being secure, efficient, and not having errors. The problem today is that because of the accelerating demands of getting solutions to market, security is no longer part of the whiteboard session when we are designing apps and products—it's an afterthought that gets implemented only once all the other work has been done, and often in the form of merely requiring a user ID and password. Maybe multifactor authentication, at best.

That's because businesses and consumers are demanding. They say, "I want it fast. I want it to be the coolest, latest, greatest thing. Also, I don't want to pay a lot of money for it, and I just want it to work. Oh, and I don't want to read a manual." People just expect to plug it in and go. These realities are not something that require change: The security community needs to embrace the human psyche and deliver security.

And as a result of this, every year we experience the biggest, baddest breach that has ever happened! Despite $1 trillion in investments in the most sophisticated security technology the world has ever seen, the US Office of Personnel Management (OPM), Equifax, Sony, Target, Anthem, and others have been breached. And why? Because we have built our current approach to cybersecurity around protecting old digital routines: We still use magnetic strips on ID cards (circa 1970s), we keep trying to build a better mousetrap for "user IDs and passwords" (circa 1970s–80s), and we use the same approaches to protecting email accounts (circa 1990s).

This shift in purchasing demands has created an iterative cycle of innovation that is insecure by design. This is why a similar shift in ideology must happen on the development side that requires software programmers and security engineers to design security so that human training is not our last line of defense against human error. We must shift the paradigm away from simply trusting humans to pick a good password or not click on a malicious link, because we all already know that's not going to work.

In planning and designing for human frailty, we need to consider the following realities:

- The threat of cybercrime has created a significant increase in an organization's interest in cybersecurity, with companies spending billions of dollars to protect themselves against a rapidly evolving array of current and potential future threats. Many spend heavily on monitoring, surveillance, and software; however, they often neglect the risk created by their own people, and in this digital age, by their customers as well.

- Cybercriminals gravitate to the weakest spots in institutional defenses, and that often means going after customers.
- As money becomes more mobile, the threat from cyberattackers on the mobility attack vector is likely to increase.
- Corporate networks and systems are also a constant target of cyberattacks. While hackers may be out to steal valuable data, consumer records, account credentials, or trade secrets, the reality is that nearly 80 percent of all cyberattacks start with tricking the user.
- The introduction of new technologies such as cloud-based storage, IoT devices, Software as a Service (SaaS) adoption, and the growth of mobile devices that users are connecting to the network are all driving digital transformation, allowing organizations to compete more effectively in today's connected marketplace. While these additional capabilities and devices provide numerous benefits, it should come as no surprise that they also introduce new vulnerabilities.
- In all of this, humans continue to be the most vulnerable element in any security defense. Not only are 95 percent of all security breaches due to sophisticated attacks that we were unprepared to defend ourselves against, but human error has also caused 95 percent or more of those breaches.

THE SOLUTION: DESIGN FOR THE HUMAN PSYCHE

Never trust the security of technology, and you will never be disappointed.

Almost all technology today is open. It has to be. You would be upset if that smartphone, tablet computer, smart watch, gaming system, or other really expensive technology you just purchased could not be easily connected to online resources or automatically updated. You'd be upset precisely because you spent a lot of money on it. By design, these devices are open platforms that allow you to download the latest app quickly, update the operating system, perform sensitive transactions, load security patches, and more. But because it is open to being updated, it is also open to being hacked, no matter what we do.

One of the reasons why these devices are so vulnerable is that we have established very arcane rules to follow, such as having a 12-character password of nonrepeating numbers or letters, and so on that are so complex that they actually help attackers get in and keep legitimate users out. We've worked hard to design security systems that act more as enablers and establish rules that become restrictive for people to gain the network access they need to do their jobs. Naturally, they look for ways to circumvent those roadblocks.

When I was asked to design a security strategy for the Executive Office of the President, I knew we had to address the hearts and minds of the staff if we wanted to protect their privacy and security, and in many cases, also protect national security. Two key questions occurred to me during my first 90 days, and I knew I had to answer them or we could potentially face a major calamity:

- Why, in spite of talented security teams and significant investments in security, do breaches still happen?
- Why is it that, despite hours and hours of boring computer-based training and security campaigns, we still make mistakes and click on exploited links?

It became clear to me that we need a new line of thinking, one that kills boring computer-based training courses and bans the purchase of the latest security tool if we haven't first tried using innovation to combat the human element of our risk. The underlying path for this new approach is driven by a core principle: Design for the human.

This line of thinking is comparable to installing childproof or safety items when you have small, curious children in your home. You still tell them, "Don't touch," but just in case they do, you have already designed safety into your house with them in mind. Likewise, we need to design security for our employees using this same fundamental principle. We already know that users will access free Wi-Fi, recycle passwords, and respond to emails that are tricking them into giving up information—in fact, they will break all the security rules because they are not security employees.

And by the way, I am going to let you in on a little secret: Security employees break the rules too! They get bored and sloppy when reviewing log files or when configuring or patching dozens of devices. They leave ports open or create backdoors so they can get some work done later when they are offsite. In the worst-case scenario, their username is *admin* and their password is *admin*.

WINNING SECURITY STRATEGIES

I have been looking at cybersecurity challenges my entire career, and I have found that there are six critical approaches that security professionals and the entire security industry need to adopt if we want any chance of getting and staying ahead of the cybercrime challenge:

Life is a Happy Meal. Getting someone to do something they may not want to do often requires adding a "prize" to their lunch box. You have to start by owning the hearts and minds of the people you are trying to protect and whose behavior you are trying to shape. You do that by being seen as an enabler and problem solver. You listen carefully, promise to solve their problem, and then follow through with more than you promised. Then, when you need their help in addressing a security issue, they are already motivated to support you.

Segment to save it. An open network only needs to exist in the eye of the beholder. While you can design networks so that people have access to the tools they need to do their jobs, you also need to establish clear network segmentation. That way, when attackers inevitably compromise a device or group of devices, you already have controls in place to protect critical data and resources, especially when that threat attempts to spread laterally.

Redesign access. Username and password and even multiauthentication access controls are approaching the end of their life cycle. And in many cases, that expiration date was reached long ago. Access needs to be reconsidered based on a number of criteria, including location, type of device, and even behavioral analytics. If a user attempts to access a certain set of data they never requested before or tries to connect from a new location, whether from another part of the world or simply from the wiring closet on the other side of the building, doing so should automatically trigger additional access controls. And once any access is granted, that device needs to be automatically directed to a specific network segment where it can be logged, tracked, monitored, and even quarantined.

Implement a digital shredding strategy. When something is deleted or discarded, it needs to really be deleted. We not only need to follow strict rules about the disposal of old or no longer useful or relevant digital data, but that process also has to be automated so that human error doesn't leave critical information sitting on a hard drive somewhere waiting to be stolen or exploited.

Establish a real education and awareness program. Most security training programs are their own worst enemy. Rather than having the entire company go through the same boring computer-based training (CBT) security program, customize programs for different groups and job functions. Create rewards for participation. Bring groups together for hands-on training and make it an event they look forward to. Include easy and rewarding reporting as part of your security awareness strategy. While human frailty is a real problem, humans can also be critical security allies. Phishing attacks, for example, will continue to slip past security systems. Rather than simply waiting for one of these attacks to be triggered, put in a reward system for employees who notice them and forward them back to the IT team.

Leverage automation and machine learning wherever possible. Things like AI, automation, and machine learning can be critical human safety nets. Hand over as many of the redundant, boring, tedious, labor-intensive jobs to machines as possible to free up humans to do the sort of higher-level processing they are much better at performing. If people are likely to click on a malicious email attachment, identify and remove the risk before it gets to them. If people create simple-to-guess passwords to circumvent complex password requirements, use behavioral analytics and existing data to provide better security while making access to the resources they need to do their job as easy and seamless as possible.

ABOUT THE CONTRIBUTOR

Theresa Payton – Founder and CEO, Fortalice

Theresa Payton is an authority on Internet security and intelligence, cybercrime, and fraud. As the first female White House CIO, she managed the IT enterprise for the President and staff of 3,000 persons. Prior to her time at the White House, Payton was a senior executive in banking, spending 16 years providing solutions. Payton founded Fortalice in 2008, and lends her expertise to government and private sector organizations to help them improve their security posture. Payton was also featured as the Deputy Commander of Intelligence Operations in CBS's hit show "Hunted." *Security* Magazine named her one of the top 25 Most Influential People in Security, and she was recently named the 4th most influential global security expert by IFSEC Global.

THE FUTURE

"We must move from threat prevention to the greater challenge of securing hyperconnectivity."

Michael Xie,
Fortinet

"There is virtually no area of cybersecurity that won't be transformed by AI and ML."

Ken Xie,
Fortinet

How is it that humans have gone from wooden spears, a few tens of thousands of years ago, to the ability to send people to the moon and back? What other animal has progressed at that pace? What is the implication of this pace of change for the digital big bang and cybersecurity?

Well before recorded human history, something happened to the human brain. Many scientists believe that mutations, either random or caused by the environment, changed our brain's physiology, opening the door for us to communicate with one another much more robustly and to think more abstractly. Or it could have been the opposite: that the ability to communicate and think abstractly grew to a tipping point, accelerating a change in our brain's physiology. Either way, our future was forever changed.

The digital big bang has and will continue to serve as an analogous accelerant, driving our future at a breathtaking pace. While some fear the future simply because it's unknown, others worry that technologies will overtake people—that cyborgs will emerge and outpace the development of the human brain's marvelous physiology. But this is a book about science, not fear. We need not fear the future or the technology that serves it; our inventions are neither inherently good nor evil. People have the responsibility and opportunity to steer the application of technology toward good.

What is the definition of success—of "good"—in cybersecurity? Is it 7 billion people online with security that is inadequate, or only 2 billion online but with adequate security? Which is better? I don't know. Cybersecurity is unlikely to be the great equalizer, providing everyone access to the same degree of security, but it should be a tide that floats all boats—the level of security should increase on average. The earlier sections of this book identify the required elements and formulas that, if used with rigor, will achieve broadly accessible, high-quality security. But how do we scale those elements to billions?

How do we measure whether the adoption of scientific rigor—optimization around the core elements of speed and connectivity, recognizing the enduring shortfalls, implementing the fundamental and advanced strategies, and embracing the higher-order dimensions—has in fact taken hold? Let's look at some potential ways, some guideposts for the future, to get there.

UNIFYING FORCES

Creating a world of broadly accessible, high-quality, and scalable security starts with leveraging the intellect and momentum of over 7 billion people.

How do we do that?!

It's not as hard as you'd think. We can look backward to understand how similar tasks have been done before on a large scale.

Somehow, societies make the governance leap from small tribes and villages of about a hundred people or so to much larger entities where one leader governs hundreds of millions of people. Universal shared values can serve as unifying forces and provide a scalable means to govern large organizations and shape the behaviors of societies.

It's worth noting that shared beliefs and values don't have a price tag—an imposing capital investment—that is required. Values also can be invented at will. Once created and adopted, those "inventions" become the source of usually helpful stability. Of course, the voluntary mass adoption of the values is the key challenge.

A good example to follow might be environmentalism, a concept where humans believe in the responsibility to protect the planet and where norms of behavior have been established, nurtured, and generally followed. We need "cyberspace environmentalism," a set of shared beliefs, norms, and shared experiences among people—a culture of security. To change culture, we need to change people's shared experiences.

Establishing shared values is essential, just as it was following the cosmic big bang. Examples of such shared values could include an agreement that governments should not attack one another's critical infrastructure, should not steal IP from companies, and should cooperate with international law enforcement investigations. To date, we haven't created and agreed upon such issues, and we are suffering because of it. This must change.

Guidepost for the Future: Unifying Forces
Near-term, in the next 5 to 10 years, we need to invent, nourish, and solidify a culture of security on the Internet reinforced by international norms of behavior. Shared culture won't develop overnight but must be nurtured.

RELATIONSHIPS

Is social media an answer? Social media allows information to flow in ways that were unimaginable only 100 years ago. That's a good thing. But some may argue that social media also has severely eroded the strength of the connections we make. The support from 500 so-called friends or connections online may be far less than I would have gotten from just 10 friends a century ago. Our relationships in cyberspace need to have consequences—good and bad—just as our relationships do in other domains.

> **Guidepost for the Future: Relationships**
> We need to create trust-based cyber-relationships that can serve as a model for future collaboration. At a personal level, cyberspace can't be a place to sow mistrust, where semi-anonymous people spew falsehoods and stir up hate. The digital world needs to live up to its potential to be a vehicle of free speech for all—a great equalizer—not a new place to, without accountability, cry "fire" in its virtual crowded theater. A crowdsource-oriented trust rating system, relied on in different ways today by the ratings systems of eBay and Amazon, might serve as an example of how to build the foundation of trust that's needed, one virtual brick at a time.

INFORMED OPTIMISM

Without insight and optimism that the future has the potential to be better, digital transformation will forever be hindered. Cybercriminals and adversarial nation-states will not go away, so it's up to cybersecurity leadership to create trust in the platform so that the future looks promising enough to those who seek to do something ambitious with cyberspace.

The credit card industry serves as a good example. Retailers trust that a credit card used today will result in a payment that arrives tomorrow. Similarly, individuals trust that if the worst happens (their credit card number is compromised despite reasonable precautions), their liability and risk are limited and relatively small. As a result, retailers, individuals, and the banks that serve as intermediaries all benefit, resulting in increased spending, convenience, happiness, and profitability—which translate into confidence in the future.

Eleanor Roosevelt said, "We gain strength, and courage, and confidence by each experience in which we really stop to look fear in the face...we must do that which we think we cannot." The future of trust on the Internet will be built one brick at a time. The science of the technology foundations of that trust has been described in previous chapters, and just around the corner is the more widespread use of cyberinsurance to help compensate for the unexpected. Both technical and insurance-based solutions are needed to create and sustain trust in the future.

Guidepost for the Future:
Confidence That the Internet Will Be Better

The perception of Internet security can't be fatalistic, limited by the expectation that compromise is inevitable or by assumptions that civility is forever absent, followed by widespread acceptance of bad behaviors. We must work to instill confidence in the Internet's future.

PURSUIT OF FACTS AND WISDOM

Science is often portrayed as moments of sudden breakthroughs, but perhaps the most important breakthrough was neither sudden nor an obvious leap forward. This critical breakthrough was a deliberate leap backward, when scientists recognized that we don't have all the answers. In previous centuries, leaders governed by claiming unique insights into the mysterious knowledge of unseen gods, using that power to control those labeled as ignorant of such insights. But today, scientists admit they don't know what existed before the cosmic big bang and are therefore doggedly pursuing that knowledge. That's the real value of science: acknowledging we don't know it all and rigorously pursuing answers.

The premise of this book is that we need to treat cybersecurity like a science, and then leverage the understanding of that science to enable a brighter future. That means we must freely admit there is a lot we do not know and have yet to figure out. We should not settle for "the one-eyed man leading in the land of the blind."

The beauty of treating cybersecurity like a science is that established truths of science are not controversial. These truths don't require picking winners and losers, are agonistic to country boundaries, and, to paraphrase Neil deGrasse Tyson, are true whether you believe them or not.

Looking back at history, science—for example, biological research—was used for very different purposes in military-oriented governments compared to economic-oriented governments. Nevertheless, the science of cybersecurity—for example, solving the Internet's authentication problem—can and should proceed. The science of cybersecurity should be both secure in its accomplishments and eager to discover new wisdom, reduce ignorance, and find even better methods.

Guidepost for the Future:
Cybersecurity Is a Science, Not an Art
Our cultural heroes of the future Internet are those who, with wisdom, dogged pursuit, rigor, and a degree of unselfish collaboration, create the tools and rules for our digital big bang universe.

MACHINES THAT SERVE PEOPLE

How far away are we from having the ability to alter what defines us as humans? Few people today would argue against titanium joints for the infirm, pacemakers to steady a heartbeat, or brainwave-detecting sensors for commanding the paralyzed limbs of spine injury patients. Today, we are already capable of altering the genetic makeup of people to change the physical direction from which we grow. In animals, scientists have discovered genes that control not only physical traits but certain behaviors as well.

The abilities to change human physical composition, reprogram our behaviors, and gain access to seemingly limitless computing and storage capacity to make real-time decisions are potentially the building blocks of a new race, made up of modified and computerized humans—smarter, stronger, more moral, and so on. We may not even be that far from determining how to store human intelligence and consciousness inside a computer, to live a life virtually (or if that's too bold, to serve as a backup copy in case the all-flesh version is damaged).

Heady stuff (pun intended).

Those who worry about AI fear that not only will computers be more agile and deeper thinkers than humans, but that computers will also create objects that will supplant humans, either by creating robots that take over the space in the physical world or by dominating key resources for their own use (for example, electric power to run and water to cool).

In cybersecurity, we're using the tool of storytelling to construct our strategies and architectures just as ancient civilizations spun elaborate stories to explain the importance of good over evil. But we shouldn't let narratives about a potentially dark future—cyberspace scare tactics or horror stories—drive our cybersecurity behaviors. We need to wean ourselves from cybersecurity evangelists who talk of cybersecurity good and evil. Instead, we need to attach our cybersecurity wagons to the language of scientists, identifying the behaviors and data flows through precise scientific terms, where the intentions of the humans who define cybersecurity policy are automatically translated into the language of machines.

The guidepost for the future is *technology that serves humankind.*

Today, cybersecurity is mostly seen as a self-licking ice cream cone: You implement security to achieve better security. To succeed, cybersecurity has to make the leap from being tolerated as a necessary evil—a cost of doing business—to becoming a means to do business with greater efficiency or effectiveness. Transformative. Just like when humans figured out they could transform one type of functionality—speed—into an entirely different one—lift—by combining speed with an airfoil wing. That's how airplanes were invented and we learned to fly in the physical world. In the digital world, we need to invent the airplane equivalent by combining cybersecurity with the strategic intent of business owners.

Infusing human intent into security is a major revolution that will allow security strategy and solutions to grow, scale, and adapt dynamically and economically to meet today's problems of speed and scale, while becoming the foundation for economic and personal success. Intent-based security obeys and implements the science of cybersecurity—the rules and formulas—to create safe and secure cybersecurity science at speed and scale. The end result will be machines that serve people, rather than people serving machines.

There are a number of paths down which security will continue to evolve. Hoping to survive a cataclysmic event is highly risky. The preferable, more prudent action is to future-proof your environment now as much as possible and build in opportunities for future inspiration and agility.

CONCLUSION

The hallmarks of the organisms, ideas, and technologies that have managed to survive in the cosmic big bang have something in common: endurance, agility, inspiration, wisdom, a willingness to evolve, and most importantly, an externally enforced obedience to the laws of science ("you can't fool Mother Nature"). In our data-centric future, the science of cybersecurity should serve as the foundation. But it also requires that we recognize the moment to ensure that our species doesn't get left behind and forgotten in the dust of the digital big bang.

WHY CYBERSECURITY NEEDS AI

Michael Xie, Fortinet

All over the world, the power of artificial intelligence (AI) and machine learning (ML) are being put to work to make existing systems more powerful. In many cases, AI and ML help systems do their current jobs better. In others, the systems are able to do tasks never before possible. In still others, the whole system must be redesigned because AI and ML have changed the game.

In cybersecurity, AI and ML will be used in all three of these ways to such an extent that soon it will be redundant to speak of AI- and ML-powered cybersecurity. It will be impossible to deliver adequate cybersecurity without AI and ML for several reasons:

- First, the attack surface has become so wide, so deep, and so tall that humans working on their own just won't be able to keep up.
- Second, the sophistication of attackers keeps pace with and at times exceeds that of defenders. Zero-day attacks that conceal themselves and are constructed to work differently each time will not be detectable without AI and ML.
- Third, to implement zero trust and intent-based security, the level of automation and the sophistication of the automation will need to expand rapidly in ways that can only be delivered through AI and ML.

A sophisticated, layered approach is required to properly implement AI and ML for cybersecurity. Different types of AI and ML will be required for different tasks. The results of one type of AI and ML will be passed to the next. Here's a brief overview of the hierarchy of AI and how the layers will work together:

- Deep learning is a form of ML in which data is filtered through self-adjusting networks of math loosely inspired by the structure of neurons in the brain. This type of learning, also called artificial neural networks (ANN), surfaces patterns and anomalies from huge amounts of data.

- ML uses data to refine how computers make predictions or perform a task. Systems can learn to make predictions and then to make decisions on their own.
- AI enables a system to make intelligent choices that mimic human behavior.

These layers work together and complement each other to allow systems to process huge amounts of data, sort through and detect what is important, and then react. A vital part of getting this right is using the appropriate way to train the AI and ML. Three methods are most promising for cybersecurity:

Supervised Learning This initial model begins the training of the AI by feeding it a vast amount of labeled data, clearly identifying the characteristics of each labeled data set, and then repeatedly applying those characteristics to unlabeled data.

Unsupervised Learning In this next phase, the algorithm has no known solution set to follow. Instead, it recognizes patterns learned in phase one that enable it to label data without human help. At this point, new data can be slowly introduced to force it to deal with data it hasn't seen before and make new decisions.

Reinforcement Learning The results of supervised and unsupervised learning are then "tested" by scoring the system's performance with unlabeled files and "rewarding" the system for good results. Training then continues to cycle between these three learning strategies on an ongoing basis.

Just getting an AI and ML system working is an immensely difficult task. But it is even harder to make AI and ML systems work in the real world. Anyone who tells you it just works like magic doesn't have a system that can stand up to the messy difficulties of the cybersecurity battlefield. The fact is that AI and ML need guide rails and human supervision so that they can work their magic, but then recognize when the magic is not working, and human intelligence or rule-based approaches are needed. At Fortinet, we are six years into our journey to make AI and ML work in real-world cybersecurity systems. While we are happy with our progress, it is clear that there is virtually no area of cybersecurity that won't be transformed by AI and ML. There is so much yet to learn and we are looking forward to the journey.

ABOUT THE CONTRIBUTOR

Michael Xie – Founder and CTO, Fortinet

Michael Xie has more than 15 years of experience in the network security industry. Previously he held positions as software director and architect for NetScreen. He was honored with a 2009 Tech Innovator Award by Everything Channel's CRN. He was also named a 2006 Northern California Entrepreneur of the Year by Ernst & Young and a Top Technology Innovator by *VARBusiness* Magazine in 2004. Xie has an MS degree in electrical and computer engineering from the University of Manitoba as well as an MSc degree in automobile engineering from Tsinghua University.

THE FUTURE OF CYBERSECURITY

Ken Xie, Fortinet

This book represents a milestone because it so clearly explains the history of cybersecurity and sets the stage for what will be done in the next phase of the industry. For my entire career, I have been working on solutions to address the challenges that Phil Quade and the contributors describe in this book. We have seen how speed and connectivity have driven the adoption and massive value created by the Internet, and how cybersecurity must serve and amplify those forces, not get in the way.

When we founded Fortinet, Michael and I had a vision for how cybersecurity would truly align with forces that drive the success of the Internet, address the elementary shortfalls described, and go beyond what has been achieved in the fundamental and advanced strategies that have been presented and analyzed.

We believe that increasingly, security will be consolidated into infrastructure and applications, based on a security fabric controlled by intent-based intelligence and automation. The vision we have for a new security framework will provide an architecture that both aligns and keeps pace with the power of speed and connectivity that continues to expand uses of the Internet to new domains. Using AI and automation, the vision embraces and orchestrates the technologies used to address elementary shortfalls into a security fabric.

If we get this right, we will no longer be playing catch-up. Instead, we will have the foundation for a new Internet, one that is designed to be truly secure, with security built in at every level in a way that handles the technology aspects but also addresses the persistent challenges of the higher-order dimensions of human frailty, privacy, and complexity management.

This is of course a tall order, but we feel that, building on the story told in this book, we can now show the way forward to a qualitatively superior architecture for cybersecurity that can be the foundation for a whole new type of Internet.

WHAT HAPPENED IN THREE GENERATIONS OF CYBERSECURITY

The landscape of cybersecurity has now reached a point where we can start thinking about how all of the pieces work together. This is only possible because we now have solutions that implement fundamental and advanced strategies that cover so many of the elementary shortfalls. These solutions act as control points that allow us to detect and guide what is happening with the underlying endpoints, network, and other computing infrastructure.

Cybersecurity didn't start out with such a broad set of solutions. When I founded my first security company 27 years ago as a graduate student at Stanford, the first generation of security was focused on connectivity. Firewalls, the initial control points, were placed at the network edge and controlled who and what could connect to the network. A few years later, those firewalls were combined with VPNs to encrypt traffic, and tools like IDS and IPS soon followed to better monitor and secure traffic because threats had become more complex.

But these new security solutions were resource intensive, which had an impact on business operations. This is why I built the first ASIC-based firewall appliance a few years later, redesigning the firewall from the ground up. ASICs (application-specific integrated circuits) are special-purpose chips that can be adapted for cybersecurity processing. Just as NVIDIA designed the graphics processing unit (GPU) and Google designed the tensor processing unit (TPU), this customized ASIC allowed firewalls to run up to 10 to 100 times faster than software alone, enabling organizations to run their businesses without compromising on either performance or protection.

The second generation of network security began when threats began to target applications. Content became much richer and more powerful. It was not just text or passive documents being passed between connections, but content that could be programmed to become vectors of agent-based attacks. Fortinet was founded to provide organizations with a second-generation antivirus firewall that could identify, inspect, and secure application-layer transactions and content—something that first-generation firewalls were not able to do. This sort of comprehensive examination of content, which came to be known as unified threat management, turned out to be hugely resource intensive, requiring up to 30 to 100 times the computing power required to just examine network routing data. ASIC-powered hardware, which can provide a 100-fold boost in performance, was developed to keep up with this challenge. However, most other security practices stayed the same because network perimeters remained clearly defined, devices were still owned and controlled by the corporation, and traffic volumes and speeds were predictable.

Antivirus firewalls, which were the initial focus of Fortinet, implemented unified threat management by adding massive hardware power and also finding ways to embed security as deeply as possible in the computing and networking infrastructure, a job that continues to this day and just gets more complex.

Network, storage, and computing infrastructure has become more programmable and orchestrated. The movement toward software-defined everything means that all of these infrastructure components can meaningfully participate in cybersecurity systems, if those systems have the requisite forms of automation and the smarts to put them to work.

But another major shift has happened. Because so many of us have powerful movable devices and work in many arenas, not just inside the cocoon of safety inside a company, it is no longer possible to assume all actors inside the firewall are good. Every person and every device inside and outside the firewall is assumed to be a threat until proven otherwise. In this era, the border protected by firewalls disappears and the trust zone is gone. We need a much more sophisticated environment inside the firewall, a security fabric that brings together and coordinates capabilities to work together responsively to meet our needs.

Speed and connectivity are driving the use of the Internet into a huge number of domains, including the IoT, medical devices, a vast array of mobile apps, and so many more. Each of these domains will also have solutions that can act as control points and are also software defined. These control points and the associated infrastructure will also become part of the security fabric and make each domain more secure using smart and powerful cybersecurity.

The third generation of cybersecurity is coming to life as a smarter, more orchestrated security fabric. To handle the zero-trust cybersecurity paradigm, the security fabric must adapt to contain threats as they emerge. In addition, this type of intelligence makes it possible to include security concerns from the start of creating network connections rather than applying cybersecurity as an afterthought. More on this later.

While it is clear that each of these domains will have its own cybersecurity challenges, it is also clear that a general approach is emerging. The security fabric will become that approach, moving from a desire to responsively integrate and orchestrate capabilities to a new type of cybersecurity architecture, one that will require progress in a variety of dimensions.

HARDWARE AND SOFTWARE NEEDED FOR BUILDING SECURITY INTO THE NEW INFRASTRUCTURE

The Internet has always been distributed, and to some extent cybersecurity has been as well. But the rise of mobile applications, 5G, software-defined wide area networking (SD-WAN), and edge computing, as well as cloud computing, are leading to a radical expansion of the distribution of data and computing across the Internet. The realm of mission-critical operational technology represents another frontier.

The majority of data no longer stays inside company networks where it can be protected by edge firewalls. Instead, global networks and data connect everything, including transactions, services, and social interactions, through borderless businesses, connected homes, and increasingly autonomous devices.

Because data is the new currency of today's business, it is a more valuable target than ever. In such a world, shortening the time to detect and respond to threats, while providing clear visibility and protection across distributed environments, is essential. At the same time, organizations need to comply with stricter regulations, such as new privacy laws. And this is all happening in the midst of a global cybersecurity skills shortage.

To meet these challenges, the world needs a third generation, a security-driven network designed to follow data and workloads as they move between flexible ecosystems of interconnected networks and devices. Organizations also need to be able to see and secure all infrastructures and devices, from endpoints and IoT devices to on-premise physical and virtual systems, and out to complex multicloud ecosystems, through a single lens.

This third generation of security must provide organizations with something that is sorely needed: the ability to express in a clear and detailed way what they want their cybersecurity policies to be. The policies will not just be about blocking access in the manner of first- and second-generation firewalls. Rather, they will be advanced playbooks to handle complex situations and responses required in a zero-trust world. The result won't be a moat, but more like the immune system in the body that moves around to block and neutralize threats.

To make this work, massive processing capabilities for cybersecurity must be built into the distributed nodes of the Internet. Right now, much cybersecurity processing takes place on the same hardware that is running the applications. As the security fabric grows, more and more computing will be needed to analyze and protect every device, application, and service running on the Internet. If we assume that the application and cybersecurity components will share available computing resources, we will soon hit a wall.

The design of a new Internet, which means not only the routers and networking systems, but also devices, applications, and general-purpose computing platforms, will include dedicated hardware and memory for cybersecurity. In addition, a wide variety of security solutions will be distributed. These solutions, along with the software-defined infrastructure, constitute the security fabric and must be ready for integration and orchestration. At first, vendors will lead the design and orchestration of this fabric by making their own components work together. Eventually, it is likely that the security fabric will be based on standards. Either way, the result will be a new type of Internet, one with cybersecurity designed in. This will transform the world.

As briefly noted earlier, one of the largest changes in this new Internet will be a change in one of the most fundamental paradigms of networking: the way network connections are made. Right now, when someone or something wants to connect to a resource, the network connection is created to maximize speed and connectivity and then cybersecurity rules are applied afterward. In a new, security-aware Internet, the connection will be optimized for speed, connectivity, and security. Connections will be created in a way that not only serves the intended networking purpose but also is guaranteed to be safe. My name for this concept is *security-driven networking*.

Adding this level of intelligence will allow a new sort of awareness of security to become available. I can imagine a security threat index that indicates the safety of various parts of the Internet, marking them with red for danger, yellow for problematic, and green for safety. When making a connection, the routing algorithm can be security aware and choose a network path that goes through the safest parts of the Internet. It is possible to imagine many other sorts of indicators and optimizations as well in this new world.

THE POWER OF INTENT-BASED SECURITY TO ORCHESTRATE THE SECURITY FABRIC

The massive expansion and distribution of the Internet will soon make second-generation security technologies inadequate. A security fabric serves as a foundation for continued innovation that can keep pace with technology disruptions like 5G. But another dimension will be needed.

As just pointed out, a computing capability must be distributed throughout the Internet for cybersecurity components to have sufficient power to do their jobs. But remember, we have a growing set of components that will just grow larger and more and more programmable infrastructure at every level. Will every single component be applied to every single packet of traffic? It is clear that would be unworkable. We must have an AI- and ML-powered orchestrating brain that can figure out how to control the security fabric to deliver the security needed in any instance. As Michael's contribution pointed out, we just will not be able to meet the current challenges of cybersecurity without sophisticated mastery of AI.

What is often missed in discussions of cybersecurity is that there are huge variations in the type of security policies needed across different segments of an organization. The security policies and remediations needed in a distributed workforce or in branch offices may be completely different from what is required to protect the mission-critical systems and IP crown jewels in the central office.

In addition, security systems must have expanded capabilities for using the security fabric to predict the actions of hackers, to analyze live traffic in real time, and to inspect unstructured data.

They also need to automatically correlate intelligence collected from specialized security devices to baseline behaviors and patterns. This constant monitoring and coordination of resources enables integrated security solutions to anticipate security threats and proactively respond to bad intent before resources are compromised, regardless of where those events occur.

Modern cybersecurity systems must be able to accept high-level instructions and then translate that intention into the tactics implemented by the security fabric. That is the mission of intent-based security: to allow a high-level expression of intent to be implemented through the complex configuration of the cybersecurity solutions and infrastructure of the security fabric. In my view, the orchestrating brain should work as follows:

1. The computing landscape is tagged and identified in various ways so that we can make statements about it. For example, we could tag all low risk servers as green, all medium risk as yellow, and all high risk as red.

2. The CISO can then tell the orchestrating brain to apply certain policies to green and yellow servers and different ones to red servers.

3. The orchestrating brain then configures all the cybersecurity components and infrastructure to implement the policies.

This is just a simple expression of the power of intent-based segmentation. In practice, the orchestrating brain is able to move the practice of cybersecurity to a higher level. The policy language that is provided to CISOs to describe their intent can include concepts and playbooks that involve orchestrating many different components and infrastructure. Rich descriptions of concepts and playbooks for automating monitoring, responses, and remediations can be defined and used to allow intent to be described in simple terms. For example, intent-based security could create playbooks for high-level needs such as border security, asset separation, compliance, and risk mitigation. In essence, the CISO is provided with a declarative language to express what is desired. The orchestrating brain instructs the security fabric in how to make it happen.

As our dependence on data-driven digital connections increases—from multicloud networks to mobile devices and the IoT—security must move from threat prevention to the greater challenge of securing hyperconnectivity as traditionally isolated systems and infrastructures begin to converge. A security fabric orchestrated by intent-based security can make use of a deep understanding of security fundamentals, business requirements, and human behaviors to enable that evolution. That's why the fundamentals explained in this book by some of the top CISOs and thought leaders in the industry are more relevant—and valuable—than ever before.

Understanding the critical role that speed, integration, and automation will play in data protection, combined with having the right people and processes in place, will enable us to prepare for the new threats we will face over the next decade. Doing this requires security leaders to keep pace with evolving threats, technical innovations, and best practices. That also includes their ability to address the business—and human—requirements that are fundamental to their success.

Increasingly, cybersecurity is global security. To a great degree, the success of the digital transformation of our society depends on how effectively we implement the fundamentals outlined in the pages of this book.

ABOUT THE CONTRIBUTOR

Ken Xie – Founder and CEO, Fortinet

A cybersecurity expert and successful entrepreneur, Ken Xie founded and built three cybersecurity companies that have shaped the cybersecurity industry. In 2000, Xie founded Fortinet, which today is among the top three cybersecurity companies worldwide and one of the fastest-growing network security companies. In 2018, Fortinet crossed an innovation milestone of over 500 issued patents worldwide, with an additional 240 pending patent applications, a record among similar security vendors.

Previously, as founder, president and CEO of NetScreen, Xie led the company to develop the industry's first ASIC and dedicated hardware systems for high-performance firewalls and VPNs. NetScreen was acquired by Juniper for $4 billion.

Xie earned an MS degree in electrical engineering from Stanford University and BS and MS degrees in electronic engineering from Tsinghua University. He is a member of the National Academy of Engineering. Xie also represents Fortinet as a member of the board of directors of the Cyber Threat Alliance and a founding member of the Center for Cybersecurity for the World Economic Forum.

INDEX

INDEX